Capitalism & Disability

MARTA RUSSELL (December 20, 1951–December 15, 2013)
Photo by John Scheele.

Capitalism & Disability

SELECTED WRITINGS
BY MARTA RUSSELL

Edited by Keith Rosenthal

Haymarket Books
Chicago, Illinois

© 2019 Keith Rosenthal
Introduction © Marta Russell and Ravi Malhotra

Published in 2019 by
Haymarket Books
P.O. Box 180165
Chicago, IL 60618
773-583-7884
www.haymarketbooks.org
info@haymarketbooks.org

ISBN: 978-1-60846-686-3

Distributed to the trade in the US through Consortium Book Sales and Distribution (www.cbsd.com) and internationally through Ingram Publisher Services
International (www.ingramcontent.com).

This book was published with the generous support of Lannan Foundation
and Wallace Action Fund.

Special discounts are available for bulk purchases by organizations and institutions. Please call 773-583-7884 or email info@haymarketbooks.org for more information.

Cover design by Rachel Cohen.

Printed in the United States.

Entered into digital printing, July 2020.

Library of Congress Cataloging-in-Publication data is available.

10 9 8 7 6 5 4 3 2

TABLE OF CONTENTS

VI. Body Politics: The Missing Link

Editor's Preface

The present volume is a systematic and representative collection of the uniquely insightful writings of the late author and activist, Marta Russell (December 20, 1951–December 15, 2013).

Russell was born in the heart of the Mississippi Delta and grew up on her family's cotton farm. By the time she had reached young adulthood, the civil rights movement of the 1960s was in full swing across the South, and Russell gravitated to the center of it. She soon found herself in Jackson, Mississippi, volunteering for the American Civil Liberties Union (ACLU) in the struggle against racial segregation. There she witnessed the full brutality of the Jackson Police Department—beatings and arrests of friends and comrades; destruction of underground newspapers and organizations.

Russell was growing increasingly politicized during this period, but she did not yet think of disability in political terms, nor in connection with the struggle for civil rights taking place around her. Indeed, although she was born with cerebral palsy (and attendant mobility impairments), she was well into her thirties before such thoughts crossed her mind. Russell moved to Los Angeles, California, in the mid-1970s. There she began a career working in the film industry and, shortly thereafter, raising a daughter. In the late 1980s, Russell developed further mobility impairments, and she began using a wheelchair. Before long, she found it increasingly prohibitive to continue working in the industry and eventually came to rely on Social Security Disability Insurance (SSDI) payments as a means of supporting herself and her child.

Slowly Russell met more disabled people, in particular, more disabled activists, who introduced her to the notion of disability as a political concept. She became involved with disability activist organizations such as ADAPT (American Disabled for Accessible Public Transit, later renamed simply to the word

ADAPT) and Not Dead Yet. She organized protests against the economic oppression of disabled people as carried out by both political parties in Washington. She also continued her activism with the ACLU and participated in demonstrations against the 2003 US war on Iraq.

Simultaneously, Russell rapidly developed her political ideology. She engaged in extensive studies of the works of Noam Chomsky, Howard Zinn, Frances Moore Lappé, Angela Davis, Karl Marx, and a plethora of other left-wing intellectuals. In 1994 she produced an award-winning documentary, *Disabled and the Cost of Saying 'I Do,'* on the structural injustices faced by SSDI recipients considering marriage (injustices which remain unresolved to this day). In 1998 she published her first and only book, *Beyond Ramps: Disability at the End of the Social Contract*, which brought her the attention and praise of such pioneering socialist disability theorists as Vic Finkelstein and Mike Oliver.[1]

Over the next seven to ten years, Russell further developed, refined, and reformulated her arguments on the nature of disability oppression under the system of capitalism. She authored a slew of essays which appeared in an array of publications. Those essays comprise the subject and contents of this book.

Marta Russell was by no means the first to explore the connection between capitalism and disability—or the notion that disability itself is a form of oppression conditioned by the historical-material circumstances of society. Rather, her genius resides in the scope and depth with which she excavated such phenomena.

In particular, Russell went further than anyone else in specifically rooting disability oppression under capitalism in explicitly Marxist terms. For Russell, the oppression of disabled people in the modern (i.e., capitalist) world is no mere historical accident or tangential "symptom" of the dominant social system. Rather, capitalism and disability are structurally, necessarily, and ontogenetically linked in a dialectical process of mutual reinforcement.

Utilizing Marx's concepts regarding the nature of classes, wage labor, exploitation, the rate of profit, market competition, the reserve army of labor, and the bourgeois state, Russell identified the oppression of disabled people as an inextricable constituent component of the operation of the capitalist mode of production itself.

Drawing out the strategic implications of such a theoretical analysis was Russell's other major political contribution. Russell fully supported all legislative reforms and programs that in any way protected, aided, or advanced the interests of disabled people in the US. Nonetheless, she maintained profound criticisms of the ultimate efficacy of a liberal civil rights-based approach which eschewed confrontation with the rooted structural relations of capitalism.

The Americans with Disabilities Act (ADA) of 1990 often figures as a centerpiece of Russell's critiques in this vein. Given that the ADA is hailed as a landmark piece of civil rights legislation, akin to the Civil Rights Acts, it makes sense that disabled people and disability rights advocates would have high expectations of this putatively-sweeping reform. Sadly, upon close scrutiny, the ADA has fallen far short of any grandiose emancipatory hopes.

Though some have mischaracterized Russell's position as being wholly dismissive of anything worthwhile in the ADA,[2] this is demonstrably not the case. In chapter 4 of this book, Russell provides an extended example of how the more progressive aspects of the ADA can be used as an instrument to highlight and even remedy rampant instances of disability discrimination. The problem, according to Russell and other like-minded critics, is that the ADA is so infrequently utilized to this end, and, in those cases where it is brought into play, is so frequently interpreted in the most narrow and feckless manner—if not outright defied with relative impunity. Moreover, the progressive aspects of the ADA are arguably overwhelmed by the many flaws, caveats, and contradictions which are contained within the law as conceived and written.

In the years since Marta Russell wrote the enclosed pieces, some of the shortcomings of the ADA have come under revision by Congress. In response to two decades in which US courts had interpreted nearly all meaning and applicability out of the ADA, President Bush signed into law the ADA Amendments Act (ADAAA) of 2008. The stated purpose of the ADAAA was to redefine the term disability itself in a more expansive manner than hitherto. While this more inclusive definition is certainly welcome, the ADAAA in fact promised and delivered little in terms of correcting the misuses and abuses of the ADA.

As others have since pointed out, the ADAAA does not address a number of the most glaring inconsistencies and problems in the original language of the ADA.[3] Nor has its track record in the legal system proven substantially better than that of the original ADA. For these reasons it can confidently be stated that, despite changes in the law, Russell's critiques of the ADA herein remain just as relevant and apt as ever.

Beyond economic theory or polemics regarding more oft-discussed topics, Russell's contributions further shone as her gaze swept across an expansive field of issues. She addressed herself to questions of housing, mass incarceration, environmental inequality, imperialism, the welfare system, eugenics, and euthanasia. To all these concerns she brought to bear a characteristically searing, systemic, and edifying analysis.

Along these lines, Russell had a notable capacity to effectively present her arguments to an incredibly wide and diverse set of audiences. Her writing carried equal sharpness and intelligibility whether it appeared in a more esoteric academic journal or in an anarchist webzine; whether engaging in "high" theory or "low" muckraking. Among other things, this book has attempted to collect writings that demonstrate this variety.

Although the pieces in this book were originally written separately, at different moments and for different publications, they have been conjoined here into a coherent whole. As editor, I have selected, arranged, and slightly adapted the following essays in such a manner that they are best read as successive chapters of a single cumulative argument or thesis. While it is possible to read the individual chapters in isolation to adequate effect, this book is not intended as a mere anthology.

To this end, I have taken the liberty of editing the pieces so that they complement each other without producing needless redundancies. I have made no excisions whatsoever to the political content of the pieces. I have only made cuts where entire paragraphs, passages, or sections were repeated verbatim in multiple essays. This has been done for the sole reason of making the reading of this book as a whole a less cumbersome or tedious experience. The end result is that anything that has been cut from a given individual chapter can still be found in its entirety in another part of the book. Such cuts are indicated throughout this book by bracketed ellipses, like so [. . .]. Any editorial commentary or citations that I have added will be found in the text and endnotes, like so [—Ed.].

There is one additional editorial matter that I would like to draw the reader's attention to. Marta Russell was at her most prolific between the years of 1998 and 2005, and all of the pieces found in this book are dated from that period. Thus, much of the specific topical data and statistics she posits are from fifteen to twenty years ago. However, after cross-referencing current and updated figures, I have decided to leave all of it untouched as in the original. There are three reasons for this.

First, much of the data she deployed has remained unchanged (e.g., disability unemployment and poverty rates). Second, in those instances in which the precise numbers have changed, the trajectory or tendency that Russell advanced a given data set as proof of has remained constant (e.g., depicting an increase or decrease in a particular vector over time).

Third, it is simply the case that the enduring potency and relevance of Russell's writings has little to do with the specific data she employs (all of which she anyhow extracted from other readily available sources). Instead, the importance of Marta Russell's writings, then as now, resides in the overarching theoretical, analytical, and polemical arguments she develops; the manner in which she relates the general and manifest phenomena of capitalism and disability as such, rather than in the particulars or ephemera.

Nevertheless, I have appended to this book a more current collection of disability statistics. These include updates to many of the original figures found in Russell's pieces, as well as some additional figures of intersecting relevance. Those who are coming to this book with little to no existing knowledge of the subject matter may actually find it quite helpful to begin by reviewing the appendix before approaching the main body of this text.

Finally, I would like to extend special thanks and mention to the family and friends of Marta Russell who helped make this book possible. First among them is Russell's daughter, Georgia Scheele, whose feedback has been vital at every step and in every aspect of this book's production; Russell's friend and partner, Steve Weiss, who provided essential biographical, political, and historical background information; and Russell's colleague and co-thinker, Ravi Malhotra, editor of the eulogistic symposium, *Disability Politics in a Global Economy: Essays in Honour of Marta Russell* (New York: Routledge, 2017), whose encouragement, critiques, and intercessions were central to this book's maturation.

Capitalism and the
Disability Rights Movement

Marta Russell and Ravi Malhotra

Having a disability is conventionally regarded as a personal tragedy which the individual must overcome, or as a medical problem to which the individual must become adjusted. In 1976, however, the Union of the Physically Impaired Against Segregation (UPIAS) in Britain made a significant advance when it pointed out that "disability is something imposed on top of our impairments by the way we are unnecessarily isolated and excluded from full participation in society."[1] Among those concerned with disability it soon became common ground that "it is society which disables persons with impairments."

This social model of disability[2] necessitates a rethinking of prevalent definitions. Leaving aside biological or physical-anthropological definitions of disability which make it appear that impaired persons are *naturally* and, therefore, justifiably excluded from the *labor force*, even mainstream definitions have serious shortcomings. The World Health Organization (WHO), for instance, defines impairment (the condition of being deaf or blind, or having impaired mobility or being otherwise impaired) as the physiological "problem"; disability as restricted functions or activities resulting from an impairment; and handicap as the "disadvantage resulting from the impairment or disability, that limits or prevents the fulfillment of a role."[3] This terminology has been criticized by social model theorists of disability because it relies primarily on medical definitions and uses a bio-physiological definition of normality. Further, "the environment" within which this "disadvantage" is located, "is represented as 'neutral,' and any negative consequences of this approach for the person with an impairment are regarded as inevitable or acceptable rather than as disabling barriers."[4]

Reconceptualizing disability as an outcome of the political economy, however, also requires acknowledging the limitations of the *minority* model of disability, which views it as the product of a disabling social and architectural environment. In this view the fundamental source of the problems encountered by disabled persons is prejudicial or discriminatory attitudes, implying that by erasing mistaken attitudes society will accept *difference* and equality will flourish.[5] This approach diverts attention from the mode of production and the concrete social relations that produce the disabling barriers, exclusion, and inequalities facing disabled persons.

In contrast, we take the view that disability is a socially created category derived from labor relations, a product of the exploitative economic structure of capitalist society: one which creates (and then oppresses) the so-called *disabled* body as one of the conditions that allow the capitalist class to accumulate wealth. Seen in this light, disability is an aspect of the central contradiction of capitalism, and disability politics that do not accept this are, at best, fundamentally flawed strategies of reform or, worse, forms of bourgeois ideology that prevent this from being seen.

Capitalist Beginnings and the Commodification of the Impaired Body

The primary oppression of disabled persons (i.e., of people who could work in a workplace that was accommodated to their needs) is their exclusion from exploitation as wage laborers.[6] Studies show that disabled persons experience lower labor-force participation rates, higher unemployment rates, and higher part-time employment rates than non-disabled persons.[7] In the US, 79 percent of working-age disabled adults say they would prefer to work,[8] yet in 2000 only 30.5 percent of those with a work disability between ages sixteen and sixty-four were in the labor force and only 27.6 percent were employed; while 82.1 percent of non-disabled persons in this age group were either employed (78.6 percent) or actively seeking work for pay.[9] Though having a job does not always translate into an above-poverty-level existence, disabled persons' historical exclusion from the labor force has undoubtedly contributed to their poverty. Disabled persons are nearly three times as likely to live below the current poverty line—29 percent live in poverty, compared to 10 percent of non-disabled people.[10] In the US fully one third of disabled adults live in a household with an annual income of less than $15,000,[11] while the 300 to 400 million living in developing countries have even less chance of employment and exist in abject poverty, usually with no social safety nets at all.[12]

Historical materialism provides a theoretical base from which to explain these conditions and outcomes. Under feudalism, economic exploitation was direct and political, made possible by the feudal concentration of land ownership. While a few owners reaped the surplus, many living on their estates worked for subsistence and disabled people were able to participate in this economy to varying degrees.[13] Notwithstanding religious superstition about disabled people during the Middle Ages, and significant persecution of them, the rural production process that predominated prior to the Industrial Revolution permitted many disabled people to make a genuine contribution to daily economic life.[14]

With the advent of capitalism, people were no longer tied to the land, but they were forced to find work that would pay a wage—or starve; and as production became industrialized, people's bodies were increasingly valued for their ability to function like machines.

Bosses could push non-disabled workers to produce at ever increasing rates of speed. [. . .] As work became more rationalized, requiring precise mechanical movements of the body, repeated in quicker succession, impaired persons—the deaf, blind, mentally impaired, and those with mobility difficulties—were seen as—and, without job accommodations to meet their impairments, were—less "fit" to do the tasks required of factory workers, and were increasingly excluded from paid employment.[15] And so "the operation of the labour market in the nineteenth century effectively depressed handicapped people of all kinds to the bottom of the market."[16]

Industrial capitalism thus created not only a class of proletarians but also a new class of "disabled" who did not conform to the standard worker's body and whose labor-power was effectively erased, excluded from paid work.[17] As a result, disabled persons came to be regarded as a social problem and a justification emerged for segregating them out of mainstream life.[18] [. . .]

After World War II the expansion of the welfare state in most industrialized countries gave rise to two contradictory trends for disabled people. On the one hand, there was increased state provision of social services. On the other hand, there was also a greater attempt to regulate the lives of the recipients of these services. This was particularly the case in Britain and other European countries. The Beveridge Report in Britain symbolized this project and it clearly envisaged an "ableist" and patriar-chal system in which white male able-bodied workers were the primary breadwinners, married women worked in the home, and disabled people were defined as a medi-cal problem and relegated to the expertise of specialists.[19] However, even in the US, which adopted a relatively modest welfare state, one saw increased provision of social programs such as segregated sheltered workshops which exploited disabled workers in part by paying below-minimum wages. This was a component of the "dictatorship over needs" inherent in the bureaucratism of the welfare state which transformed people into objects of state policy called "clients."[20]

The "medicalization" of disablement and the tools of classification clearly played an important role in establishing divisions between the "disabled" and the "able-bodied." Disability became an important "boundary" category whereby people were allocated to either a work-based or a needs-based system of distribu-tion. [. . .] The disability category was essential to the development of an exploit-able workforce in early capitalism and remains indispensable as an instrument of the state in controlling the labor supply today.[21] By focusing on curing so-called abnormalities and segregating those who could not be cured into the administra-tive category of "disabled," medicine cooperated in shoving less exploitable work-ers out of the mainstream workforce.[22]

So, just as capitalism forces workers into the wage relationship, it equally forcefully coerces disabled workers out of it.[23] Disabled workers face inherent eco-nomic discrimination within the capitalist system, stemming from employers' ex-pectations of encountering additional production costs when hiring or retaining a nonstandard (disabled) worker as opposed to a standard (non-disabled) worker who has no need for job accommodations, interpreters, readers, environmental modifications, liability insurance, maximum health care coverage (inclusive of at-tendant services), or even health care coverage at all.[24] "Disability" is a social cre-ation which defines who is offered a job and who is not, and what it means varies with the level of economic activity. [. . .]

An employee who is too costly (i.e., significantly disabled) to add to net prof-its at the current level of output will not likely become (or remain) an employee at all.[25] US Census data consistently show that, as compared with the four-fifths of working-age persons with no disability who have jobs, only just over one-quarter of people with a significant disability do so.[26]

Employers and investors rely on the preservation of the status quo labor sys-tem which does not require them to absorb the nonstandard costs of employing disabled workers under the current mode of production, let alone the 800 million people who are totally or partially unemployed worldwide. Consequently, disabled individuals who are currently not in the mainstream workforce, who are collecting disability benefits and who could work if their impairments were accommodated, are not tallied into employers' costs of doing business.[27] The disability benefit system thus serves as a socially legitimized means by which the capitalist class can avoid hiring or retaining nonstandard workers and can "morally" shift the cost of supporting them onto poverty-based government programs—thereby perpetuating their poverty.

Being categorized as "disabled," however, and the subsequent impoverishment that so many face when struggling to survive on disability benefits,[28] serves another class function: it generates a very realistic fear among workers of becoming disabled. At base, the inadequate safety net is a product of the owning class's fear of losing full control of what they do with the means of production;[29] the American work ethic is a mechanism of social control that ensures capitalists a reliable workforce for making profits. If workers were provided with a social safety net that adequately protected them through unemployment, sickness, disability, and old age, laborers would gain a stronger position from which to negotiate their conditions of employment. American business retains its power over the working class through a fear of destitution that would be weakened if the safety net were to actually become safe.

Disabled persons who do not offer a body which will enhance profit-making as laborers are used to shore up US capitalism by other means. Entrepreneurs and rehabilitation specialists have made impaired bodies of use to the economic order by shaping disablement into big business[30] and turning the disabled body into a commodity around which social policies get created or rejected according to their market value.[31] The corporate solution to disablement—institutionalization in a nursing home, for instance—evolved from the realization that disabled people could be made to serve profit because public financing guaranteed the revenue (in the USA, Medicaid funds 60 percent of the cost, Medicare 15 percent, private insurance 25 percent). [...]

Despite the efforts of the disability rights movement to deinstitutionalize disabled populations and shift policy towards the provision of in-home services, the logic of capital reasserts itself via the recommodification of the disabled body in the home (insofar as public funding permits—with the advent of "managed care," trying to limit costs, there is an increased financial motive to underserve). Corporations have taken an interest in the money-making potential of the in-home services field, and indeed promote the in-home services model as they build their new "home-care" empires. As Jim Charlton puts it, "the transformation of people into commodities hides their dehumanization and exploitation by other human beings: it becomes simply an economic fact of life."[32]

It is also evident that the definition of disability is not static but fundamentally linked to the needs of capital accumulation. Hence, when the welfare state entered into "crisis," governments attempted to narrow the definition of disablement and to cut entitlement levels. There have also been widespread closures of the institutions that warehoused disabled people, but without an allocation of adequate resources and services to enable them to live independently. Yet this withdrawal of the state from certain types of benefits does not entail any rupture in the intervention of the state in the lives of disabled people. The state's interventionist role remains but is refocused on the ruthless cutting of social expenditures, including services and income support programs to disabled people, in the name of neoliberal efficiency.[33]

The rise of capitalism has thus seen dramatic changes in the ideological classification and treatment of disabled people. Yet while socialists have considered the relationship between the rise of capitalism and, for instance, the enactment of the English Poor Laws,[34] the classification, marginalization, and oppression of disabled people have been largely ignored. Speaking generally, the rise of capitalism clearly had contradictory outcomes for disabled people. On the one hand, there were positive effects in terms of better medical technology that lengthened the life span and increased the quality of life for those who could afford it. On the other hand, there were some very negative effects, including classification into rigid and arbitrary diagnostic categories and incarceration in oppressive institutions. Exclusion from exploitation in the wage-labor system, as the "deserving poor," lies at the core of disabled peoples' oppression in every aspect of modern life. [. . .]

Disability Rights Movements: Prospects and Limitations

While new social movements fighting against racism, patriarchy, and homophobia were gaining prominence in many Western countries in the 1960s,[35] movements of disabled people, with more or less coherent programs and ideologies, also slowly emerged. Unlike other social movements, the various disability rights movements[36] to date have received relatively little attention from socialists, union activists, or academics, even in the US, which arguably has one of the strongest and oldest disability rights movements.[37] Yet an examination of their various trajectories suggests useful insights that those seeking to challenge capitalism in other struggles can learn from and incorporate in them. To the extent that widespread accommodation to the needs of disabled workers would necessarily transform the workplace and challenge expectations of ever-increasing productivity rates, the disability rights movement can be seen as radically democratic and counter-hegemonic in potential and scope.

An important analytical distinction must be made between charitable organizations established for disabled people, sometimes by parents of disabled children, and organizations directly controlled by disabled people. In the former category, the organizations, usually based on a diagnostic category linked to impairment, do not necessarily reflect the views and experiences of disabled people themselves, notwithstanding that they may do occasional work that is beneficial. In fact, the implicit ideological agenda of these paternalistic organizations is that disabled people are unable to advocate on their own behalf.[38] Moreover, the fact that their mandate rests on usually arbitrary diagnostic categories places unwarranted emphasis on medical issues and not enough on the barriers imposed by the physical environment and the class system. The resulting fragmentation— splintering disabled people into literally hundreds of different categories—also works to make cross-disability solidarity that much more difficult. Just as importantly, these organizations, like NGOs in other sectors, are often directly tied to the state through funding arrangements. Consequently, they are extremely limited in their ability to criticize government policy, even if they were so inclined, for fear of losing funding and access to decision-makers. In fact, organizations run for disabled people dramatically outnumber those controlled by disabled people, and receive far more generous funding.[39] The severe limitations of their politics should come as no surprise, given the questionable and co-opted record of NGOs in all contexts.

In sharp contrast, organizations run by disabled people have at least the potential for more radical politics. In the late 1960s, the Independent Living (IL) movement emerged in Berkeley, California, spearheaded by a disabled students' group known as The Rolling Quads. It sought to promote the empowerment of disabled people and focused attention on the structural barriers imposed by the built environment, not on the impairments of individuals. The first Independent Living Center (ILC), based on the social-political model of disablement, was founded in Berkeley and sought to broaden struggles for empowerment to include students and non-students alike. Within a few years, a network of hundreds of ILCs had sprouted across the United States, as well as a number of other countries including Britain, Canada, and Brazil.[40]

The emergence of the IL movement was unquestionably a step forward for the disability rights movement. The shared sense of consciousness fostered by collective action is an important first step in the building of any social movement. By redefining as political issues requiring redress by society at large what had been previously regarded by most people as private troubles (just as the women's movement had done), the IL movement provided a basis for a vital social movement;[41] and the vitality of the women's movement, the Black civil rights movement, the gay and lesbian movement, the Chicano movement, and other new social justice movements created an opening in which the case for eradicating disability oppression could also get a hearing.

Nevertheless, there were and are serious contradictions in the IL philosophy. On the one hand, it seeks to promote autonomy and self-determination for disabled people. On the other, it implicitly accepts the foundations of free market ideology by framing the debate in terms of the right of disabled people as consumers to receive equal treatment from the marketplace. The ability to access the marketplace is cold comfort to the huge proportion of disabled people living in poverty or near-poverty conditions. In a capitalist society, after all, access to the marketplace is predicated on having the purchasing power to buy the services in question. A strategy of disability liberation politics entirely dependent on that purchasing power is so impoverished as to be of assistance to only a tiny fraction of the most privileged disabled people. It also tends to marginalize the concerns of women and minorities. By accepting free market principles as a given the IL movement undermined its radical potential to truly empower disabled people. In the worst cases, some IL centers, afraid of rocking the boat and losing state funding, have become little more than venues for peer counseling and organizing picnics. Only by questioning the very basis of the rules of the market can there be liberation for disabled people.

Yet there have always been some strands of the disability rights movement that have resisted the dangers of state co-optation and engaged in militant, in-your-face tactics that demonstrate the possibility for resistance and broader social change. For example, decades before the emergence of the IL movement, the League for the Physically Handicapped, a group of some three hundred disabled pensioners in New York, engaged in civil disobedience during the Great Depression to protest their discriminatory rejection from the employment offered by the Works Progress Administration (WPA).[42] Much later, in 1970, an organization called Disabled in Action (DIA) was founded and adopted the tactic of direct political protest. During the 1972 presidential election DIA militants joined with disabled and often highly politicized Vietnam veterans, clearly an influential base of support, to demand an on-camera debate with President Nixon. They also organized a demonstration at the Lincoln Memorial after President Nixon vetoed a spending bill to fund disability programs.[43]

Perhaps the most memorable moment in recent disability rights history in the US came during the struggle in 1977 to have the regulations pursuant to section 504 of the Rehabilitation Act of 1973 issued. The regulations were to outline how it was illegal for federal agencies, contractors, or public universities to discriminate on the basis of disability. They had been delayed by previous administrations but there was an expectation that the new Carter administration would fulfill its promise to issue the regulations. When it became obvious that policy makers were stalling and wanted to substantially modify the regulations so as to permit continued segregation in education and other areas of public life, disability rights activists mobilized in a number of cities across the US. While most demonstrations ended fairly quickly, in Berkeley the movement took on a truly extraordinary trajectory. There, disability rights activists occupied the Department of Health, Education, and Welfare (HEW) federal building for some twenty-five days, culminating in total victory: the issuing of the regulations without any amendments.[44]

In the process, the participants in the occupation found themselves transformed by the experience. They discovered their ability to change the world through political action. Whereas divisions along arbitrary diagnostic categories based on a flawed medical-model approach to disablement have often created serious tensions in building social movements, in this instance people with different impairments were able to unite around a common strategy and build solidarity in what was clearly a key turning-point. Links were also forged with other social movements.

For instance, unions and civil rights organizations donated food for the demonstrators, and it was prepared by the local branch of the militant Black Panther Party. It is clear, however, that the HEW protests built on the legacy left by the pioneering work of the IL movement, notwithstanding its structural and ideological limitations.

In both the USA and Britain, a small cadre of militant disability rights activists have continued a tradition of struggle from below. In 1983 a new organization, the American Disabled for Accessible Public Transit (ADAPT), was established by disability rights activists in several important cities in the US to highlight the inaccessibility of public transportation for people with mobility impairments. It quickly became known for its confrontational and often successful tactics. For instance, it repeatedly disrupted the conventions of the American Public Transit Association, leading to mass arrests, in protest against their unwillingness to implement modifications to make public transportation more accessible. They also demonstrated a dramatic flair when they engaged in symbolic forms of protest, like crawling up the numerous stairs at the entrances of public buildings to highlight their inaccessibility.[45] It is hardly surprising that more moderate disability organizations have largely shunned or even attacked ADAPT; a coalition of IL centers in Michigan went so far as to condemn its actions in a letter to the state's governor.[46] More recently ADAPT has switched its priorities to securing better funding for a national attendant services program that would permit disabled people to live in the community as opposed to being institutionalized.

Yet, ultimately, even the most grassroots disability organizations in both the US and Britain appear theoretically ambiguous in their ideological formulations. They have yet to adopt an anti-capitalist agenda that sees disablement as a product of the class system. Moreover, in both the US and Britain the passage of disability rights legislation, which is individualistic at base, removes an element of coherence from the political praxis of even the most militant disability rights organizations. A failure to see their common links with other marginalized members of society, including the reserve army of the unemployed, welfare recipients, the increasingly large segment of society working in part-time jobs or in jobs that do not pay a living wage, and others, may result in the squandering of the promise of the various disability rights movements on the shoals of identity politics—or, worse, on postmodern discourse whose theorists refuse to name capitalism as a cause for their oppression. A turn to class politics and historical materialism, fully cognizant of its risks and limitations, is what the disability rights movements need most. [. . .]

I.

The Political Economy
of Disability

CHAPTER 1

Marxism and Disability

Any movement for social equality, or freedom from oppression, has something in common with Marxism. In liberal capitalist economies, such social movements often consist of reform efforts to enact civil and human rights legislation. The very perception that there is a need for legal rights to protect marginal classes of persons suggests that oppression exists, for if members of a particular group were not oppressed, they would not have barriers to remove nor rights to be gained. Marxists identify structural injustices that need rectifying and seek to change society through action.

From here, however, Marxism parts ways with traditional liberalism. Liberal solutions, Marx would argue, must fall short of remedying oppression because liberalism fails to acknowledge the central role of productive activities and labor relations in history. Specifically, liberalism fails to expose either the way society is organized for the production of the material conditions of its existence or that the mode of production plays the chief causal role in determining oppressive social outcomes. Marxism posits the principal motive for historical change is the struggle among social classes over their corresponding shares in the harvest of production. With respect to the social condition of disablement, the focus is on the struggle of the class of disabled persons for the right to enter the labor force and on the place the disabled body occupies within the political economy of capitalism. The term *disabled* is used to designate the socioeconomic disadvantages imposed on top of a physical or mental impairment.[1] Bypassing biological or physical anthropological definitions that make it appear that impaired persons are naturally and, therefore, justifiably excluded from the labor force or that one is handicapped by ableist biases reflected in the physical environment, this article takes the view that disability is a socially created category derived from labor relations. For this reason, *disabled persons* is the nomenclature of choice rather than *people with disabilities*. *Disabled* is used to classify persons deemed less exploitable or not exploitable by the owning class who control the means of production in a capitalist economy.

This article presents an overview of Marxism, from the theory of labor power relations to capitalism's role in defining disability, to show that our economic system produces the state of disablement and that the prevailing rate of exploitation of labor determines who is considered disabled and who is not. The article then explains how class interests perpetuate the exclusion of disabled persons (and others) from the workforce through systemic compulsory unemployment. Disability is conceptualized as a product of the exploitative economic structure of capitalist society; one that creates the so-called "disabled body" to permit a small capitalist class to create the economic conditions necessary to accumulate vast wealth.

The Primacy of Production:
Profits and the Nonconforming Body

The man who possesses no other property than his labor power must, in all conditions of society and culture, be the slave of other men who have made themselves the owners of the material conditions of labor. He can only work with their permission, hence live only with their permission.

—Karl Marx, *Critique of the Gotha Programme*[2]

Marx's most significant contribution to history was to pinpoint the primary cause of oppression as economic: The capitalist class exploits the working masses (wage earners) for profit to the detriment (alienation) of the working class. Private property relations entail an exploiting owning class that lives off the surpluses produced by an exploited non-owning, and thus, oppressed class. Feudal and slave-based modes of production also had exploitative relations of production, though different than those of capitalism. The surpluses are extracted by different methods in capitalism, feudalism, and slavery.[3] Exploitation, in strict Marxist terms, refers to the appropriation of surplus value through the wage relationship.

A primary basis of oppression of disabled persons (those who could work with accommodations) is their exclusion from exploitation as wage laborers. [. . .]

A class analysis makes apparent that it is neither accident nor a result of "the natural order of things" that disabled persons rank at the bottom of the economic ladder. Capitalism has certain disadvantages, such as persistent vast inequalities.[4] A chief disadvantage is that many people are unemployed, underemployed, and impoverished against their will. Although capitalism has sometimes held the promise of expanding the base of people benefitting from it, for disabled persons it largely has been an exclusionary system.

Economic historians, such as Karl Polanyi and E. P. Thompson, have pointed out that capitalist beginnings required a major change in the concept of human labor. The effects on the disabled population can be explained by tracing how work evolved under capitalism. In precapitalist societies, economic exploitation, made possible by the feudal concentration of land ownership, was direct and political. Although a few owners reaped the surplus, the many living on an estate worked for subsistence. With the advent of capitalism, the discipline of labor was now economic, not political. The worker was "'free' in the double sense that he or she was no longer tied to a given manor and had the right to choose between work and death."[5]

Under Marx's *labor theory of value*, the basis of capitalist accumulation is the concept of *surplus labor value*.[6] The worker's ability to work—Marx calls this labor power—is sold to the capitalist in return for a wage. If the worker produced an amount of value equivalent only to her wage, there would be nothing left over for the capitalist and no reason to hire the worker. But because labor power has the capacity to produce more value than its own wages, the worker can be made to work longer than the labor-time equivalent of the wage received.[7] The amount of labor-time that the worker works to produce value equivalent to her wage, Marx calls necessary labor. The additional labor-time that the worker works beyond this, Marx calls surplus labor, and the value it produces, he calls surplus value. The capitalist appropriates the surplus value as a source of profits.[8] So writes Marx, "the secret of the self-expansion of capital [of profit] resolves itself into having the disposal of a definite quantity of other people's unpaid labor."[9]

To Descartes, the body was a machine; to the industrialist, individuals' bodies were valued for their ability to function like machines. As human beings were gathered into the "satanic mills" (William Blake) to accomplish the task of capital accumulation, impediments were erected to disabled people's survival. New enforced factory discipline, time-keeping, and production norms worked against a slower, more self-determined and flexible work pattern into which many disabled people had been integrated.[10] [...]

Reproducing Disablement

Despite the availability of advanced assistive technology and an information-age economy that has expanded the realm of jobs disabled persons could readily perform, body politics under standard business practice are still a part of the employment struggle of disabled persons. Economic discrimination—the structural mechanisms that permit and even encourage a systemic discrimination against disabled workers—has not been fully confronted.

Productive labor under capitalism refers to the production of surplus value near or above the prevailing rate of exploitation. Because the material basis of capitalist accumulation is the mining of surplus labor from the workforce, the owners and managers of the businesses necessarily have to discriminate against those workers whose impairments add to the cost of production. Expenses to accommodate disabled persons in the workplace will be resisted as an addition to the fixed capital portion of constant capital. In effect, the prevailing rate of exploitation determines who is disabled and who is not. [...]

Any executive knows that employer-capitalists will resist any extraordinary cost of doing business. For example, a leading economist in the Law and Economics movement, Richard Epstein, states that the employment provisions of the Americans with Disabilities Act (ADA) are a "disguised subsidy" and that "successful enforcement under the guise of "reasonable accommodation" necessarily impedes the operation and efficiency of firms."[11] [...]

Disabled workers face inherent economic discrimination within the capitalist system, stemming from employers' expectations of encountering additional nonstandard production costs when hiring or retaining a nonstandard (disabled) worker as opposed to a standard (non-disabled) worker with no need for accommodation, interpreters, environmental modifications, liability insurance, maximum health care coverage (inclusive of attendant services), or even health care coverage at all.[12]

The category of "disabled" as applied to the labor market is a social creation; business practices determine who has a job and who does not. An employee who is too costly due to a significant impairment will not likely become (or remain) an employee.[13] Census data tends to support this view. For working-age persons with no disability, the likelihood of having a job is 82.1 percent.[14] For people with a non-severe disability, the rate is 76.9 percent; the rate drops to 26.1 percent for those with a significant disability.[15] According to the 2001 National Organization on Disability/Harris Survey, employment rates are 19 percent for those with a severe disability, 51 percent for those moderately disabled, and 32 percent for those with any disability.

Data from the Equal Employment Opportunity Commission (EEOC) suggests a strong relationship between disability onset and employer firings. The most prevalent cause of complaints disabled workers file with the EEOC are over involuntary termination of employment upon disablement.[16] Of the 171,669 employment discrimination charges filed with the EEOC for the period of July 26, 1992, through February 28, 1998, 53.7 percent involve the issue of discharge, and another 32.1 percent involve the failure to provide reasonable accommodation.[17] The ADA itself explicitly states that employers are not required to provide an accommodation if it would impose an "undue hardship" on the business. The disabled person's theoretical right to an accommodation is really no right at all; it is dependent upon the employer's calculus.

Managers and owners, in general, have only tolerated the use of disabled workers when they could save on the variable portion of cost of production, resulting in lower wages for workers. The sheltered workshop is the prototype for justifying below-minimum wages for disabled people. [. . .] According to the *Washington Post*, 6,300 such US workshops employ more than 391,000 disabled workers, some paying 20 percent to 30 percent of the minimum wage: as little as $3.26 an hour and $11 per week.[18]

Census Bureau findings substantiate that disabled workers' pay in the regular labor market also falls to the low end of the wage scale. [. . .] Over a lifetime, the disparity in earnings represents tens of thousands of dollars lost to disabled workers (and pocketed by business).

In liberal capitalist economies, redistributionist laws like the ADA are necessarily in tension with business class interests, which resist such cost-shifting burdens. Representatives of small and medium businesses, such as the US Chamber of Commerce, the National Association of Manufacturers, the American Banking Association, and the National Federation of Independent Business, opposed the ADA. [. . .]

Marxian political economy tells us that disability oppression has less to do with prejudicial attitudes than with an accountant's calculation of the present cost of production versus the potential benefits to the future rate of exploitation. Discrimination can be ameliorated, but not eliminated, by changing attitudes. Only a system of material production that takes into account the human consequences of its development can eliminate discrimination against disabled persons. [. . .]

Class Interests Regulating the Labor Supply in Disability Policy

It is often claimed that disabled persons are invisible, disregarded by mainstream society, and irrelevant to the workings of society. This analysis has attempted to explain that the "unemployables" have been deliberately shut out of the labor force due to a capitalist economy that so far has dictated their exclusion by measure of economic calculations that favor the business class. It further posits that disabled persons are further oppressed in capitalist societies by having been purposely shifted onto social welfare or segregated into institutions for similar reasons—to keep workers who could not be profitably employed out of the mainstream workforce but also to exert social control over the entire labor supply.

Marx explains that capitalism is a system of "forced labor—no matter how much it may seem to result from free contractual agreement."[19] It is coercion because capitalists own the means of production and laborers do not. Without ownership of factories and other means of production, workers lack their own access to the means of making a livelihood. By this very fact, workers are compelled to sell their labor to capitalists for a wage because the alternative is homelessness or starvation or both. Deborah Stone in *The Disabled State* convincingly argues that in order to restructure the workforce for the demands of early capitalist production, it was first necessary to eradicate all viable alternatives to wage labor for the mass population.

Labor is a resource to be manipulated like capital and land. Stone writes, "The disability concept was essential to the development of an exploitable workforce in early capitalism and remains indispensable as an instrument of the state in controlling labor supply."[20]

Regulating the composition of the labor force through social policy became key to ensuring an ongoing exploitable labor supply. Disability became an important boundary category through which persons were allocated to either the work-based or needs-based system of distribution. In the United States, disability came to be defined explicitly in relation to the labor market. For instance, in some workers' compensation statutes, a laborer's body is rated by impairment according to its functioning parts.[21] In Social Security law, disabled means medically unable to engage in work activity.[22]

Our institutions (particularly medical and social welfare institutions) have historically held disablement to be an individual problem, not the result of economic or social forces.[23] They have equated disability with physiological, anatomical, or mental "defects" and hegemonically held these conditions responsible for the disabled person's lack of full participation in the economic life of our society. This approach presumed a biological inferiority of disabled persons.[24] Pathologizing characteristics such as blindness, deafness, and physical and mental impairments that have naturally appeared in the human race throughout history became a means of social control that has relegated disabled persons to isolation and exclusion from society.[25] By placing the focus on curing the so-called abnormality and segregating the incurables into the administrative category of disabled, medicine bolstered the capitalist business interest to shove less exploitable workers with impairments out of the workforce.

This exclusion was rationalized by Social Darwinists, who used biology to argue that heredity (race and disability status) prevailed over the class and economic issues raised by Marx and others. Just as the inferior weren't meant to survive in nature, they weren't meant to survive in a competitive society. For nineteenth-century tycoons, Social Darwinism proved a marvelous rationale for leaving the surplus population to die in poverty. Capitalism set up production dynamics that devalued less exploitable or non-exploitable bodies, and Social Darwinism theorized their disposability. If it was natural that disabled persons were not to survive, then the capitalist class was off the hook to design a more equitable economic system—one that would accommodate the body that did not conform to the standard worker body driven to labor for owning-class profit.

Social analysts describe the disability needs-based system as a privilege because "as an administrative category, it carries with it permission to be exempt from the work-based system."[26] In conservative terms, disability can be described as "an essential part of the moral economy."[27] In the public debate over redistribution of societal resources, public assistance is viewed as legitimate for those deemed unable to work, but the disabled individuals on public benefits under US capitalism do not have any objective right to a decent standard of living, even with privileged status, nor is the definition of disability etched in stone. As Stone pointed out, the definition of disability is flexible; the state (which evaluates disability status) controls the labor supply by expanding or contracting the numbers of persons who qualify as disabled, often for political and economic reasons.[28]

Neither privilege nor morality theories adequately describe the function of the needs-based system. A political economy analyst would ask what role do public disability benefits play to further the machinations of production and wealth accumulation?

The vast majority of those on Social Security Disability Insurance (SSDI), the deserving workers involuntarily severed from their wages, are not privileged. They are financially oppressed by less than adequate aid. Public disability benefits hover at what is determined an official poverty level. In 2000, the Department of Health and Human Services set the poverty threshold for one at $8,350. Because $759 was the average per month benefit that a disabled worker received from SSDI and $373 was the average federal income for the needs-based Supplemental Security Income (SSI), the annual income of more than 10 million disabled persons on these programs was between $4,000 and $10,000 that year. The extremely low SSI benefit was set up for those with no work history or not enough quarters of work to qualify for SSDI: the least valued disabled members of society.

It would not accurately describe the depth of poverty faced by those on disability benefits, however, without explaining that the current system of measuring poverty dates back to the 1960s. Government has never adjusted the equation to take into account the sharp rise in housing, medical care, and childcare costs of the following decades that have altered the average household's economic picture. The Urban Institute concluded that in order to be comparable to the original threshold, the poverty level would have to be at least 50 percent higher than the current official standard. If basic needs were refigured to the modern market, almost a quarter of the American people would be deemed to be living in poverty.[29]

Most important, public policy that equates disablement with poverty means that becoming disabled (a nonworker) translates into a life of financial hardship, whether one has public insurance or not, and generates a very realistic fear in workers of becoming disabled. At base, the inadequate safety net is a product of the owning class's fear of losing control of the means of production. The all-encompassing value placed on work is necessary to produce wealth. The American work ethic is a mechanism of social control that ensures capitalists of a reliable workforce for making profits. If workers were provided with a federal social safety net that adequately protected them through unemployment, sickness, disability, and old age, then business would have less control over the workforce because labor would gain a stronger position from which to negotiate their conditions of employment, such as fair wages and safe working conditions. American business retains its power over the working class through a fear of destitution that would be weakened if the safety net were to actually become safe. This, in turn, causes oppression for the less valued nonworking disabled members of our society; those who do not provide a body to support profit making (for whatever reason) are relegated to economic hardship or institutionalized to shore up the capitalist system.[30] Nursing homes, for instance, have commodified disabled bodies so that the least productive can be made of use to the economic order.

A materialist analysis suggests that capitalism has created a powerful class of persons dependent upon the productive labor of some and the exclusion of others. Business owners and Wall Street investors rely on the preservation of the status quo labor system (not having to absorb the nonstandard costs disabled workers represent in the current mode of production or the reserve army of unemployed). [...] The US work-based/needs-based system is a socially legitimized means by which business and investors can economically discriminate and "morally" shift the cost of disabled workers onto poverty-based government benefit programs rather than be required to hire or retain the unemployables as members of the mainstream workforce.

Consequently, disabled individuals currently not in the workforce collecting SSDI or SSI who could work with an accommodation are not tallied into employers' cost of doing business. Employers do not pay direct premiums for Social Security disability programs. (The cost of direct government and private payments to support disabled persons of employable age who do not have a job is estimated to be $232 billion annually). Instead, disabled persons have no right to a job. Civil rights laws do not intervene in the labor market to mandate employment of disabled persons (not even to adhere to affirmative action, much less to a quota system like Germany's); rather, these costs are shifted onto the shoulders of the working class and the low middle class who pay the majority of Social Security taxes while business and our economic system is absolved of responsibility. This analysis is not suggesting that benefits be dissolved; employment discrimination is related to reliance on public aid because those who experience labor market discrimination are also more likely to need public assistance.[31] It does suggest that capitalism is a system that forces non-disabled persons into the labor market but also just as forcefully coerces many disabled persons out. Oppression occurs in either case.

Lingering Questions

A Marxian analysis demonstrates that the employment predicament of disabled persons is produced by the economic and social forces of capitalism. The mode of production is key to explaining the organization of society, to preserving existing class relations of production. It is neither arbitrary nor irrational that disabled persons have been excluded from education, transportation, and other social spheres. Rather, it is logical that such a state of affairs would exist as long as disabled persons have little value as workers to the capitalist class.

The civil rights model holds that disabled persons need the protections afforded by the ADA to help shrink the pervasive gaps that still exist between them and non-disabled Americans. This equal opportunity approach, however, assumes that the employment needs of disabled people can be solved under our present economic system. [. . .] The economy dictates that large numbers of the disabled population will be left jobless or working at subminimum wages regardless of disability civil rights laws. Is this acceptable? Is the disability rights movement's goal only to see that some, not even all, disabled persons are "free" to be boldly exploited like everyone else?

Liberalism presumes a free, rational, autonomous human can exist under capitalism, but oppression is a permanent factor of any class-based economic system. Marx saw capitalism as a block to workers' autonomy. Economic change, he deemed, was necessary for the full realization of each person's human potential. Marx's final goal, however, was not economic revolution, but human change.

Erich Fromm points out that "the goal of [Marx's] atheistic radical humanism was the salvation of man, his self-actualization, the overcoming of the craving for having and consumption, his freedom and independence, and his love for others."[32] Marx believed that individual autonomy is interwoven with and dependent upon social relations. Labor power is something that must be created and controlled in a manner appropriate to the maintenance of the capitalist social relation. Exploitation is a common feature of all modes of production that are split into classes. Alienation is a consequence of the mercantilization of human life as a whole by the capitalist relations of production. Wage labor is the transformation of human energy into a commodity like any other piece of matter. So, if the masses were to have freedom and autonomy, Marx believed there must be a transformation of alienated, meaningless labor into productive, free labor, not simply employment or employment at higher wages by a private or state capitalism.

In our society, humane concerns are subsumed by the market's tyranny, the inversion or *camera obscura* of what is needed to foster an inclusive, cooperative, and healthy society. Questions that need to be brought to the forefront might include the following: What is the purpose of an economy—to support market-driven profits or to sustain social bonds and encourage human participation? Is it acceptable to reduce the productive activities of persons to commodity wage labor? Is the capacity to produce for profit an acceptable measure of human worth? Is it defensible to hold in contempt bodies that do not produce the way the capitalist class demands, leaving disabled persons to struggle on low wages or meager benefit checks or to be institutionalized? How can the realm of work be reorganized to provide accommodations for all, and how can all members of society be embraced and rewarded whether they work or not?

The disability rights/independent living liberation struggle provides a strong motive for historical change. There is an opportunity to reconceptualize disability and to eliminate disabled peoples' oppression. We must contest the biological rationale for the exclusion of disabled persons from the realm of work and replace it with a materialistic rationale calling for drastically and justly altering the political economy.

The fundamental questions of class power raised by Marx must be addressed politically if the long-term goal of a society of equals, where "from each according to their [dis]ability, to each according to their need"[33] is to materialize.

CHAPTER 2

The New Reserve Army of Labor?

In October of 1999, Karl Marx topped a BBC News Online poll to be named the millennium's "greatest thinker" by voters around the world. Marx has survived one hundred years of scrutiny because his theories are relevant to the workings of capitalism today. Capitalism may be changing by "revolutionizing" into variations of itself—but it always remains unchanged. Take capitalism's inherent need for what Marx calls a "relative surplus population" or "reserve army of labor," which includes the official unemployed and all those parts of the population, whether part of the workforce at a given time or not, who might become part of the workforce if the demand for them grew. Marx explains the business cycle "depends on the constant formation, the greater or less absorption, and the reformation of the industrial reserve army or surplus population," because the economic system dictates that larger numbers of workers must be seeking work than employers will ever recruit.

Traditionally, disabled people have been considered irrelevant to the modern political/economic system, and placed in the category of people Marx designated the "stagnant" surplus population—those unable to work and the least likely to be employed. But now that more disabled persons can work with a reasonable accommodation as called for by the ADA, there is the potential that this stagnant group may join the "active" reserve army of labor.

Upon passage of the ADA in 1990, *Business Week* suggested that "one of the hidden keys to profitability may be a large and growing bloc of Americans—

people with disabilities." It projected ". . . in a decade in which willing and able workers will be increasingly hard to find, the nearly nine million working age Americans with disabilities now outside the job market may be one of the best sources of new employees—period."[1] Disabled persons represent a possible influx of hundreds of thousands of job seekers to newly compete with, and join the ranks of, labor. Seven out of ten working-age disabled persons who are not employed, for example, say that they would prefer to be working.[2] [. . .]

Recently, President Clinton has used his bully pulpit to place employment of disabled persons on the national radar screen. He has, for instance, ordered federal agencies and departments to hire these potential workers, which in turn, he says, will set an example and provide a model for private industry to follow. Business, however, so far has resisted hiring and retaining workers with disabilities by vigorously fighting ADA discrimination cases in the courts. [. . .] Unlike non-disabled employees, disabled workers may need reasonable accommodations, and the cost of providing their health care may exceed the norm (insurers charge exorbitant rates for those who have a history of a disabling condition). Americans with disabilities face a distinct form of economic discrimination, inherent in capitalism, in which the costs of nonstandard (disabled) labor are weighed against standard (non-disabled) labor, and employers discriminate accordingly.

The president's call to private industry is accompanied by support for legislation that would remove one such economic barrier. Rather than tackling the powerful and fragmented health care industry, where private health insurance companies are in the business to make money as opposed to guaranteeing health care, government is enacting legislation (Work Incentives Improvements Act) that would publicly subsidize the health care of employed disabled persons by allowing them to buy into Medicare or Medicaid. Instead of the employer paying for a disabled worker's health care, government will offer paid health care as an incentive to potential employers.

Why, after some twenty years of activists' efforts to get government to reform such systemic problems which restrict disabled persons' freedom to work, and twenty-five years of government noncompliance with affirmative requirements under the previously enacted Rehabilitation Act [of 1973—*Ed.*], has the government chosen 1999 to become active? The recent emphasis suggests there is more to the president's actions than advancement of the civil rights of disabled persons. There is, in fact, another dimension to the president's call. His administration has a macroeconomic agenda (as opposed to a singularly microeconomic matter of labor discrimination). Labor Secretary Alexis Herman told a joint meeting of national disability organizations, "The last big group of people in this country who could keep the economy going strong with low inflation are Americans with disabilities . . . who are not in the workforce." President Clinton clarified how the new reserve army fit into macroeconomic planning on his poverty tour: "[T]here are a couple of options [for ways to keep America's economy growing without inflation]. You can bring more people from welfare or from the ranks of the disabled into the workforce. . . ."

Clinton's comment came upon the heels of discussion in economic circles as to whether the Federal Reserve Bank would raise interest rates or not. Their concern: how much growth and how low the unemployment rate could go before the combination set off an explosion of inflation due to rising labor costs, which Clinton and mainstream economists fear would kill the recovery. Although the Humphrey-Hawkins Act directs the Federal Reserve to adhere to goals of full employment, Federal Reserve monetary policy is based on the theory that a certain level of unemployment is healthy for the economy; it caters to investors' interests by manipulating interest rates to quash growth, which, in turn, cools down hiring. This, they rationalize, controls inflation but, more importantly, it protects profits and investments on Wall Street.

Disabled persons are the last identity group to enter the workforce, seeking the right to share in the wealth of the nation at a time when unemployment levels are as low as they have been in nearly forty years, and may be below what the investor class traditionally will tolerate. The employment expectations of disabled persons are likely to outstrip material gains due to the limits economic policy makers place on growth. The administration's primary intent is to use the new army of labor to put downward pressure on the now rising wages in a tight labor market. After nine years of lax enforcement of disabled persons' civil rights, and relative inattention to the unemployment predicament of disabled persons, those representing the investor-capitalist class now have an incentive at this stage in the business cycle to utilize them to meet Wall Street ends. Ironically, the unemployment predicament of disabled persons may improve, not because of civil rights laws, but because the macro economy demands enlarging the active reserve army.

Macroeconomic Matters: Reserve Armies, Compulsory Unemployment, and Wall Street

Under Marx's General Law of Capitalist Accumulation, unemployment is not an aberration of capitalism; rather, it is a built-in component of the market economy that requires many people be unemployed against their will. There are many sources of the reserve army of labor. Some of them, like the destruction of precapitalist societies, the detailed division of labor, and mechanization, are internal to the process of capital accumulation; and others, such as the manipulation of credit availability by the US Federal Reserve System, are international mechanisms of state policy. I want to focus my attention on the role of the state in augmenting the reserve army.

US monetary policy as carried out by the Federal Reserve—a system of quasi-independent banks overseen by a board of governors appointed by the president, which sets interest rates, and for many years now has essentially been running the economy of the nation—illustrates how US capitalism preserves the reserve army of labor. Before we continue, it is important to remember that the reserve army is much larger than the officially unemployed. For example, the Bureau of Labor Statistics put official unemployment at 5.5 million in April of 2000, but another 3.1 million people work part time when they would rather have a full-time job, and 4.4 million who need jobs are off the recording charts because they gave up looking and are not counted. The real jobless rate is closer to 13.0 million or 8.9 percent of the population—more than twice the official rate.

Large numbers of people are left jobless because mainstream economists believe that a threshold of unemployment is necessary to avoid inflation and maintain the health of the American economy. The theory of a "natural rate of unemployment," or nonaccelerating inflation rate of unemployment (NAIRU) has dominated macroeconomics for about twenty-five years. The Full Employment and Balanced Growth Act of 1978 (the Humphrey-Hawkins Act) mandates that the Federal Reserve Bank promote full employment, but the Federal Reserve connects low unemployment with inflation in disregard of the Humphrey-Hawkins Act. Since the 1970s, the Fed has instead assumed the task of fighting inflation by raising interest rates, slowing economic growth, and keeping unemployment in check. When the unemployment rate drops, the Fed adjusts interest rates upward to discourage more growth (employment) with the intent of preventing inflation.

There are central bankers who reject the NAIRU theory, and these have adopted the "Taylor Rule," making their anchor of economic policy the "sustainable rate of growth." Under this theory, growth becomes unsustainable when unemployment gets below 3 percent. Under either theory, mainstream economic policy makers assume the need for a reserve army of labor, holding that at least 3 to 6 percent of the population must be unemployed at all times.

Underlying the Fed's maintaining a ratio between employment and unemployment or enlarging the active reserve army of labor, is its desire to regulate wages. Marx explains:

> [Wages are not] determined by the variations of the absolute numbers of the working population but by the varying proportions in which the working class is divided into an active army and a reserve army, by the increase or diminution in the relative amount of surplus population, by the extent to which it is alternatively absorbed and set free.[3]

Tight labor markets—a "labor shortage" or smaller active reserve army—mean pressure for wage increases from labor; as unemployment goes down, labor costs go up because there is more pressure for wage increases.

Before Marx, Adam Smith, observing such a mechanism, originated the truism that the power relationship between workers and capitalists changes with the employment rate. Smith wrote that "the scarcity of hands occasions a competition among masters, who bid against one another in order to get workmen, and thus voluntarily break through the natural combination of masters to not raise wages."[4] A shortage of labor forces capitalists to raise wages.

There is solid empirical evidence for the negative correlation between wage levels and unemployment. Two mainstream economists, David Blanchflower and Andrew Oswald, have produced evidence that, all things being equal, unemployment depresses wages.[5] Economist James Galbraith has also shown that power, and particularly market or monopoly power, changes with the general level of demand, the rate of growth, and the rate of unemployment. He explains that "in periods of high employment, the weak gain ground on the strong; in periods of high unemployment, the strong gain ground on the weak."[6] Even Alan Greenspan, the chairman of the Federal Reserve Bank, the mouthpiece for Wall Street investors, admits a class relationship: a primary purpose of US monetary policy is to keep wages down.[7]

When the unemployment rate gets too low, wages will rise. So, in terms of the political economy, enlarging the active reserve army of labor is "good" for business because it disciplines labor. Having more people desperate for work keeps competition for jobs high and workers' wages down, thereby protecting the corporate profit margins which are sacred to the interests of capital.

How many disabled persons are there to potentially join the active reserve army? The Economic and Social Research Institute finds 2.3 million disabled who are not working could now be working with workplace accommodations.[8] But this is surely an underestimation of the disabled in the reserve army. There are 17 million working-age disabled persons, 5.2 million of whom are working.[9] This leaves 11.8 million either officially unemployed or not in the labor force. According to the 1998 National Organization on Disability/Harris Survey, seven out of ten among those with disabilities age 16 to 64 who are not employed say that they would prefer to be working.[10] Thus, as many as 8.3 million workers could be enlisted in the active reserve army. But further, there are indications that disabled persons may be significantly underemployed, preferring to work full time when they are only employed part time. Between 1981 and 93, the proportion of disabled persons working full time declined by 8 percent, while the number of disabled working part time for both economic and noneconomic reasons increased disproportionately.[11] All in all, there is a large pool of disabled persons to utilize as buffers against higher wages and lower profits.

Of course, the administration's objective is not to assimilate the millions of disabled persons wanting a job into the workforce. The omission of a jobs creation program that might achieve such an end is a clear signal that government's intent is to use the disabled (along with those transiting from welfare to work) to protect the interests of investors by keeping inflation and wages in check. Both inflation and higher wages decrease the value of financial assets and weaken the fortress of class privilege—Wall Street.

The administration's ultimate aim is to prevent the collapse of the "new economy," which has delivered primarily to the investor class while working-class people have slid further behind. Over the past twenty years, for instance, real wages have fallen for 60 percent of the workforce. Seven years into the recovery, the inflation-adjusted earnings of the median worker in 1997 were 3.1 percent lower than in 1989,[12] the worst performance since the Great Depression. By contrast, the "new" economy has delivered for capital; it is consolidating money into the hands of the few. The stock market, for example, rose by a staggering 60 percent in 1995 and 1996 alone, but according to economist Edward Wolff of New York University, an estimated 42 percent of the benefits of the increase in the stock market (between 1989 and 1997) went to the richest 1 percent.[13] The richest 1 percent of households now controls 40 percent of the nation's assets, twice what they had twenty years ago. Since 1983, the value of the stock market has increased thirteen-fold, but less than half of the population owns any form of stocks, and the vast majority of those who do—three quarters of the stockholders—have less than $5,000 invested in the market. The administration and the Federal Reserve are not about to upset this economic juggernaut, this capitalist golden egg, by allowing wages to rise too much.

Microeconomic Obstacles: Business Resistance to Employing Disabled Persons

Can the government employ a strategy to successfully use disabled persons to fight inflation? Here, the microeconomic interests of business may be in conflict with investors' macroeconomic interests. [. . .]

As Marx outlined, and as any businessperson knows, business exists to make profits. The basis of capitalist accumulation is the business use of surplus labor from the workforce in a way which makes it money. Typical business accounting practices weigh the costs of employment against profits to be made. Productive labor, or exploitation of labor, means simply that labor is used to generate a surplus value which is based on what business can gain from the productivity of workers against what it pays in wages, health care, and benefits (in other words, the standard costs of having an employee). The surplus value created in production is appropriated by the capitalist. The worker receives wages, which cover the worker's subsistence, (theoretically) making it possible to reproduce labor-power every working day.

To business, the hiring or retaining of an employee with a disability represents nonstandard extra costs when calculated against a company's bottom line. Whether real or perceived in any given instance, employers anticipate increased costs in the form of providing reasonable accommodations, speculate that disabled workers will increase their workers' compensation costs, and project extra administration costs to hire an unknown quantity, the nonstandard worker. Employers, if they provide health care insurance at all, expect extra premium costs for health insurance for workers with disabilities. Insurance companies and managed care health networks often exempt "pre-existing" conditions from coverage for periods of time, or make other coverage exclusions based on chronic conditions, charging extremely high premiums for the person with such a medical history. Employers, in turn, look for ways to avoid providing coverage to cut costs. In addition, employers characteristically assume that they will encounter increased liability and lowered productivity from disabled workers, either from decreased capacity or absences from work.[14] [. . .]

How could a government now interested in bringing more workers with disabilities into the active army of labor to fight inflation make the pendulum swing in the other direction, so that business, in fact, could profit from and be compelled to hire disabled people? One way is through public subsidies to employers. Government has already moved to subsidize disabled workers' health care by allowing them to retain their public health care while on the job by buying into Medicare and Medicaid. This may reverse one disadvantage: it means business will not have to pay for these laborers' health care, and non-disabled people's health care will seem the more expensive prospect. It could subsidize the cost of reasonable accommodations or provide other subsidies to make it more palatable to business. The Labor Department could include disabled persons as a part of its mandatory affirmative action program (currently it only *urges* employers to hire them).

Other incentives might include officially lowering the price of disabled persons' labor. Economist Richard Epstein, for instance, says that "[disabled persons] have been subject to unfair treatment in the marketplace," but holds that this is due to government interference with the control of their labor in the competitive process. Epstein argues that "the disabled should be allowed to sell their labor at whatever price, and on whatever terms, they see fit." Pointing to the free market as the appropriate mechanism, he states that "the minimum wage laws and various kinds of ostensible safety and health regulations can impose a greater burden on them [disabled persons] than on others. Repeal those laws as well."[15] Epstein believes that in a deregulated competitive market, disabled persons' labor would fall below minimum wage because it is worth less.

Despite the fact that the ADA prohibits wage discrimination, wage gaps are readily found in the "regulated" market for the 5.2 million workers with disabilities who have a job. [. . .] Further, there is a precedent for justifying below-minimum wages for disabled persons. Section 504 of the Rehabilitation Act of 1973 provides that federally financed institutions are required to pay a "fair" wage to disabled workers, but they are not required to meet even minimum wage standards. The traditional sheltered workshop is the prototype, based on the theory that disabled persons are not able to keep up with the average widget sorter. Any employer is allowed to pay below minimum wage to disabled employees under federal law, if the employer can show that the disabled person has "reduced productive capacity."

Six years after passage of the ADA, Republican legislator Scott Baugh (CA) latched onto the subminimum wage concept for disabled workers by introducing legislation in 1996 that would allow employers to hire disabled workers at a "special minimum wage," without the minimal and very subjective "protection" of having to show that the prospective employee is "less productive" than a non-disabled one. Any disabled person could be considered "less productive," and theoretically a subminimum wage or wage below non-disabled in any pay category could be used to not only hold down the wage floor, but lower it.[16]

When Clinton signed the Personal Responsibility and Work Opportunity Reconciliation Act of 1996, government ended federal welfare entitlements and made moving people from welfare to work a primary goal of federal welfare policy. By ensuring that between two and twelve million new workers would be forced onto the job market, the government has used the welfare population to control inflation and depress wages. By July of 1999 seven million women had transited from welfare into low-wage, in many cases below poverty rate, jobs. Many disabled persons fall into a similar work grouping because they generally have low high school graduation rates, and many students with disabilities do not continue their education at postsecondary institutions.[17] Theoretically, welfare reform and disability Return-to-Work programs could result in an overall lowering of the cost of labor. The Economic Policy Institute, for instance, warned that the low-wage labor market is already suffering greatly, and proposals to put welfare recipients to work will drive the wages of the working poor down further. It estimates that to absorb all the welfare workers, the wages of the bottom third of the labor force would have to fall by 11 percent nationally.[18]

The tight labor market, alone, may reverse businesses' reluctance to hire disabled persons. In labor shortages, employers are more likely to hire workers they would ordinarily discriminate against simply because they need them. The National Urban League, for instance, finds African American employment and income have been raised to "unprecedented levels" in the current labor market.[19]

Microsoft Corp., for one, has recently taken note of the employment potential of disabled persons. It is leading a group of twenty-one major North American corporations in establishing a program dubbed "Able to Work," in an effort to share strategies aimed at finding jobs for disabled persons. Microsoft knows how to use the marginalization of certain groups of workers to its advantage. It has, for example, utilized prison labor at the Twin Rivers Correctional Center in Monroe, Washington, to pack Windows and Microsoft Office software, as well as thousands of Microsoft mice, through a subcontractor, Exmark. Prisoners are paid low wages, and Microsoft has no overhead, no medical costs, no retirement benefits, no local taxes, no workers' compensation, because the taxpayers absorb the costs of doing business. Disabled persons, formerly excluded from having a steady paycheck and eager to have jobs, similarly offer employers a reliable, partially subsidized workforce.

A tight labor market may temporarily produce more jobs for those previously excluded from the workforce, but in the long run there is little security. A

Wisconsin study of the welfare-to-work transition period conducted by John Pawasarat of the University of Wisconsin at Milwaukee, found 75 percent of those hired lost their jobs within nine months.[20] Only 28 percent sustained projected annual earnings of $10,000 for two consecutive quarters, and such work was often part-time, low-paying, and quick to end. When the Children's Defense Fund and the National Coalition for the Homeless reevaluated the status of former welfare recipients in 1998, they found that only about 50 percent to 60 percent of those who leave welfare are working, and those who work typically earn just $5.50 to $7 an hour—too little to lift a family out of poverty.[21] During World War II, American industry recruited women and physically limited persons in large numbers to keep production going while the able-bodied male population was fighting overseas. As the war ended, many of these workers, particularly those with disabilities, lost their jobs to returning soldiers. It remains to be seen if the ADA can protect disabled workers who may be hired at the peak of this business cycle from firings and layoffs.

As Marx explains, "The reserve army belongs to capital as if the latter had bred it . . . a mass of human material always ready for exploitation."[22] The stagnant category, being the most disposable, can be rendered superfluous at the slightest downturn of the business cycle.

These scenarios, however, are "solutions" which promote conflict between groups of disadvantaged workers, rather than making it a right of every citizen to have a living-wage job and health care. Whether the unemployment rate is at 4 percent, 6 percent, or 10 percent, the capitalist system produces jobless casualties, much like a pyramid scheme where a percentage of the population gets left out of the game at all times. The reserve army of unemployed—including welfare recipients and those who could work with a reasonable accommodation but remain on disability benefits—are the unsung heroes of the capitalist system. By living in abject poverty, they buoy the entire system.

Neither civil rights, affirmative action, nor ending economic discrimination against disabled persons will assure a living-wage job for all who need one. Capitalism cannot consider the human consequences of its development, because those concerns are not included in its historical role as a transitory form of material production. Basic changes must be made in the economic, social, and political structure in order to advance economic solutions that reach beyond capitalism's instability. The reserve army, itself, must be made a disposable concept.

CHAPTER 3

Disability and Capitalist Globalization

It was predicted by *Business Week* in the 1990s—and assumed by disability groups—that in the "Information Age" disabled workers would get a shot at improving their employment lot. Technology makes it possible for significantly disabled persons to use computers, while Information Technology (IT) promised plenty of office deskwork.

One spin *Business Week* put on the Americans with Disabilities Act in its early days was that disabled people would "become a strategy for profitability—a new competitive advantage in the search for capable workers."[1]

What happened instead is that government and the corporations abandoned American workers, including disabled workers, leaving them in the dust in search of cheaper labor made possible by that very technology. Privatization of government jobs and IT outsourcing—sending jobs overseas—has become a popular means to lower the cost of labor committed to perform computer-related functions.

The corporations, with the approval of the Bush administration, are shipping prospective jobs overseas to India, Malaysia, Eastern Europe, and soon to China where workers can be hired for about 10 percent the salary of an American worker. Banks, corporations, Wall Street, and governments have all jumped on the outsourcing bandwagon.

The White House Council of Economic Advisers released its Economic Report of the President in February stating, "When a good or service is produced more cheaply abroad, it makes more sense to import it than to make it or provide it domestically."[2]

Economist Gregory Mankiw, who chairs the Council, called outsourcing which usually comes hand in hand with firing Americans and sending their jobs overseas "a good thing."

To the Bush administration it makes good economic sense to outsource jobs that could be going to unemployed American workers. This administration has no allegiance to the nation's unemployed. Rather Bush's people take Calvin Coolidge's statement as a given: "The business of America is business." What's good for the corporations is not to be tied down by pesky regulations that would place a premium on hiring Americans. It is profit maximization they are after.

In praising the merits of outsourcing, Bush's administration is following the lead of CEOs such as General Electric's Jack Welch who shifted software development and back office jobs to India years ago. Today firms such as McKinsey & Co. and A. T. Kearney have shifted the bulk of their research divisions to places such as Bombay and Chennai, India. J. P. Morgan Chase & Co. has hired junior stock analysts and other research staffers in its Bombay office. US banks such as Citibank, brokerages such as Merrill Lynch, mutual companies, and other financial services companies are planning to relocate five hundred thousand jobs offshore, or 8 percent of their workforce over the next few years. Deloitte Research forecast in April last year that about 15 percent of financial jobs worldwide would be moved to countries sporting cheap labor.

If it can be done sitting in front of a desk it is game for outsourcing.

The trend is not limited to corporations. Bush's White House plans to subject at many as eight hundred and fifty thousand federal jobs to competition from the private sector including desk jobs that can find their way overseas to politically well-connected contractors with offices in India, Malaysia, the Philippines, and perhaps Russia.

Forty states have already hired foreign workers in other countries to perform such jobs as answering questions about food stamps or welfare programs. India is a favorite contracting country because people there speak English. Public and private call centers are being off-shored en masse. India now has a booming industry of telemarketers and phone banks, taking information economy jobs from the US.

Technology has backfired on disabled job seekers. Capital has taken off with IT to make as large a profit as possible.

There are other factors involved in the poor labor market. Massive layoffs, a de-skilling of the American labor force into low-paying service sector jobs, downsizing, factory shutdowns, outsourcing of jobs overseas, and NAFTA have all contributed to the 65 to 70 percent disabled unemployment rate.

Of course, this is serious trouble for all US workers, 14.7 million of whom have no job. The administration likes to point to the fact that there was a recent decline of the official unemployment rate but it fell two tenths of a percentage point not because more people got jobs but because five hundred and thirty-eight thousand workers left the labor market and are "not in the labor force." Discouraged, they gave up looking for a job and aren't counted as unemployed anymore.

The nation's official jobless rate is 5.9 percent but that figure tells only a part of the story of the labor market.

To begin with, there are the 8.7 million unemployed, defined as those without a job who are actively looking for work. However, 4.9 million part-time workers say they would rather be working full time—the highest number in a decade.

There are also the 1.5 million people who want a job but didn't look for one in the last month. Nearly a third of this group says they stopped the search because they were too depressed about the prospect of finding anything. Officially termed "discouraged," their number has surged 20 percent in a year.

Add these groups together and the jobless total for the US hits 9.7 percent, up from 9.4 percent a year ago.

In fact, payroll jobs are down well over two million since George W. Bush moved into the White House. Bush's economic policies have not added enough jobs to compensate for the loss. Despite Bush's [January 20, 2004—*Ed.*] State of the Union Address citing need for focus on jobs, in January the economy only added one thousand jobs, making this a jobless recovery.

The jobless recovery may well be a permanent job loss "recovery." According to Doug Henwood, a Federal Reserve Bank study confirms that job losses over the last few years were "structural and not merely cyclical."

Usually a recovery is accompanied by the return of jobs. Layoffs are temporary and workers are recalled when the economy performed well. Henwood notes, "In the current cycle, almost all of the job losses have been the result of positions being eliminated."[3]

Structural changes bode ill winds ahead for would-be disabled workers. If the American labor force is shrinking, it is hard to see any room for gain. The rule of thumb for disabled workers is last one hired and first one fired.

With Presidential comments praising the merits of offshore manufacturing and hiring practices we are a long way from bringing government round to take some social responsibility for the loss of jobs in our country.

Still, our directive should be clear. There will be a greater need for unemployment benefit extensions, job creation in the public sector, and above poverty-level income support to avoid conditions of greater homelessness and poverty in the nation.

CHAPTER 4

A Brief History of Wal-Mart and Disability Discrimination

Wal-Mart was recently busted for disability discrimination in hiring—again. In January [2004—*Ed.*] the Equal Employment Opportunity Commission (EEOC) filed a lawsuit against the retail giant for discriminating against Steven J. Bradley when he applied for a job at Wal-Mart in Richmond, Missouri. Bradley has cerebral palsy and uses crutches or a wheelchair as mobility aids.

Wal-Mart refused to reach a settlement, so the EEOC filed suit using the ADA seeking lost wages and benefits, compensatory and punitive damages, and a job for Bradley.

It was just back in 2001 that Wal-Mart and the EEOC reached a $6.8 million consent decree which resolved thirteen lawsuits the commission had pending against the corporation in eleven states, including Missouri.

Ten years after passage of the ADA, Wal-Mart's illegal pre-employment questionnaire, "Matrix of Essential Job Functions," violated employment discrimination provisions (ADA) by seeking disability-related information from applicants before making conditional offers of employment.

Title I of the ADA prohibits private employers, state and local governments, employment agencies, and labor unions from discriminating against qualified individuals with disabilities in job application procedures, hiring, discharge, advancement, compensation, job training, and other terms and conditions of employment. Unfortunately, that tag, "qualified," applies to disability discrimination cases; it rightly does not to gender or age-related civil rights law.

As part of the settlement, Wal-Mart agreed it would change its ADA policies and procedures, create an ADA coordinator position, provide training in ADA compliance and offer jobs to certain disabled applicants.

It wasn't long before a judge slapped Wal-Mart with major sanctions for violating the Consent Decree in May of 2001 in the US District Court for the District of Arizona. The court sanctioned the corporation $720,200 and ordered it to produce a TV advertisement stating that Wal-Mart had violated the ADA and referring people who believe they have been discriminated against. The court also ordered Wal-Mart to reinstate William Darnell, a hearing-impaired employee, to a full-time receiver/unloader position and directed the corporation to accommodate Darnell's disability in all activities of his job.

Wal-Mart was found in violation of the Decree because of its failure to create alternative training materials for use nationwide by hearing-impaired employees. The materials include a sign-language version of its computer-based learning modules used to train entry-level employees. In addition, EEOC contends, and Wal-Mart admitted, that it had failed to provide court-ordered training on the ADA to its management employees.

"It is extremely unusual for EEOC to have to ask a court to hold an employer in contempt," said C. Emanuel Smith, acting regional attorney for EEOC's Phoenix District Office, which has jurisdiction for Arizona.[1]

Then in June 2001 the EEOC filed its sixteenth ADA suit against Wal-Mart for violating the ADA again. The EEOC accused the world's largest retailer of failing to reasonably accommodate an employee with a disability at its Peoria, Arizona, store.

The lawsuit alleged that Wal-Mart discriminated against Alice Rehberg by refusing to provide a reasonable accommodation for her disability. Rehberg is severely limited in her ability to stand for extended periods of time. Wal-Mart refused Rehberg's request for permission to occasionally sit down while performing her duties as a People Greeter, failed to engage in the interactive process required by the ADA, and constructively discharged Rehberg from her position.

The suit sought compensatory and punitive damages, reinstatement, injunctive relief, and a court order requiring Wal-Mart to conduct training that will prevent further violations of the ADA.

EEOC also has won several jury verdicts against Wal-Mart in other disability discrimination suits. In one case, a jury found that Wal-Mart intentionally refused to hire an applicant as a cashier because he used a wheelchair, and awarded him more than $3.5 million in damages (which was subsequently reduced by the court to comply with the ADA's statutory caps; again, caps do not apply to other protected minorities). In another case, a jury awarded $157,500 to an applicant due to Wal-Mart's unlawful pre-employment inquiry and refusal to hire him because of his disability, an amputated arm. The verdict included a $100,000 punitive damage award, the largest ever levied against a company for asking an unlawful medical question under the ADA.

To wit, private sector-government resolutions must be watchdogged to assure compliance.

Why, under such a hostile environment, would anyone want to work at Wal-Mart anyway? Aside from disability discrimination, Wal-Mart is dragging wages and benefit levels back to nineteenth-century standards—Wal-Mart workers are paid $2 to $3 an hour less than union members who perform similar jobs. $6 per hour is about the average wage for unskilled workers these days.

Contrast that to five relatives of the late Sam Walton, founder of Wal-Mart Stores Inc., who retained five of the top ten spots of the wealthiest people in the world. Their net worth increased to $18.8 billion each from $17.5 billion in 2001, thanks to consumers buying the cheaper food, cheaper shirts, cheaper sheets, jeans and motor oil—in short, cheaper everything—and the corporation's dubious labor practices.

The company has been found to ask employees to work longer than the standard forty-hour workweek without overtime pay.[2] It has often harassed or fired non-disabled workers who have not been viewed as sufficiently cooperative with management.

Workers who did not believe that Wal-Mart had been adequately accommodating of their needs could fear losing their jobs if they discussed this fact with a reporter. William Darnell lost his job at Wal-Mart for demanding deaf-related accommodations from management.

Wal-Mart, America's largest retailer, employs 1.14 million workers at nearly four thousand facilities worldwide. Only about one in three adults with significant disabilities is working. Many live on below-poverty disability benefits. In a shrinking job market under the Bush administration, the job hunt has gotten fierce. In the view of some significantly disabled persons and indeed non-disabled workers, any job is a job worth having these days.

That is the way of it.

II.

Civil Rights and Retreats

CHAPTER 5

Backlash and Structural Inequality

Introduction

The Americans with Disabilities Act (ADA) is both a civil rights [. . .] and an economics bill intended to increase the relative wages and employment of disabled people by "leveling the playing field."[1] However, just as the Civil Rights Act of 1964 produced a backlash by those who feared that minorities and women would take jobs away from them, the ADA has been subject to recent backlash by the public, our elected officials, and the courts.

The most prominent hostility towards the ADA has come from business, though this may not technically be a "backlash," given that the business sector largely opposed the Act from the start. [. . .] Ongoing resistance from business interests is nonetheless significant in that it exposes the economic nature of opposition to enforcement of the Act. The year the ADA was signed, the Cato Institute, a conservative think tank, called on President George H. W. Bush "to ask Congress to reconsider" the ADA since, from the standpoint of free enterprise, it represented a re-regulation of the economy that was harmful to business.[2] [. . .] Rick Kahler opined in a piece entitled "ADA Regulatory Black Hole" that "the ADA make[s] getting out of business look more profitable all the time,"[3] while Trevor Armbrister wrote that the ADA "has produced spectacular injustice and irrationality."[4] In 1995, the director of regulatory studies at the Cato Institute wrote:

If Congress is serious about lifting the regulatory burden from the economy, it must consider major changes in, if not outright repeal of, the ADA. And if Congress is to undo the damage already done by the act, it should consider paying reparations to cover the costs that individuals, private establishments, and enterprises have suffered under the ADA's provisions.[5]

This paper explores the backlash and hostility to the ADA by examining the relationship between politics, policy, and economics—particularly with regard to the interests of business. I argue that the backlash to the ADA has been prompted by capitalist opposition. This opposition has not only stifled any potential benefits that might have resulted from ADA enforcement, it has promoted the backlash among groups of workers who have become fearful that their own interests are in jeopardy as a result of the Act's enforcement powers.

In making this argument, I claim that liberal policy explanations, whether in progressive or conservative form, fail to adequately create the conditions necessary for economic and social justice. In contrast, radical theory, which analyzes the sociohistoric process of the political economy under capitalism, asserts that capitalism cannot be directed (reformed) towards a social-ethical end (which to be ethical must be stable and redistributive/collective).[6] To succeed in reforming disability discrimination, the economic system itself must undergo serious change. As will be explored here, the economic system is a crucial contributing factor to a backlash against civil rights laws (the ADA in particular), the poor enforcement of those laws, and the lack of economic advancement of disabled people.

Despite an expanding US economy, the neoliberal age has brought rising inequality, a decline in workers' standard of living, greater job insecurity, and growing economic anxiety. Income and wealth disparities are at their highest levels since the Great Depression. Poverty and hardship remain a persistent blight on the American landscape. This paper will detail how the structurally flawed political economy, sustained by a self-serving decision-making class, perpetuates poverty, inequality, underemployment, and systematic compulsory unemployment. It will demonstrate that this flawed economy which does not provide for the material needs of all, in turn causes divisions amongst groups of workers locked in intense competition over the scarcity of decent paying jobs, health care, and shrinking benefits. And lastly, it aims to delineate why a different approach is vital to remedying the predicament.

Equal Opportunity Ideology and Persistent Wage and Employment Gaps between Groups of Workers

In the United States civil rights laws have been enacted to surmount obstacles faced by the less powerful and minorities—women, people of color, disabled people and others. Historically such groups have experienced vast differentials in pay, income, and employment opportunities.[7] In the United States, seventeen million working-age people are identified as disabled.[8] Since there are expectations that the ADA will foster economic parity for disabled workers, it is essential to examine whether more than thirty years of efforts to ensure civil rights for all have been able to bring about the expected wage and income equality and economic parity for minorities and women.

Women, minorities, and disabled people have experienced both employment and wage discrimination resulting in their confinement to the bottom of the socio/economic pyramid. Discrimination occurs when two groups of workers with equal average productivity earn different average wages[9] or have different levels of opportunity for employment. Poverty is disproportionate amongst the 54 million Americans who have some level of disability. [. . .] The 1998 National Organization on Disability/Harris Survey of Americans with Disabilities found that fully a third (34 percent) of adults with disabilities live in a household with an annual income of less than $15,000 compared to one in eight (12 percent) of those without disabilities.[10] Furthermore, the gap between disabled and non-disabled persons living in very low-income households has remained virtually constant since 1986 (four years prior to passage of the ADA).[11]

But the NOD/Harris Survey annual income cutoff at $15,000 doesn't paint a complete picture of the depth of poverty some disabled people endure. For example, since $720 is the average per month benefit that a disabled worker received in 1998 from Social Security Disability Insurance (SSDI) and $480 is the average federal income for the needs-based Supplemental Security Income (SSI), the real income of over ten million disabled people[12] on these programs is between $5,000 and $10,000—far below the $15,000 mark.

Most analysts attribute these gaps largely to discrimination and seek to provide a remedy based on "equal opportunity," or equal access to employment and pay. The Civil Rights Act of 1964,[13] affirmative action, the Equal Pay Act of 1963,[14] and the Americans with Disabilities Act[15] were enacted to provide a legal means to eradicate sex, race, and disability discrimination in wage-setting and employment procurement systems.

Yet what does the data show at the end of the century? The Census Bureau's Current Population Survey shows that the income gap was most recently altered for the Black population between 1993 and 1997, when Black median family incomes rose from 57 to 61 percent of white levels and the bottom 80 percent showed wage gains relative to the rest of the population.[16] But the gap widened for Hispanic workers who saw their median family incomes fall from 69 to 60 percent of white levels between 1979 and 1997.[17]

Studies show that there were periods of substantial progress after passage of the Civil Rights Act of 1964 and adjunct affirmative action programs leading to declining racial discrimination between 1965 and 1975.[18] But the movement toward racial equality stagnated and eventually weakened after the mid-1970s.[19] From 1972 (the earliest year available) to 1999, the unemployment rate for Blacks has fluctuated between 7.1 percent and levels as high as 21.7 percent.[20] During the same period, white unemployment ranged from a high of 10.2 percent to a low of 3.3 percent, while Hispanic unemployment ranged from 16.9 percent to 6.1 percent.[21] Blacks and Hispanics continue to experience higher levels of unemployment and receive lower wages than whites. While the median white worker earned $19,393 in 1997, the median Black earned only $15,348 and the median Hispanic even less, $13,150.[22]

Although the wage gap between men and women is shrinking, this change cannot be attributed to equal pay laws. Since 1973, much of the change in the wage gap has resulted from the fall in men's real earnings; white and Black men's earnings have gradually moved down while white women's earnings have gradually risen, exceeding the earnings of Black men in 1991.[23] The US Department of Labor reports that after the recession in the early 1990s, women's earnings failed to show the steep gains exhibited during the 1980s in comparison to wages earned by men[24] and concludes the movement towards pay equity has slowed. A telling measure of pay equity can be found in median hourly wages; the median woman earned $9.63 per hour in 1997, while the median man earned $14.39.[25] Narrow or wide, the wage gap has persisted for more than forty-five years, during which the Equal Pay laws were active for thirty-six.[26]

Wage gap studies do not traditionally trace comparable data for disabled people, but unpublished data from John McNeil of the Census Bureau shows a negative association between earnings and disability. In 1995, workers with disabilities holding part-time jobs (disabled people are more likely to work part time) earned on average only between 72.1 percent and 72.6 percent of the amount non-disabled workers earned annually.[27] Such wage differentials were observed for disabled people working full time. Median monthly income for people with work disabilities averaged between $1,511 (women) and $1,880 (men) in 1995—

as much as 20 percent less than the $1,737 to $2,356 earned by their counterparts without disabilities.[28]

Of greater significance is the chronic unemployment of disabled people. A 1998 Harris Survey found that among working-age adults with disabilities (ages 18 to 64), three out of ten (29 percent) work full or part-time compared to eight of ten (79 percent) of those without disabilities—a gap of fifty percentage points.[29] The unemployment rate for disabled people remains much higher than for the population as a whole, with only one-quarter of persons with severe disabilities working.[30] The overall combined (severe and non-severe) disabled unemployment rate is 65–71 percent.[31] Among disabled people who are not employed, 79 percent of working-age disabled people report that they would prefer to work.[32] [. . .]

Material progress for women and minorities appears to be incremental at best while wage inequality among similarly skilled workers, vast income disparities, wage gaps, and poverty persist. After thirty years of federal anti-discrimination legislation, it is valid to conclude that although there is evidence that the Civil Rights Act of 1964 did make a difference in the *extent* of racial and gender discrimination, neither civil rights laws nor successful affirmative action programs have produced the complete economic equality desired by advocates of employment rights.[33] Proponents of affirmative action, who are today arguing against its abolition, say only that gains made will be *eroded,* not that the program has achieved economic parity for minorities. Affirmative action has not proven to be a major solution to poverty or a sufficient means to equality.[34]

Though only ten years have passed since the passage of the ADA, there is no reason to believe that disabled people will fare better in terms of outcomes after the ADA than did women and minorities following the passage of civil rights laws and affirmative action. The reasons are both similar and distinct.

Every redistributive measure, including civil rights laws, involves political compromise between the public and the powerful interests of big business and big government. The ADA in particular faces some extraordinary limitations as a direct result of the political climate in which it was produced and enacted.[35] The philosophical momentum for social justice which spurred the Civil Rights Act and subsequent progressive court decisions in the 1960s was well into decline by the 1990s. For example, in the era following passage of civil rights laws in 1957, 1960, 1964, and 1968, the Republicans made dramatic inroads into democratic victories which forged the civil rights movement, established the Office of Economic Opportunity and initiated the war on poverty during the Great Society.[36] Presidents Reagan and Bush dismantled the entire Community Services Administration, responsible for driving much of the 1960s social change agenda by advancing human services, occupational safety, consumer protection, and environmental laws.[37]

On the way out were civil rights and entitlements, replaced by a conservative thrust to reduce "big bad government." The dominant agenda of the 1970s and 1980s was bolstered by corporate goals which emphasized globalization and political dominance of government.[38] Increased international capital mobility and liberalized international trade have resulted in more power of management at the expense of labor.[39] Conservative forces targeted regulations for repeal or rollback which, in their view, interfered with business.[40] Economic policy in the post-1979 period "moved decisively toward creating a more laissez-faire, deregulated economy."[41] Industries such as transportation and communications have been deregulated. Social protections, including safety, health, and environmental regulations, the minimum wage, government transfer payments (welfare), and the unemployment insurance system all have been weakened. The ADA was no exception. It was watered down substantially to achieve congressional consensus and Bush's presidential approval in 1990.[42]

A 1997 comparative study between the pre- and post-ADA state and federal disability anti-discrimination laws shows that civil rights laws have not produced the gains in employment rates, wage rates, or employment opportunities for disabled people that advocates expected.[43] Nine years after the passage of the ADA, national employment surveys show no real statistical gain in employment. One study suggests that the proportion of working-age adults with disabilities who are employed has declined since 1986, when one in three (34 percent) were working.[44]

Positive outcomes from disability civil rights are further compromised by the lack of mandatory affirmative action following the ADA for disabled people. Though there is controversy over how much affirmative action contributed to the gains made by women and minorities, there is little doubt that when accompanied by adequate enforcement, affirmative action has had a positive impact in opening previously closed doors.[45] This is especially pertinent given the plaintiffs' overall lack of success in the courts where employers have been charged with disability discrimination. Studies show that in the first eight years, defendants (businesses) overwhelmingly prevailed in ADA employment cases at both the trial and appellate court levels.[46] Law professor Ruth Colker states that this outcome is "worse than results found in comparable areas of the law; only prisoner rights cases fare as poorly."[47]

To be truly "equal" all biases must be eradicated. [...] Aside from the traditional biases or social influences that determine one's access to the goods of society such as where one was educated, the family economic status, and the environment in which one was raised,[48] workers with disabilities (as distinct from women and minorities) face economic bias and labor market discrimination due to business accounting practices which weigh standard (non-disabled) costs of labor against nonstandard (disabled) costs of labor. Such business accounting calculations foreshadow the continuation of a gap in pay and employment opportunities for disabled individuals.

Despite over thirty years of liberal reform via federal equal opportunity laws, substantial race, gender, and disability-based inequality remain in the American economy. Both racial and gender employment and earnings inequalities have declined since the enactment of civil rights legislation in the 1960s, but studies show that such reductions in inequalities have been uneven, incomplete, and unstable (i.e., reversible).[49] On balance, the extent of inequality for women, people of color, and disabled people can be viewed as a measure of the political success of liberal ideology where the activities of the courts and government enforcement agencies either serve to advance or roll back liberal regulations promoting equality.

Competition: Labor Market and Structural Inequality

The common explanation given by mainstream economists for inequality of wages and employment opportunities between races and genders is twofold. First, individual workers experience differences in productivity-linked characteristics (called a *human capital gap*). Second, they experience differences in treatment due to discrimination. The dominant or human capital view is that individuals exhibit skill and educational differences due to skill-biased technological changes which cause the widening gap in pay, and that by increasing education and technological training, these differentials will be overcome.[50]

The neoclassical *supply and demand* theory of competition holds that the labor market will equalize pay and employment differentials. Pay inequality is explained as a natural result of the spread of information technologies (the computer revolution) which create differences in skills; those most trained in these new fields reap the benefits in pay from the transformation in the workplace while those without such training fall behind.[51] Supply and demand theory asserts that this is so because the pressures of the marketplace, what Adam Smith called the "invisible hand," direct the activities of individuals and serve as a self-regulating mechanism for wages, prices, and production. In practice, the demand for workers trained in technological fields will encourage more workers to seek such training, eventually equalizing wage differentials over the long run.

A substantial body of work challenges the notion that human capital, quality of education, and years of work experience can adequately explain the wage differentials and employment patterns which remain prominent in the economy.[52] For instance, research by economists Lawrence Mishel, Jared Bernstein, and John Schmitt shows that skill-biased technological change cannot account for wage disparity. Throughout the 1990s, average starting wages for college graduates, the most technically advanced and computer-literate workers in the labor market, fell by 7 percent.[53] New engineers and computer scientists were offered 11 percent and 8 percent less respectively in 1997 than their counterparts received entering the market in 1989.[54] This flatly contradicts claims that more education and skill training will equalize pay differentials. Furthermore, productivity rates, which should be exploding if the computer revolution were generating huge returns for high-tech skills, grew no faster in the 1990s than in the 1980s.[55] Economists James Galbraith, Claudia Goldin, and Lawrence Katz show that the readjustment of incomes to a wider and more equal distribution of skill levels for the overall workforce failed to happen in the past and is not happening in today's economy.[56]

Studies show that competitive market forces did not eliminate discriminatory practices in the decades leading up to the passage of the Civil Rights Act of 1964 (which remained until the federal adoption of anti-discrimination laws)[57] and that discrimination has managed to sustain itself, both in the US and elsewhere, for generations at a time.[58] Research by Martin Carnoy concludes that while Blacks narrowed the educational gap separating them from whites, they slid further behind in average earnings.[59]

Some analysts attribute inequality gaps not to individual ineptitude but in large measure to labor segregation. Estimates of the hard figures on inequality by James L. Westrich of the Massachusetts Institute for Social and Economic Research show that there is a hierarchical division of labor within the labor force. For example, women are numerous at the bottom of the economic pyramid and scarce at the top. While 23.7 percent of women earn less than $10,000 (a result of both low pay and part-time status), just 12.8 percent of men earn so little. While 58.7 percent of women earn under $23,000, the same is true for only 36.3 percent of men; and 9.9 percent of men earn over $75,000, compared to only 2.6 percent of women.[60]

A study by Donald Tomaskovic-Devey for the US Department of Labor's Glass Ceiling Commission at Cornell University found that while part of the wage gap results from differences in education, experience or time in the workforce, a significant portion cannot be explained by any of those factors.[61] His findings revealed that "differences in human capital, investments in education and training by individuals explain a small proportion of the gender gap and about a third of race/ethnic earnings inequalities, but substantial earnings inequalities are not a function of gender or race/ethnic differences in education, labor market experience or firm tenure."[62] Instead, these gaps are attributable to the social division of labor, systematic underpayment, and occupational segregation of people because of their sex or race.[63]

Tomaskovic-Devey shows that "not only is there racial and gender discrimination against individuals, but as a result of employment segregation, jobs that become associated with particular racial or gender categories tend to be organizationally stereotyped and valued accordingly."[64] As jobs become stereotypically female or minority, there is a tendency in many workplaces to provide lower wages and less opportunity for skill training and promotions. He concludes that the confinement of "many women of all ethnic backgrounds and minority men to lower quality jobs *than they can perform*" is a direct cause of gender and race/ethnic earnings inequalities.[65]

Economist James Galbraith challenges the supply and demand theory that people are, in fact, paid in proportion to the value of what they produce. Galbraith shows that power, and particularly market or monopoly power, changes with the general level of demand, the rate of growth, and the rate of unemployment.[66] [. . .] In this view, inequality is a product of differential power, rather than differential skill. This concept is consistent with Adam Smith who observed that "masters [capitalists] are always and everywhere in a sort of tacit, but constant and uniform combination, not to raise the wages of labor above their actual rate."[67] Smith keenly perceived the tendency towards monopoly power of capital, writing that "masters too sometimes enter into particular combinations to sink the wages of labor even below this rate."[68] [. . .]

Marxist economic theory provides further insight. Marx's theory of surplus value posits that profit lies in the ability of capitalists to pay less for labor power than the actual value the worker will impart to the commodities he or she helps to produce.[69] Profit, as such, essentially resides in underpaid labor. Marx defines competition as a tendency toward equalization of profit margins, leading to monopolies as the consequence of competition rather than its antithesis.[70]

Marxist interpretations link economic competition to discrimination in the work place. As economists William Darity and Patrick Mason explain, "Race and gender exclusion are used to make some workers less competitive for the higher paying positions. This approach emphasizes that the major elements for the persistence of discrimination are racial or gender differences in the access to better paying jobs within and between occupations."[71] Racial inequality, then, can be traced to the economic system that generates it.[72] Persons with disabilities encounter similar power differentials in the labor market. [. . .]

In the neoclassical view, markets are efficient ethical generators and distributors of wealth. According to this theory, blame for the phenomenon of the wage gap falls on the individual himself. If one fails to keep up with changes in the workplace, the argument goes, it is because of the individual's shortcoming rather than the functioning of the labor market. If workers are less productive, it is their fault and they do not deserve a minimum wage (and certainly not a living wage) for their labor. A materialist analysis contends that the labor market is a social construct where marginalization of certain groups works to the advantage of the business class. [. . .]

The Business Backlash, Labor, and Profits

The US Commission on Civil Rights reports that one of the most persistent criticisms of the ADA has been that employers are forced to pay too high a price to comply with employment provisions.[73] While it is clear that the disabled should not be denied civil rights simply because employers may incur costs while attempting to comply with the ADA, business objections are informative and reveal labor market mechanisms endemic to capitalism. Business practices demonstrate that the economic structure does generate obstacles to the employment of disabled people. Equal opportunity has failed in this aspect to provide a sufficient remedy for economic discrimination. [. . .]

Whether real or perceived in any given instance, employers continue to express concerns about increased costs in the form of providing reasonable accommodations.[74] [. . .] In today's highly competitive business climate, it can fairly be asserted that business managers and owners will not cut into their profits for moral, noble, or socially just purposes to lower the disabled unemployment rate. [. . .]

Civil rights traditionally demand equal treatment, requiring that disabled people be treated the same as non-disabled people. In the case of employment and disability, however, the notion of civil rights within a capitalist paradigm envisions equal treatment but fails to acknowledge the reality of economic discrimination. This fatal oversight ensures that laws such as the ADA will necessarily fall short of accomplishing employment goals. For opportunity to be *truly* equal, biases (including economic biases) must be eradicated. A government committed to providing such opportunities could "level the playing field" to compensate for economic discrimination by employers. It could ensure ongoing health care for disabled people (preferably within a disability-sensitive universal health care system not linked to employment status), subsidize job accommodations, and allow other subsidies to reimburse businesses that hire or retain employees with disabilities. Government enactment of severe and immediate penalties on employers (including government employers) who balk at providing job accommodations in a timely manner could serve as a backup measure to further advance disabled workers' access to jobs.

There is ideological tension between remedies which grant subsidies and civil-rights type remedies which legally mandate that employers comply with antidiscrimination statutes. Under the ADA, employers are required to provide access and accommodations as a matter of individual right.[75] By contrast, subsidies provide a government offset to business costs based on the notion that it is in the government's (and society's) interest to see that disabled people are employed. Disability rights groups and activists (myself included) have favored the civil rights approach over subsidies, but given the economic discrimination inherent in capitalism, can we afford to remain fixed in our belief that civil rights will provide timely relief for those disabled people seeking employment redress in the courts? Will the courts initiate an economic revolution which forces business to provide accommodations? So far, disabled plaintiffs have faced great difficulty prevailing in court on key issues. [. . .]

It is reasonable to view consistently negative court outcomes as an extension of the business backlash against the ADA, and a particularly harmful one at that. Employers remain victorious in court. The American Bar Association's Commission on Mental and Physical Disability Law reports that while employers have complained the most of unfair treatment under the ADA, "the facts strongly suggest the opposite: employees are treated unfairly under the Act due to myriad legal technicalities that more often than not prevent the issue of employment discrimination from ever being considered on the merits."[76] Ruth Colker concludes that the courts are deploying strategies that result in "markedly pro-defendant outcomes under the ADA" by "abusing the summary judgment device"; judges are making decisions that should go to the jury.[77] Procedurally, she explains, this results in pro-employer outcomes because juries, traditionally more hospitable to civil rights, are not hearing the cases.[78]

Others have written at length on these matters.[79] To briefly explain here, legitimate plaintiff cases are thwarted when medical conditions are not granted the legal standing of "disability" under the law and when courts fail to comprehend equal rights as applied to disablement or to understand the purpose of reasonable accommodations.

Workers pay a heavy personal price when employers contest disablement or refuse badly needed access modifications, reasonable accommodations and/or removal of work barriers and choose instead to put up a fight in court. When, for example, an employee cannot work without an accommodation and the employer does not readily provide one, the worker is often unable to perform her job and is fired.[80] Common sense would dictate that when the worker has a protracted court battle ahead of her to enforce her right to an accommodation but no paycheck in the mail, the last practical resort is to go onto disability benefits. Yet employers use a worker's qualification for disability benefits to undermine discrimination cases against them. Under the Social Security Administration's (SSA) definition of disablement, a worker is qualified for benefits if he/she cannot work; SSA does not consider whether the employee could continue to work if the employer provided a reasonable accommodation. The employer, contesting the worker's discrimination suit, holds that if the worker claims he or she cannot work for purposes of claiming disability benefits, he or she *cannot* work and therefore the discrimination suit is moot.[81]

In the spring of 1999, this issue was brought before the Supreme Court in *Cleveland v. Policy Management Systems*.[82] There, the plaintiff became disabled, asked for but was denied a reasonable accommodation, then lost her job due to failure to perform. The plaintiff subsequently successfully applied for Social Security disability benefits. The plaintiff sued the employer for failure to comply with the ADA. The Supreme Court granted certiorari to decide "whether an ADA plaintiff's representation to the [Social Security Administration] that she was 'totally disabled' created a rebuttable presumption sufficient to judicially estop her later representation that, for the time in question, with reasonable accommodation, she could perform the essential functions of her job."[83]

The justices ruled in *Cleveland* that application for and receipt of SSDI benefits does not automatically estop a recipient from pursuing an ADA claim or erect a strong presumption against the recipient's ADA success.[84] However, it held that to survive a summary judgment motion an ADA plaintiff cannot ignore her SSDI contention that she was too disabled to work, but must explain why that contention is consistent with her ADA claim that she can perform the essential functions of her job, at least with reasonable accommodation. Under this holding, therefore, both parties have the opportunity to present or contest the plaintiff's explanation. Furthermore, a plaintiff may argue that her SSDI statement of total disability was made in a forum that does not consider the effect reasonable workplace accommodation would have on ability to work. She may also argue that such statements were reliable at the time they were made.[85]

The Supreme Court's ruling in *Cleveland* is beneficial from the plaintiff's perspective. It does not, however, preclude the employer from firing the worker first and does not guarantee a favorable outcome for the disabled employee. The court warned that "in some cases an earlier SSDI claim may turn out genuinely to conflict with an ADA claim."[86] It remains to be seen how workers with disabilities will fare in light of this ruling.

If *Cleveland* was a step forward, the Supreme Court took two steps back with rulings in the next three ADA employment cases: *Sutton v. United Airlines, Inc.*,[87] *Murphy v. United Parcel Service*,[88] and *Albertsons, Inc. v. Kirkingburg*.[89] At issue in these cases was the meaning of disability under the ADA. Significantly narrowing the scope of the law by use of these three cases, the Court ruled that correctable physical limitations (such as near-sightedness or high blood pressure) do not qualify as disabilities under the ADA and do not entitle plaintiffs to sue under Title I, regardless of whether they were fired because of such conditions. The Court distinguished between workers whose disabilities can be mitigated through corrective equipment or medicine and those workers whose disabilities cannot.

But what does "mitigated" imply? The dissenting justices in *Sutton* did not overlook the possibility that the majority's opinion in that case could be read to include the very people the Court maintained that the ADA protected.[90] Joined by Justice Breyer, Justice Stevens suggested that under the majority's ruling, the Act would not even protect people who had lost limbs in industrial accidents or while in armed service to their country. He pointed out that:

> With the aid of prostheses, coupled with courageous determination and physical therapy, many of these hardy individuals can perform all of their major life activities just as efficiently as an average couch potato. If the Act were just concerned with their present ability to participate in society, many of these individuals' physical impairments would not be viewed as disabilities . . . [and] many of these individuals would lack statutory protection from discrimination based on their prostheses.[91]

The dissenters accused the Court of making the ADA's safeguards "vanish when individuals make themselves more employable by ascertaining ways to overcome their physical or mental limitations."

Indeed, the majority opinion in *Sutton* presents workers with an unclear pathway for future employer/worker disputes. If one is not disabled because one's condition is "correctable" with medication, wheelchairs, prostheses, hearing aids, insulin, etc., how can one expect to receive a reasonable accommodation which depends on being defined as "disabled"? Yet employers can continue to fire workers because of performance limitations caused by such un-accommodated "nondisabilities." Additionally, employers may still conclude that a person is too disabled to work, even though under the law she is not disabled enough to be protected by the ADA. The ruling thus creates a Catch-22 for ADA plaintiffs: if one is disabled enough to sue, one is too disabled to work. The employer can fire the worker with a disability and the ADA is effectively withdrawn from those left under its auspices since if one is able to work, one has no grounds to sue.

The National Chamber of Commerce Litigation Center called the decision "a major victory for employers and the business community."[92] Business groups filing *amicus curie* briefs urged the Court to consider "the impact its decision in this case may have beyond the immediate concerns of the parties to the case."[93] The National Association of Manufacturers asserted that "like sexual harassment last year, disability discrimination is the major employment law issue on the Supreme Court's docket this year. Manufacturers should not be forced to pay damages, including punitive damages, to individuals who can lead normal lives with medication or corrective lenses."[94] The American Trucking Associations and the Equal Employment Advisory Council (a nonprofit association made up of more than 315 major companies) joined the amicus brief.

Clearly, greater government intervention in this precarious period is not only justified but essential to achieve positive outcomes for workers with disabilities. Government provision of ongoing health care, reasonable accommodation costs, and other subsidies would simply remove the issue of added cost from the employer's calculus when deciding to hire or retain disabled workers. Successful intervention promises to lessen the burden on disabled people otherwise forced to litigate in courts that are hostile to the rights of disabled individuals or that view "disability equal rights" as a subsidy to unfairly be paid by business.

However, these proposals must come with two qualifiers. First, such reforms would likely be stop-gap measures that could yield more job placement for disabled people but (as the next segments will show) cannot alone significantly impact disability unemployment in the overall political economy. Second, subsidies risk augmenting acrimony and division within the labor force. [. . .]

Job Insecurity and the Fixed Pie Syndrome

According to a quarterly nationwide survey of US workers inaugurated in August 1998 by Rutgers University's Heidrich Center for Workforce Development and the University of Connecticut's Center for Survey Research & Analysis, some 59 percent of respondents say they are very concerned about job security for "those currently at work."[95] An additional 28 percent indicate they are "somewhat concerned."[96]

Reports on US job trends show that workers have reason for concern. Workers appear less likely to be able to count on long-term employment which in the past provided steady wage growth, fringe benefits, and long-term job security. Jobs have grown more insecure in the 1990s as the share of workers in "long-term jobs" (those lasting at least ten years) fell from 41 percent in 1979 to 35.4 percent in 1996, with the worst deterioration having taken place since the late 1980s.[97] Corporate mergers and downsizing have contributed to job cuts or company shutdowns which cost nearly 30 percent of US workers their jobs from 1990 to 1995.[98] [...]

Underemployment, a broader measure of lack of employment success in the labor market, hovered at 10.1 percent for 1995.[99] For some economists this is a much more troubling statistic because it represents part-time workers who could not find full-time jobs and "discouraged workers" who wanted jobs but had been discouraged by their lack of success, subsequently leaving the labor force and dropping off the unemployment rolls.

To understand job-loss anxiety, it is necessary to know what happens to a worker's material reality when he or she is fired from a job. Workers have difficulties finding new employment, with more than one third still out of a job when interviewed one to three years after their displacement.[100] Workers rarely regain the old wage and are often forced to take jobs with pay averaging about thirteen percent less than the old job.[101] Others try to make ends meet with two or more part-time jobs. In 1995 more than 7.9 million people worked more than one job.[102]

In the 1990s the "contingent" workforce has grown; almost 30 percent of workers in 1997 were employed in situations that were not regular full-time jobs—independent contracting and other forms of self-employment such as temporary agency labor or day labor.[103] The number of workers employed by temporary agencies almost doubled, rising from 1.3 percent in 1989 to 2.4 percent in 1997.[104] Temporary workers on average earn less than workers with comparable skills and backgrounds who work in regular full-time jobs and are less likely to receive health or pension benefits.[105]

Displaced workers are facing increased job insecurity, lowered career expectations, lowered wages, and less control over their financial futures. Such economic trends have been linked to intergroup tensions. Increased intergroup disparities and divisiveness arise out of worsening economic conditions and increased competition for scarce resources.[106] Job insecurity can convert to a scarcity mentality: that is, the thinking that "there is not enough to go around."

Although employers are not required to hire disabled people under affirmative action, disabled people seeking work (as many as 7.8 million) and those potentially coming off public benefit programs under the Social Security Return-to-Work program represent an influx of new competition joining the ranks of labor. Women on welfare transitioning into jobs[107] are similarly positioned, both as a group of potential workers moving from the surplus population to work and as an undereducated workforce.[108]

The Personal Responsibility and Work Opportunity Reconciliation Act of 1996,[109] which ended federal welfare entitlements and ensconced welfare-to-work as a primary goal of federal welfare policy, illuminates the backlash experience. Welfare reform can be viewed through the lens of the zero-sum game theory, holding that under US capitalism one group benefits absolutely at the expense of the other. When some workers gain, others will lose; when some workers get a job, others will be displaced. Radical or Marxist theory asserts that employers deliberately exploit existing racial tensions and to divide the workers, increase profits, and keep the wage floor down.[110]

Two years after the enactment of welfare reform, both worker displacement and increased worker exploitation are already having an impact. Jon Jeter reported that women coming off welfare are competing with, and in some cases, displacing other low-wage workers under the "subsidized employment" plan.[111] Under this plan, the state pays a company to hire someone in the program at minimum wage. At the Omni Inner Harbor Hotel in Baltimore, for instance, social service workers placed thirteen jobless women into welfare-to-work jobs. During her ninety-day probation, each woman wipes, dusts, and vacuums on eight-hour shifts, five days a week, just as regular housekeepers paid $6.10 per hour. In return, she receives $410 a month in welfare benefits from the state and a $30 weekly stipend from the Omni Inner Harbor Hotel. The hotel saves the difference.[112]

According to Jeter, the entry of subsidized workers has increased coworker tension at the hotel where regular low-wage employees have formed a union among the 300 bellmen, housekeepers, doormen, and kitchen workers to improve their wages and benefits.[113] Jeter explains the twofold threat to coworkers: not only can subsidized welfare workers undercut regular worker wages and possibly interfere with union goals of better wages and benefits, but they raise the question of whether management will hire the welfare recipient as a permanent worker and displace a regular employee.[114] The welfare-to-work program has added even more uncertainty to an uneasy coexistence between groups of working poor in Maryland and across the nation, who fear the loss of their jobs to a cheaper workforce.

Welfare advocate Laura Riviera explains the effect of subsidized employment under the Wisconsin welfare-to-work program, called a model for welfare reform by the Clinton administration. "Women are introduced to other employees as 'the W-2 [welfare-to-work] participant.' Knowing that this person is required to work at the company for free, employees automatically feel threatened by this person," says Riviera. "This sets up a situation where it is very difficult for that person to get along well with other employees no matter how hard she tries."[115]

Riviera reports that she has heard from many women who were working and barely making ends meet until welfare reform began. "They were pushed out of their minimum wage jobs by these less expensive employees provided by the state and are now in the W-2 program."[116]

Similar job displacement has occurred under the workfare grant program in New York City, where the recipient receives a predetermined amount of money and in turn must work in a "volunteer" position assigned by the caseworker. When Steven Greenhouse conducted interviews with more than 50 workfare workers and visited more than two dozen work sites, he found that many workfare participants had taken the place of city workers.[117] He reports that:

> In many municipal agencies, the city has shrunk its regular workforce and increased the number of workfare participants. The Sanitation Department's workforce slid from 8,296 in 1990 under Mayor David N. Dinkins to 7,528 in early 1994, when Mr. Giuliani took office, then down 16 percent more last year, to 6,327. Today, the department employs more than 5,000 workfare laborers, who wear bright orange vests, sweeping streets and doing other tasks around the city.[118]

According to Greenhouse, workfare recipients are doing much of the work once performed by departed city employees. The 34,100 people in the city's Work Experience Program constitute a low-cost labor force that does a substantial amount of the work that had been done by municipal employees before Mayor Rudolph W. Giuliani reduced the city payroll by about 20,000 employees, or ten percent.[119]

Jon Jeter reported similar conflicts in the *Washington Post*. In Baltimore, officials at Patterson High School decided last year not to renew the contract with the janitorial company that cleaned the building and are now looking for welfare recipients to do the work, in part because "their rates would be cheaper."[120] A job-training program in Alabama requires some welfare recipients to work for more than four months without pay for employers such as Continental Eagle, a cotton gin manufacturer near Montgomery.[121]

Other sources of workfare labor are being sought as well. In New York City, for example, the Giuliani administration plans to extend workfare to homeless shelters, making workfare and other requirements a condition of shelter for the 4,600 families and seven thousand single adults in New York City's homeless shelter system.[122]

While the stated intent of welfare reform is to move those on welfare into work and thereby lower federal and city welfare outlays, participating businesses receive a net gain from welfare reform: having a captive workforce who can be pushed into lower wage jobs, whether permanently or temporarily, keeps wages low and increases business profit margins. An insidious fiscal benefit to government has also emerged—undercutting regular worker salaries cuts city service budgets and generates a surplus at the expense of the poorest parts of the workforce.[123] [. . .]

While the majority of reports focus on the initial success of welfare reform in terms of numbers of people dropped from the rolls, there is a growing realization amongst state and county officials that placing all recipients into jobs is unrealistic. [. . .]

There are not enough living-wage jobs available for women being forced off welfare, and there will not be enough jobs for disabled people wishing to work or to transition from public benefits into a job. The welfare reform experience indicates that subsidies to business can elevate coworker tension, yet, in the case of disability and employment, subsidies for reasonable accommodations and health care *will be necessary* to level economic discrimination inherent in business accounting practices. Just as women coming off AFDC (Aid to Families with Dependent Children) create increasing competition for jobs and increasing job insecurity, disabled job seekers must be aware that they too can generate resentment amongst those lacking job security who may view subsidies to disabled workers as a threat to their employment.

Though many disabled people will be entering the workforce at lower pay levels akin to the welfare-to-work population (due in part to the fact that large numbers of disabled people lack access to higher education), the global economy makes job insecurity a factor in the traditionally more secure educated class as well. Evidence of change can also be found in the incidence of displacement within the elite workforce. The President's Council of Economic Advisers reports that "further analysis shows that job displacement rates rose for more educated workers . . .

although blue collar and less educated workers remain more likely to be displaced than others, displacement rates have clearly risen among those workers who had been previously immune from the threat of job dislocation."[124]

Economists are beginning to see trends which indicate that white collar workers are no longer immune to neoliberal policies which emphasize free market production and increase the labor pool. As economists Anne Colamosca and William Wolman explain, globalization has produced an economy in which "the rapid worldwide spread of available skilled labor" is set "in head-to-head competition with their American counterparts."[125] Furthermore, the globalization of financial markets has served to lower the wage floor as employers search for low labor costs in far corners of the globe and American workers' wages shrink in response. "Capital migrates to low wage areas and the only way that it can be kept in the developed world is if wages in the developed world are kept low."[126]

Summary and Unresolved Solutions

In part, the ADA backlash stems from the design of our economic system. Differentials in pay, income, and employment opportunities persist in the labor market despite anti-discrimination laws. Civil rights, though still necessary to counter individual acts of prejudice and discrimination, have only the power to randomly distribute the maladies of unemployment and income and wage inequality throughout the population. If everyone were equally educated and trained for jobs and civil rights were strictly enforced, millions would remain unemployed and underemployed in any capitalist system. Anti-discrimination laws cannot bridge the systemic employment gap, and individual rights cannot reach the root of the parity predicament created by the economic structure. Neither the market nor civil rights laws can undermine the structure of inequality nor prevent its reproduction. [...]

To be effective, any solution to the backlash must address the very nature of social relations.[127] It must ask: What is work, who controls it, and what is its purpose? If work is controlled by the Federal Reserve, investors, and Wall Street, all looking to make ever-higher profits from people's labor rather than trying to make the system work for all, the paradigm itself must be challenged. It then becomes imperative to ask what an economy is for—to support market-driven profits, or to sustain community bonds and elevate human participation?

To stem the tide of the backlash, which promises to grow as more workers are displaced in the global economy,[128] it is essential to reassert the basic radical principle that an economy only works if it works for people; if it delivers health care, a living wage, and a secure livelihood and income for every person. The exclusion of even 3 percent of the population from employment in the liberal definition of "full employment" is simply intolerable.[129] Since private industry views unemployment as an integral part of the "normal" capitalist system (which keeps wages and inflation low and makes unemployment compulsory), people must bypass private industry and insist that government recognize the fundamental right of each person to a livelihood (full employment at a minimum of a living wage and quality disability-sensitive universal health care). This must be the very cornerstone of our economic policy.

A government guarantee of full employment would require reorganizing the economy to allow everyone free choice among opportunities for useful, productive and fulfilling paid employment or self-employment. Base compensation must be set at a living real wage below which no remuneration for disabled or non-disabled workers is allowed to fall.

The wide variety and range of disablement means that some disabled people may never be hired by businesses but would nevertheless like to be productive in their communities. In order to bring more excluded persons into the workforce, it will be necessary to expand the work environment beyond the capitalist profit motive and ensure that federal and state governments act as the employers of last resort. In addition, those unable to work for pay or find employment must have a government entitlement to an adequate standard of living which rises with increases in the wealth and productivity of society.

Problems of Power

Gregory Mantsios writes:

> [T]he class structure in the United States is a function of its economic system—capitalism, a system that is based on private rather than public ownership and control of commercial enterprises, and on the class division between those who own and control and those who do not. Under capitalism, these enterprises are governed by the need to produce a profit for the owners, rather than to fulfill collective needs.[130]

Inequality is traceable both to the economic system[131] and to the interaction between private interests and government. Liberal remedies that seek change by requiring government to enact sustained full employment, raise the minimum wage, lower interest rates, and initiate price stability still rely on the premise that these controls can occur with capitalism intact in a democratic society, when hierarchical power relations remain a crucial impediment to realizing such positive outcomes.

Many have questioned the relationship between political power, monetary policy, and wealth inequality in our democracy. There is consensus amongst these theorists (some liberal, some radical) that government has failed to stop rising inequality and contributed to the decline of labor power because it has been derelict in its duty to exercise power over private capital. The degradation of workers occurs in this age of mergers and acquisitions, bolstered by the power of speculative capital and unregulated by government precisely *because capital has control of government*.[132] The enormous power of private capital over government is evident in business's backlash against the ADA, Federal Reserve inflation management strategies primarily aimed to benefit Wall Street, the millions of dollars spent by the insurance industry to prevent a universal health care program, and both the passage and content of welfare reform legislation passed by Congress and signed by President Clinton in 1996.

After several centuries of capitalism, our society still shows no signs of allowing sustained full employment. If history provides any guide, it is safe to assume that the decision-making class will *never* allow it. In the 1940s the US experienced the lowest unemployment rate in its history (one percent); directly on its heels came McCarthyism, an organized attack on socialist ideals of equitable distribution. In the 1970s, drops in wages and the standard of living occurred at the same time as a decline in the power of labor unions.[133] Economist Michal Kalecki's observation that labor must be kept weak to preserve profits and the class dictatorship of capital seems undeniable.[134] Government enactment of full employment under capitalism can only result in an even greater crushing of labor so as to reinstate "stability" and reassert control over the economic lives of workers.

Capitalist measures—whether the type promoted by free market conservatives or that of welfare liberals—fail to respond to the discrimination faced by millions of disabled Americans. Only measures that account for the existence of systemic and long-standing economic inequality will provide the necessary protections against further workplace discrimination. The present reality, however, is that disabled people are the last legally protected class to enter the workforce. They seek economic equality at a time when unemployment levels are low and downsizing and market globalization are in full force. It is in such a "positive" economic environment, when business has obtained both the legal and political legitimacy necessary to discriminate in the name of workplace and market efficiency, that our battle for distributive justice becomes the toughest of all.

CHAPTER 6

What Disability
Civil Rights Cannot Do

Introduction

In the US it is now evident that disability civil rights do not equate with a lowering of the disabled unemployment rate. Despite a growing economy—the best possible scenario for increasing the employment of disabled persons—and a low aggregate national official unemployment rate (4–5 percent) presiding over much of the nine years that the ADA employment provisions have been in effect, the unemployment rate for working-age disabled population has barely budged from its chronic state—hovering at 70 percent.[1] [. . .]

According to a recent study, while many Americans reaped higher incomes from an economy that created a record number of new jobs during seven years of continuous economic growth (1992–1998), the employment rates of disabled men and women continued to fall so that by 1998, they were still below the 1992 level.[2] A *Boston Globe* headline news story, "Access and Closed Doors: Despite Federal Act, Number of Disabled with No Job is Rising," noted that pollster Louis Harris & Associates found that 71 percent of people with disabilities who are of working age were unemployed in 1998, 5 percentage points higher than in 1986, when the study was first conducted.[3]

What does the empirical data show has happened to employment during the economic expansion of the 1990s with full implementation of the ADA's employment provisions? The Congressional Research Service found that the employed share of eighteen-to-sixty-four-year-olds with disabilities who reported they were able to work grew from 70.2 percent in 1992 to 72.3 percent in 1996. Over the same period, the proportion of the non-disabled working-age population who were employed rose from 78.5 percent to 80.5 percent. The job prospects for the disabled population improved to the same degree as the non-disabled population, meaning the gap in employment rates did not narrow. Study author Linda Levine concludes, "this suggests that the ADA did not provide an extra boost to the employment situation of working-age adults with disabilities through the mid-1990s."[4]

The disability rights movement (DRM) in the US has largely conceptualized disability as a minority group, which is disadvantaged and denied majority rights status.[5] Identifying the source of disabled persons unemployment in discriminatory attitudes of employers and physical barriers in the work environment, the DRM has sought to alter the historical exclusion of disabled persons from the workforce through the establishment of individual legal rights and remedy under the liberal theory of "equal opportunity" to employment—which essentially means equal access to a job not available to all.

The ADA[6] is both a civil rights bill intended to end employer discrimination and a labor economics bill, intended to increase the relative wages and employment of disabled persons. The Act states, "[T]he Nation's proper goals regarding individuals with disabilities are to assure . . . economic self-sufficiency[.] Discrimination . . . costs the United States billions of dollars in unnecessary expenses resulting from dependency and nonproductivity."[7] The ADA bans discrimination on the basis of disability through the establishment of constitutional law and regulations which are geared to "level the playing field" for disabled job applicants and to induce employers to accommodate impairments on the job. It gives disabled persons redress against work-based disability discrimination in the courts and through the Equal Employment Opportunity Commission (EEOC).

There is consensus, however, amongst scholars and analysts that the US courts have failed to enforce the ADA as civil rights proponents intended and that EEOC enforcement has fallen short. A study by the American Bar Association's Commission on Mental and Physical Disability Law, for instance, shows that disabled workers bringing discrimination suits are unlikely to succeed in court.[8] Of the more than twelve hundred cases filed under the employment provisions of the ADA from 1992 to 1998, disabled employees prevailed only 8 percent of the time. By 2000 employers prevailed 95 percent of the time. Another study by Ohio State University law professor Ruth Colker shows similar results, finding that employers successfully defend more than 93 percent of reported ADA

employment discrimination cases at the trial court level and succeed in 84 percent of cases appealed.[9]

So far, disabled plaintiffs have faced great difficulty prevailing in court on key
issues. The US Commission on Civil Rights notes that many disability experts as-
cribe the problem to judicial and administrative confusion over interpretation of the
employment statutes.[10] Professor Matthew Diller explains that legitimate plaintiff
cases are being thwarted often for nonsensical reasons (such as medical conditions
are not granted the legal standing of "disability" under the law), and that courts
are resistant to both comprehending and accepting equal rights and reasonable accommodation as applied to disablement.[11] Arlene Mayerson, an attorney with the
Disability Rights Education and Defense Fund, characterizes ADA case law as "hy-
per technical, often illogical interpretations of the ADA," which have generated a
"disturbing trend" of court precedents.[12] Robert Burgdorf Jr., one of the drafters of
the ADA, concludes that "legal analysis has proceeded quite a way down the wrong
road."[13] Burgdorf points to a judicial tendency to view ADA plaintiffs as seeking
special benefits and treatment instead of equal rights.[14] Bonnie Tucker theorizes
that there is an inherent flaw in the civil rights paradigm when it comes to equal
rights for disabled persons. She suggests that judges may be viewing the provision of
reasonable accommodation as an "extra" requirement, an expansion of traditional
civil rights concept and, consequently, rejecting the legitimacy of disability rights
under equal rights principles.[15]

To explain such outcomes, I have sought to examine the relationship between
politics, policy, and economics—particularly with regard to the interests of business. Disability scholars such as Victor Finkelstein, Michael Oliver, Colin Barnes,
Paul Abberley, Nirmala Erevelles, Lennard Davis, Brendan Gleeson, and others
have advanced the position that the capitalist system—particularly the com-
modification of labor—is a crucial contributing factor to the lack of economic
advancement of disabled people. Going back to Marx's theory of absolute impoverishment, Ernest Mandel clarifies Marx's observation that capitalism "throws
out of the production process" a section of the proletariat: unemployed, old people, disabled persons, the sick, etc.[16] Marx calls these groups a part of the poorest
stratum, "bearing the stigmata of wage labor." As Mandel says, "This analysis retains its full value, even under the 'welfare' capitalism of today."[17]

While others have made links between capitalism and disablement, my purpose has been to expose how modern capitalism perpetuates this substratum in
the face of disabled people's struggle for their place the US labor force. In this
vein I have sought to expose systemic economic discrimination against disabled

workers in a capitalist economy that the ADA cannot address or remedy and will return to this matter below. I have also argued that ADA court failures have been prompted by capitalist opposition made more powerful in a neoliberal era, where conservative forces have politically achieved a more *laissez faire*, deregulated economy, successfully targeting regulations they view as interfering with business for weakening or repeal.[18] [. . .]

The most recent evidence that these forces remain intact: the Supreme Court's weakening of the ADA in *Garrett, Sutton, Murphy*, and *Albertsons* disability employment decisions; the striking down of the Age Discrimination Act in *Kimel v. Florida Board of Regents*; and the invalidation of the Violence Against Women Act in *United States v. Morrison*.

After years of dedicated civil rights activism in the 1950 and '60s the American civil rights leader Dr. Martin Luther King Jr. outgrew the liberal view that economic justice for Blacks was possible through the enactment of civil rights laws geared to make race-based employment discrimination against the law. King realized that civil rights (even when coupled with economic expansion) could not solve the mass unemployment of Black Americans.

At the 1967 Southern Christian Leadership Conference convention Dr. King implored the movement to:

> [A]ddress itself to the question of restructuring the whole of American society. There are 40 million poor people here. And one day we must ask the question, "Why are there 40 million poor people in America?" And when you begin to ask that question, you are raising questions about the economic system, about a broader distribution of wealth. When you ask that question, you begin to question the capitalistic economy . . .[19]

For King, the theme of job creation in a capitalist economy was an ongoing and primary part of his peoples' struggle for justice. "We need an economic bill of rights. This would guarantee a job to all people who want to work and are able to work . . ."[20] Today, almost 40 years since the passage of the Civil Rights Act of 1964, no economic rights have been enacted and Black unemployment remains twice (8 percent) that of the official national rate (4.2 percent). This is so even when civil rights have been accompanied by affirmative action measures designed to promote hiring and remedy past race discrimination. The ADA was not followed by affirmative action for disabled workers. There is no reason to believe disability civil rights outcomes will fare better.

In practice, civil rights, which primarily focus on attitudes and prejudice, have not given sufficient attention to the barriers that the economic structure and power relationships erect against the employment of disabled persons. This paper explores the shortcomings of the liberalist "equal opportunity" approach to employment. [...] Class interests perpetuate the exclusion of disabled persons from the workforce through systemic business accounting practices and compulsory unemployment. If we conceptualize disablement as a product of the exploitative economic structure of capitalist society [. . .] then it becomes clear that anti-discrimination legislation, by failing to acknowledge the contradictions of promoting equal opportunity in class-based (unequal) society, is insufficient to solve the unemployment predicament of disabled persons. Instead, the liberal rights model serves to forestall criticism of relationships of power at the center of the exclusion from employment and inequality that disabled persons face. This paper will offer such a criticism.

The Relevance of the Political Economy

Political economy is a term used for nearly three hundred years to express the inter-relationship between the political and the economic affairs of the state. In terms of economics, liberals tend to believe that the current system is basically just, and that injustices and unemployment, low pay, inequality and poverty that occur within that system are mere unintended consequences of an otherwise beneficent economy. They are reformists who believe that gross inequalities can be leveled through legislation and other measures aimed at correcting "market failures." In the US and elsewhere the DRM similarly has largely accepted the foundations of free market ideology by framing the terms of the justice debate as the rights of disabled people entitled to receive equal treatment from the existing labor market.[21] In contrast, left political economy looks to the laws rooted in the ongoing reproduction and expansion of this system of material accumulation as the source of the ills. Radical economists believe that the economic system itself is the problem: the system of profit does not create hardship as the unfortunate mishap of an otherwise just social order; rather, the pain experienced by people under such a system is very much integral to that system, and is required by it in order to function. People, including many disabled people, are excluded from work in such a system, and thus poor and even destitute, not because the system is breaking down, but because it is working exactly as intended.

The notion of the US as a meritocracy where individual failings are deemed the result of personal shortcomings is a seductive ideological posture. The appeal to rugged individualism—that we can be anything we want if we persevere—is an American tradition and perhaps a comforting notion, but barriers to advancement and achievement are often unrelated to individual effort, ability, or motivation. Disability civil rights laws (or any civil rights) do not subject that assumption to a challenge. Civil rights, for instance, are based on the premise that the individual citizen is an equal actor in the judicial process with the legal power to redress injustice through court challenges to discrimination; but what if the individual, due to her class position, lacks the money to hire an attorney, or has not the education or circumstance to secure those rights? Gender and race are also known determinants of lack of access to the courts. Furthermore, rights depend upon court interpretation. What if the political climate of the courts is such that her rights are likely to be thwarted by judges acting in opposition to the ideological premise of those rights? What if rights are in direct class conflict; if for instance, the business class has amassed such political power that the civil right has essentially become moot through defeat after defeat in the courts and few attorneys will risk taking such cases because they have little prospect of winning (and getting paid)?

In these instances, individual action and individual "right" is blocked and annulled by class and politics outside the control of the individual.

> [. . . when "rights-bearing persons"] lack the power and resources to properly "compete," rights can do nothing but reinforce the status quo, as those left powerless can do nothing [but] make sporadic and/or symbolic claims.[22]

The economic system presents a similar set of obstructions. The founding principle for the dominant economic model of our day or "pure economics" (what is falsely referred to as neoclassical economics[23]) is "methodological individualism," which treats society as nothing more than the apolitical aggregate of its component individuals, and strips the economic structure of any social dimension except the interaction of sole individual activity and projects. While both pure economic and left economic theories might allow that individuals can act independently and according to their wants, left economists recognize that behind these private wants stands an objective structure of reproduction whose requirements dominate the individual in the carrying out of her private interests. While the pure economists hold onto their theory that maximization of well-being occurs because of individual merit, left economists recognize that structural barriers dominate individual wants. As the economist Samir Amin, notes "real society, far from being built up out of direct encounters among individual behaviors, is an infinitely more complex structure combining social classes, nations, states, big businesses, collective projects and political and ideological forces."[24]

A left economic perspective does not concede disablement as a socio-attitudinal construct that can be corrected by erasing incorrect attitudes or prohibiting prejudiced-based employment discrimination. It places a different set of questions at the apex of concern, as Dr. King posed. Why are there millions of persons both with and without impairments who are willing to work left unemployed in our economy? Why in the richest nation in the world are people still impoverished and working at below living wages, and why are "deserving" disabled persons severed from the means of making a livelihood and subjected to bare survival on at-or-below-poverty disability benefits? Left political economy reflects on the limits of the market as an institution for want satisfaction and that is the approach taken here.

Compulsory Unemployment

The capitalist economy inherently restricts the liberal application of "equal opportunity" to employment for all because unemployment is not an aberration of capitalism; rather, it is a built-in component of the market economy that requires many people be unemployed against their will.[25] Not every person will be employed, not every person's material needs will get met through employment. [. . .] Large numbers of people are left jobless in part because mainstream economists believe that a threshold of unemployment is necessary to avoid inflation and maintain the health of the American economy.[26]

From 1999 to May 2000, for instance the Federal Reserve raised interest rates about two points. As Federal Reserve Chairman Alan Greenspan explained it, the economy was too healthy, unemployment had fallen too low, and wages had started to inch upward, thereby raising the specter of inflation.

Greenspan told congress:

> At some point in the continuous reduction in the number of available workers willing to take jobs, short of the repeal of the law of supply and demand, wage increases must rise above even impressive gains in productivity. This would intensify inflationary pressures or squeeze profit margins, with either outcome capable of bringing our growing prosperity to an end.[27]

It became necessary, according to the view of the Federal Reserve, to raise the cost of borrowing money, thereby cooling off the expansion and hiring, and nudging the unemployment numbers back up to slow wage increases. This deserves repeating. The Federal Reserve sought to raise (not lower) the unemployment rate, to put a halt to both hiring and better wages for workers.

Why? Tight labor markets—a "labor shortage" or a smaller active reserve army—mean pressure for wage increases from labor; as unemployment goes down, labor costs go up because there is more pressure for wage increases. [...]

Since full employment undermines labor discipline and the social position of management, political economist Michal Kalecki posits that capitalists accept unemployment "as an integral part of the normal capitalist system."[28] Economist Michael Piore explains government's reluctance to pursue full employment objectives; they believe that such policies would create rising expectations among workers—expectations that would not be met and so result in social and political instability.[29] Positive unemployment rates, then, become the outgrowth of class struggle over the distribution of income and political power.[30] [...]

How does this affect the disabled unemployment rate? The implications of a decision-making class engineered slowdown are perhaps greatest for disabled persons, whether one is seeking a job or already employed. The existence of an extremely tight labor market is generally a positive environment for previously unemployed populations to get a job. This is because a low supply of workers forces business to hire and train workers that they may not have been willing to hire or might have avoided at another point in the business cycle.[31] A downturn of the economy, however, means that disabled workers who have a job may be laid off. [...] Overall, persons with significant disabilities are hurt by negative changes in the economy evidenced by the fact that disability benefits claims rise during recessions.[32] [...]

Essentially, about twenty million working people are condemned, by federal anti-inflationary policies which ration employment, to either compulsory unemployment or employment at low wages. This demonstrates clearly that economic suffering, low wages and poverty are not the result of individual moral failings or a pathological "dependency" nor a decline in the Protestant work ethic, but rather, are built in to the structure of modern capitalism. It is easy to see why Nobel laureate William Vickrey, in his presidential address to the American Economic Association in 1993, called the "natural" unemployment rate "one of the most vicious euphemisms ever coined."[33] Pure economics rationalizes unemployment—as "voluntary"—without addressing the economic system or social relations that create it.

Microeconomic Matters: Capitalist Calculus

Mainstream economists have traditionally devoted (and limited) themselves to the "trade-offs" between equality and market efficiency. [...] Liberal society promotes equality by establishing social and political rights that are, in theory, but rarely ever in reality, distributed equally and universally. That is individual rights are considered to be above the rules of the market. There is, however, an interrelationship between market institutions, inequality, and equal opportunity.

Policy makers are keenly aware that rights affect the functioning of the economy and at the same time, their operation is affected by the market. An entitlement, for instance, is more likely to be established as a right when it has a relatively low cost. When Congress enacted the ADA, it recognized that the traditional civil rights model would not serve to provide equal opportunities for disabled people in the labor force. The DRM articulated the need for accommodations in the workplace and Congress determined that the provision of a "reasonable accommodation" was a necessary component of civil rights for disabled persons in order that they might be integrated into mainstream employment.

Considerable discussion flowed during the ADA debates over the cost that equal rights for the disabled population posed. Senator Paul Simon stated during the congressional hearings, for instance, that Congress was going to "do the right and decent thing" by enacting the ADA despite the costs that would be incurred.[34] Former President George Bush was intent upon "containing the costs that may be incurred."[35] Indeed, the right to a "reasonable accommodation" was watered down significantly with the injection of the "undue hardship" clause to alleviate business concerns. The employer is not mandated to pay for an accommodation if doing so would create "undue" financial hardship on the business; the disabled worker's theoretical "right" is not a right, it is dependent upon the employer's calculus. This and other exemptions in the ADA catering to the business class has led me to refer to the ADA as a free-market civil rights bill[36] because the business owner's right to property (wealth) is weighted more heavily than the disabled individual's "right" to accommodation on the job and, hence, to employment.

Even so [. . .] Paul Craig Roberts, a supply-side economist at the Center for Strategic and International Studies in Washington, warned on the day the Act was signed that "[the ADA] will add enormous costs to businesses that will cut into their profits."[37] [. . .]

Capitalism is a system of social relations in which profit-maximization and a constant need to revolutionize the forces of production are basic and inescapable conditions of survival, as they have never been in any other social form. Capital is only interested in labor that will increase material wealth. [. . .]

Pure economic theorists conclude then that if disabilities among the direct producers add to the cost of production without increasing the rate of profit, owners and managers will necessarily discriminate against them. Expenses to accommodate "disabled" persons in the workplace will be resisted as an addition to the fixed capital portion of constant capital.[38] [. . .]

Ruling for the employer-defendant in the Seventh Circuit in 1995, Judge Richard Posner relates the business schematic of cost/benefit analysis to the ADA:

> If the nation's employers have potentially unlimited financial obligations to forty-three million disabled persons, the Americans with Disabilities Act will have imposed an indirect tax potentially greater than the national debt. We do not find an intention to bring about such a radical result in either the language of the Act or its history. The preamble actually "markets" the Act as a cost saver, pointing to "billions of dollars in unnecessary expenses resulting from dependency and nonproductivity" ß12101(a)(9). The savings will be illusory if employers are required to expend many more billions in accommodation than will be saved by enabling disabled people to work.[39] [. . .]

Civil rights laws have historically demanded equal treatment designed to remedy the "irrational" acts of employers. In the case of employment and disability, civil rights laws operate within a capitalist labor market where profit maximization is "rational." Civil rights laws envision equal treatment, but do not acknowledge the full impact of competition and efficiency governing capitalist economies. The market transgresses on nearly every liberal right, including the right to a job accommodation. Furthermore, it needs to be recognized that productivity is at the center of capitalist accumulation. Capital holds labor as always, *a priori*, the retarding factor of productivity because labor can never produce fast enough or equivalently, at a low enough valued rate, to suit the expectation of an accelerating profit curve. Therefore, it is likely that impaired persons' labor will continue to be perceived as less than what is desirable to maximize profit.

Equal opportunity laws such as the ADA must fall short of remedying disabled peoples' employment predicament. For equal opportunity to be truly equal, biases (including economic biases) must be eradicated.[40] However, historically, capitalism has not been a system of material production that has taken into account the human consequences of its development. It is unlikely that disability discrimination can be eradicated under the current mode of production.

Beyond Equal Opportunity

Some economic theorists,[41] ignoring the damaging capitalist superstructure, have sought to alter the way neoclassical economics treats disability by attempting to show that it miscalculates the value of disabled workers. In this view, the capitalists need to "correct" their irrational (stereotypical) approach to avoid market failure. What galls these theorists is the "unfairness" of particular markets. They hope through information dissemination to employers to act rationally and create "fair" markets of perfect competition. However well intended, this seems a futile ploy in a fixed game where disabled workers are at the bottom of the competitive labor market and that labor market is, by design, structured to leave millions of workers underemployed and unemployed.

Further, says economist Amin, pure economics is not rational, it is a para-science (not a science as it claims to be), which needs replacing with a reality-based approach. Why give it any credence by persuading business they aren't acting "rationally"? Politically, pure economics is based on a single preoccupation. Amin writes:

> [Pure economics is] a preoccupation with showing that "the market" rules with the force of natural law, producing not merely a "general equilibrium" but the best of all possible equilibria, guaranteeing full employment in freedom, the "social optimum" and this preoccupation is nothing but the expression of a fundamental ideological need, the need to legitimize capitalism by making it synonymous with rationality—which, in conformity with bourgeois ideology, is seen as nothing more than the use of technically rational means for the individual pursuit of mercantile profit.[42]

By contrast, left political economy holds

> no prior assumptions attributing to the system any tendency toward equilibrium. It does not hold that class struggles upset any really existing equilibrium, or even a really existing, yet provisional, disequilibrium. In sum, Marxist political economy is realistic—whereas there is no realism at all about pure economics, which abstracts from reality (classes, states, the global system) so that its discourse, emptied of reality, is left a mythical fable.[43]

The ADA and equal opportunity (a fable) is a "demand-side" solution for a capitalist society, wherein the disabled workers and would-be workers, by definition, do not have the social or political power to realize their economic wants. Power lies at production, with the owners of capital. Productive capital is privately owned and owners are not forced to make capital available for the employment of the labor of others. Denial of access, therefore, is an important property right of capitalists to which workers do not have an equal legal rebuttal, since there is no "right to a job."

The failure of liberalism forces the need for a new discourse of liberation. We need a radically different approach. Disability, being a reflection of social class—in this instance, proletariats shoved out of the labor force—presents an opening to force a broader discussion about the legitimacy of the organization of work and our economy. We cannot ignore private ownership of the social economy. There is no "equal opportunity" when the most important economic decisions about investment, choice of technology, work processes, and the organization of work itself are in the hands of a tiny elite of corporate owners and monetary policy makers. Nor can economic (or any other) democracy be realized when this elite can effectively block progressive public policies by threatening or carrying out disinvestment from the progressive jurisdiction as has happened in the conservative US courts with the ADA employment provisions.

Both pure economics and liberal civil rights law remedies are based on the "atomistic individual" and as such need to be seen as products of bourgeois ideology.

Perhaps then disabled peoples' struggle for an equal place in the realm of work will be met with the class consciousness necessary to challenge the current disabled unemployment predicament.

CHAPTER 7

Supreme Injustice: Disability and the Judiciary

Part I

Listening to Elouise Cobell of the Blackfeet Nation on *Democracy Now!*[1] describe how Native Americans have been cheated out of their government-run trust fund income by the federal government, it occurred to me that Native American people and disabled people share a common grievance when it comes to government enforcement of the law.

Laws are made by Congress but other branches of government do not necessarily uphold the law. Legislation is enacted but government often does not adequately enforce it. Government conveniently ignores laws—in some instances unintentionally and out of incompetence but in others, government (in its many varied institutions) intentionally does not to abide by the law. Rather it evades it, bypasses it, weakens it, or makes it obsolete.

Instead of competent government regulation we have civil litigation. The process of civil litigation to enforce the ADA has been an arduous one, prone before a hostile Supreme Court.

As legal cases work their way to the Supreme Court, the court has seen fit to narrow the reach of the act on local government. A year ago [in 2001—*Ed.*], for instance, the Supremes ruled that state workers cannot use the civil rights law to win money damages for job discrimination. The court held that the disability rights law does not trump states' constitutional immunity against being sued for damages in federal courts (*Garrett v. Alabama*).

Over ten years after passage of the ADA, Jeffrey Gorman, a paraplegic who lives in Missouri, was badly injured while being taken to jail for trespassing at a country-western bar, because the Kansas City police department had not complied with ADA regulations. Gorman, who uses a wheelchair, warned officers that they did not have an accessible van to transport him safely to jail. According to Gorman's lawyer, the officers ignored Gorman, removed him from his wheelchair, propped him on a bench, and tied him to the vehicle's wall with his own belt. During the trip to the jail, Gorman fell and injured his shoulder and back. He had surgery due to the injury. None of these facts are contested.

Just think of it like this. If a non-disabled person could not be transported to jail because there were no seats for him/her in a patrol car, and the police strapped him to the top of their squad car using the belt from his clothing and the person fell off the car and injured themselves to the extent that he required surgery, would a jury punish that police department with a huge monetary award? You bet it would. It would seek punishment to avoid having the same egregious act reoccur. Would the lawyers for the city come around and try to undo that award? It is unlikely city politicians would risk public outcry.

In Gorman's case, the jury did award him compensatory and punitive damages. Kansas City did not contest the compensatory damages but appealed the punitive damages, taking the case to the Eighth District Court. It agreed with Gorman that punitive damages were in order but noted that the Sixth District Court had ruled differently in a similar case, an unfortunate signal that the Supreme Court, so hostile to disability rights, would settle the question.

Gorman hoped the Supreme Court would rule that "they [Kansas City] are not above the law even though they're the government."[2] Local government wanted protection from lawsuits when they broke the law. The Kansas City defense even asserted at the jury trial that since Gorman was mobile with the use of a corrective device, the wheelchair, he was not disabled under the ADA (Federal Rights Project). Some disabled persons have been dismissed as illegitimate ADA plaintiffs because their disabilities can be mitigated by drugs, devices, what have you. It is a bit nauseating to know that lawyers for Kansas City used the argument that Gorman was not technically disabled and had no right to sue under the ADA because his wheelchair mitigated his disablement.

[In mid-2002—*Ed.*] the Supremes agreed with Kansas City in *Barnes v. Gorman* and threw out the punitive damages holding that such damages are unavailable in private suits brought under the ADA and the Rehabilitation Act. When

Congress passed the ADA, it did not specify that people could collect punitive damages for violations, but since the ADA was fashioned like the Civil Rights Act of 1964, there was congressional understanding of the availability of punitive damages under Title VI.

Lawyers for the local government in Kansas City and the Bush administration, however, argued that Congress never intended for cities to face large jury judgments. Justice Scalia, writing for the court, said that adding punitive damages in ADA cases "could well be disastrous." He said recipients of federal funds probably would not agree "to exposure to such unorthodox and indeterminate liability."

The corporatist court applied contract-law analogy in throwing out the punitive damages. It held that "a remedy is appropriate relief only if the recipient is on notice that, by accepting federal funding, it exposes itself to such liability." The court reasoned that "since Title VI mentions no remedies; and punitive damages are generally not available for breach of contract," no damages are available under the ADA or the Rehabilitation Act. There are still punitive damages available to women and minorities under Title VI. How broadly will this court extend its ruling?

We in the disability community know from years of repeated problems at all levels of government that the Gorman case is not an isolated incident. The ADA was passed in 1990, yet over a decade later many local and state governments are not in compliance with its regulations. The significance of *Barnes v. Gorman* is broader than a disabled man being wrongly transported to jail. Local government is responsible for many public services: transportation, health, welfare, jails, and the local courts, to name but a few. If disabled persons are denied the right to seek punitive damages when governments violate the law, there will be little incentive for governments to get their act together and make programs and systems accessible.

Still the larger issue is that of societal exclusion—and the social relations which erect exclusion. Disability is a social experience which arises from the specific ways in which society organizes its fundamental activities. Work, transportation, leisure, education, and domestic life disable persons when they are not accessible. We are "disabled" by the way a society is organized.

With civil rights laws in place, disabled citizens are still treated like second- or third-class citizens—still shut out from full participation in the affairs and life of our communities. The Supreme Court has the power of judicial interpretation to decide the intent and scope of laws as they are applied in society in specific situations. So far, the Supreme Court, the final arbiter of law, has seen fit to continue to disable us.

Part II

In March [2002—*Ed.*], Justice Sandra Day O'Connor said the Supreme Court's 2001–2002 term will likely be remembered as the "disabilities act term" for all the cases dealing with the [ADA] civil rights law. [...]

The Supreme Court chooses which cases it will hear and which ones it will let stand. In every disability case the court agreed to hear this term, the disabled worker had prevailed at the district court or appellate court level. The Supreme Court justices could have left well enough alone. Instead the high court fulfilled its historical mandate to act as a check on the democratic majority and to protect private contract and property. The justices overturned the lower courts' decisions in favor of the disabled individual in every one of the cases they reviewed.

Ella Williams (up against Toyota) had won the right to retain another job which accommodated her carpal tunnel syndrome, Mario Echazabal (Chevron) who has Hepatitis C had won the right to work at an oil refinery, and Robert Barnett (US Airways) had won the right to a mailroom job which allowed him to continue to work with a bad back. All lost their right to a reasonable accommodation at the feet of this corporatist Supreme Court. [...]

In each of the three employment discrimination cases the loser corporations— Toyota Manufacturing of Kentucky, ChevronTexaco Corp., and US Airways— gleefully petitioned the Supreme Court to overturn the victorious workers in their quest for a reasonable accommodation on the job.

The corporations had a reason to expect victory since the Supreme Court had dealt blows to disabled workers the previous court term. Last year began the slaughter of the definition of "disabled" under the ADA. In what has become known as the Sutton trilogy, the Supreme Court narrowed the definition of disability and the numbers of persons who can seek redress under the ADA (*Sutton v. United Airlines, Murphy v. United Parcel Service, and Albertsons, Inc. v. Kirkingburg*).

The court ruled that impairments are not disabilities if they can be mitigated by lifestyle, by devices, or by medications. The lower courts, following Sutton, now disqualify people with diabetes, heart conditions, epilepsy, cancer, and "mental illness" from pursuing ADA employment discrimination claims because their impairments can be mitigated with medications.

Caught in a viscous Catch-22, workers with these conditions are "too functional" to be "disabled" yet can be fired for the "non-disabling" conditions. The Supreme Court virtually de-defined disability into thin air.

As Ruth O'Brien put it, the Supreme Court "turned the ADA on its head" by giving employers "the right to discriminate" and "the freedom to decide against hiring people who had limiting impairments."³ [. . .]

In the 2001–2002Y term the justices got another chance to come to the aid of big business and de-define disability in the *Toyota Manufacturing, Kentucky, Inc. v. Williams* case. The justices ruled that Ella Williams, although impaired, was not a qualified individual with a disability under the ADA because carpal tunnel syndrome did not "substantially limit" Williams in any major life activity since Williams could "still brush her teeth, wash her face, bathe. . ."!

These were actual examples the court gave. The justices threw out work as a "major life activity" prerequisite for ADA coverage! This meant that in the future a person should no longer be considered disabled merely because one could no longer perform their job.

In its *amicus* brief to the court, the US Chamber of Commerce and the American Trucking Associations called the Toyota decision, "keeping the lid on ADA litigation." The Equal Employment Advisory Council (a nonprofit association made up of more than three hundred and fifteen major companies) joined the *amicus*. Repetitive motion injuries accounted for more than a third of the 1.7 million workplace injuries reported in 1999, but these workers have little to no chance now to use the ADA to demand their employers accommodate them by placing them in another job that they can perform.

Robert Barnett had secured a vacant job in a US Airways mailroom after back problems left him unable to handle cargo. Later, when two employees with seniority decided they wanted to transfer to the mailroom, Barnett was bumped from his job and sued US Airways under the ADA.

When congress enacted the ADA, it recognized that the traditional civil rights model would not serve to provide equal opportunities for disabled people in the labor force. The disability rights movement articulated the need for accommodations in the workplace and Congress determined that the provision of a "reasonable accommodation" was a necessary component of civil rights for disabled persons in order that they might be integrated into mainstream employment.

Congress had included "reassignment to a vacant position" on its list of what was meant by a "reasonable accommodation." But Justice Scalia challenged, "What in the statute shows you can destroy the legitimate expectations of another employee?" (*US Airways v. Barnett*)

Attorney Claudia Center argued for Barnett that no one risked losing a job in this case. Indeed, the other employees claiming seniority already had jobs while Barnett was faced with the possibility of not having one at all. Is it "justice" to economically destroy one employee so that others can move up the corporate ladder?

Ruling against the Ninth Circuit Appeals Court and Barnett, and for US Airways, the Supreme Court held that employers can use a company (not union) seniority system to avoid accommodating disabled employees. By doing so, the court disallowed reasonable accommodation to challenge the social position of management.

In perhaps the most damaging decision of all, Mario Echazabal (*Chevron USA, Inc. v. Echazabal*) had worked successfully for some twenty years as a contract employee at a Chevron plant in Texas. However, when he sought a full-time job with Chevron, its medical evaluation determined that working at an oil refinery was too dangerous for Echazabal because he had Hepatitis C.

Echazabal's own physician had placed no limits on his work and Chevron had been fully apprised of Echazabal's health condition during all those years he worked as an independent agent. But Chevron wasn't about to give him a job which would have meant full benefits and perhaps extra insurance costs. Instead it claimed that working at Chevron was harmful to Echazabal's health and used the defense of "threat to self."

Rarely has the Supreme Court deferred to an Equal Employment Opportunity Commission (EEOC) ruling to determine the outcome of a case. In this instance the court did rely on an unfortunate EEOC regulation favoring employers which expanded their ADA defenses to include "threat to self," which was not in the ADA. The ADA had only named "threat to others" as a defense available to employers.

Is it not harmful to every human body to work in a chemical-laden environment? Why should one body be denied the right to boldly be exploited and slowly killed like everybody else?

The National Council on Disability damned the court's decision as "an impermissible act of paternalism." Marca Bristo stated the Supreme Court's decision endorsed "the assumption that people with disabilities are not competent to make informed, wise, or safe life choices," which is, "the most long standing and insidious aspect" of the discrimination that is banned by the ADA.

The US Chamber of Commerce called the Chevron decision "a major victory for the business community." And so it was. It may grow bigger.

Employers are keenly interested in eliminating certain individuals from employment opportunities based on their genetic make-up. Michael Kinsley, now retired editor of *Slate*, suggested that genetic tests should eventually be used as qualifications for employment.[4]

Kinsley resigned in February as *Slate*'s editor, some say due to Parkinson's Disease. Under his own genetic employment directive, Kinsley likely would have been discriminated against in employment. He could have been cut out of the game long before he established himself worthy of editorship anywhere.

How tilted towards business was the court? The justices voted 9–0 against Jeffrey Gorman. It voted against Ella Williams and for Toyota in another 9–0 vote, and again against Mario Echazabal and for Chevron in a 9–0 vote. The justices' vote against Robert Barnett was a 5–4 split in favor of US Airways. Two conservatives (Scalia and Thomas) and two "liberals" (Ginsburg and Souter) dissented.

Clinton's two "liberal" appointees, Stephen Breyer and Ruth Ginsburg, are resolute corporatists. Author Michael Parenti notes that Ginsburg, when serving on a lower federal court, had voted more often with the conservatives than the liberals, and she has continued to do so on the Supreme Court.[5] Breyer has been a strong supporter of big business.

As Ralph Nader put it, Breyer was "hostile to regulatory law enforcement," and that Clinton had thereby "locked the court into an anti-consumer, anti-worker, anti-environmental mode." He was proved correct.

Is there any doubt that we can now add "anti-disability mode" to the dirty laundry list?

The ADA and equal opportunity is a non-solution for a capitalist society wherein the disabled workers and would-be workers, by definition, do not have the social or political power to realize their economic wants. Power lies at production, with the owners of capital, and the Supreme Court is one manifestation of that power. [. . .]

CHAPTER 8

Handicapitalism
Makes Its Debut

While a backlash is in full gear against the ADA across the nation, the *Wall Street Journal* recently tagged disabled people as the "Next Consumer Niche."[1] Another icon of America's ruling class, *Fortune Magazine*, picked up on the "disabled Americans are a vast market" theme,[2] and soon after, Fortune 500 sponsored an infomercial on *CBS* which declared that disabled people have $1 trillion in consolidated buying power.[3] So it was that handicapitalism made its media debut.

Handicapitalism, a term coined by Johnnie Tuitel (a lecturer with a disability seeking to trademark the term), is firmly centered in free market ideology. It has nothing to do with the ADA or the right of disabled persons to employment, reasonable accommodations, and access. Rather the handicapitalist philosophy is that disabled people "should not be viewed as charity cases or regulatory burdens but as profitable marketing targets."

Citing 1995 Census data that there are 48.5 million people 15 and older with disabilities in the US, with annual discretionary income totaling $175 billion as support, handicapitalists pose that products and services ought to "be spurred by the profit potential" lying in these numbers, "not by ADA compliance."

"Targeting people with disabilities for purely altruistic reasons," Cheryl Duke, president of W. C. Duke Associates Inc., a disability-consulting firm in Virginia, explains to the *WSJ*, "isn't going to get the return on investment. If you do it because it's a moneymaking project, it will continue."[4]

Discounting the value of rights, the handicapitalists hold that in order for disabled people to be tolerated by our capitalist society, rights must be subsumed to the profit motive. Under this philosophy, social success will be ours when disabled persons gain status as consumers with enough buying power to command it. But where does the buying power reside; who really controls it and who benefits?

The handicapitalist $1-trillion-buying-power media blitz places in the public mind the illusion that disabled people, as a class of persons, have achieved economic prosperity. This flies in the face of the facts. Buying power data does not tell the story of the persistently high unemployment rate and wide income disparities that dominate the economic lives of the vast majority of disabled persons.

The majority of disabled people are not even working. Despite a growing economy and a 29-year-low unemployment rate, potential workers with disabilities remain chronically unemployed. Ten years after the passage of the ADA, national employment surveys show that the unemployment rate for the disabled population remains at 70 percent—nowhere near to achieving economic parity with the non-disabled population. [. . .]

For example: There is a wage gap between disabled and non-disabled workers. In 1995, workers with disabilities [. . .] earned on average only 72.4 percent of the amount non-disabled workers earned annually. [. . .] Poverty remains disproportionate amongst disabled Americans. Census data (1995) shows the non-disabled poverty rate to be 13.5 percent compared to a poverty rate of 20.2 percent for disabled persons. [. . .]

So where is all the consumer-driven buying power the handicapitalists rave about? There are 17 million working-age disabled people, 5.5 million of whom have a job. The employed will have some extra money to spend beyond expenses everyone must pay, such as rent, utilities, and food (the poor have *some* buying power). The rest of the 48.5 million disabled people are under 18 or over 65. Some buying power may rest with the parents of disabled children and the elderly who have had a lifetime to accumulate a bank account before they acquired a disability. It certainly does not rest with the 11 million working-age blind, deaf, developmentally disabled or mobility impaired people who are unemployed, living on SSDI or SSI, and not earning fat salaries on the upwardly mobile track.

The equally important question is how much of the money being spent on disability-specific needs and products is under the control of the disabled individual? It is most likely that the real buying power resides with government agencies who make purchases for disabled individuals under programs such as Social Security, Medicare, Medicaid, the Department of Rehabilitation, or with private insurance companies. Rather than the buying power being in the hands of the disabled "consumer" these agencies make the purchases on behalf of their disabled clients. The decision-making power is far removed from the disabled individual.

As it turns out, the *WSJ* story was spurred by [now-defunct—*Ed.*] WE Media, an Internet portal whose corporate partners include HotJobs.com Ltd., a job-search site that pushes products and real estate targeted at disabled persons. Best known for its New York City billboard proclaiming, "We've been called gimp, cripple, and our new favorite, retard," it also publishes *WE* magazine, a slick yuppie life-style publication that outs disabled persons in fashionable clothing in luxurious and chic public environments, and advertises $500 Bulova watches. Politically, *WE* seems to be equally comfortable with Mayor Giuliani as they are with Al Gore.

But who are WE? Voice of the people? WE is not even controlled by a pack of disabled entrepreneurs. I had to search far and wide to find any disabled persons associated with it. All three main movers and shakers in this enterprise are white non-disabled males, though there are some disabled persons listed on the advisory board and as contributing editors. As have other civil rights movements, the disability rights movement must question who profits from the disability-specific buying that does goes on?

Canceling his subscription to *WE*, Mike Brannick of Arkansas writes, "you put far too much emphasis on high dollar items. How many of us can travel to Europe or dine in five-star restaurants?"

Millions of disabled people like Brannick could never afford these products slickly reproduced on the pages of *WE*. Many have only acquired some disability-specific items because a government program will pay for them. WE and its philosophy of handicapitalism glorifies what amounts to a wee disability consumer constituency in the face of gross inequality, while undercutting the value of equal rights.

Rights, contrary to the handicapitalist opinion, are not "altruistic." Civil rights laws, though certainly not a complete remedy for the inequality described here, are an important element in the struggle in building oppressed groups' economic parity under capitalism.

There is a gaping hole in the handicapitalists' vision. Employers do not see disabled people as "a moneymaking project" when faced with the nonstandard costs of providing reasonable accommodations, higher health insurance premiums and other expenses that may arise. They come to view the disabled employee as a liability and want to unload them. The unregulated labor market has not rectified the high disabled unemployment rate, yet, as is necessary under capitalism, the consumer market cannot grow without more disabled people making the money to buy products. The consumer market, then, depends on advancing the employment of disabled persons.

If the courts continue to rule against disabled plaintiffs in employment discrimination cases (studies show employers win by wide margins), states continue to challenge the constitutionality of the ADA where employees have brought suit against them for disability discrimination, and the EEOC continues its lax enforcement of our employment rights—our economic condition will continue to stagnate. How might the handicapitalists' much anticipated "Next Consumer Niche" fare then?

Disabled people (an eighth of the world population) remain the most impoverished, the least likely to rise above subsistence in *every* nation in the world. The wee middle class of disabled persons in the US does not exist in many countries. In the underdeveloped nations disabled people have no rights, no ADA. They can be found sleeping on sidewalks without wheelchairs, crutches, or other goods they need to live a life with dignity (not that we don't have this in the US, too). There are no curb cuts in Africa or Asia and very few in Western Europe. There are no accessible buses to provide transport to a job. Disabled people in the US only have what little we have now because we have struggled for our rights. Holding up yuppie lifestyle consumerism—handicapitalism—as a solution to disabled people's problems in the face of such reality is a terrible hoax.

Making their debut, here are a few wealthy people with corporate sponsorship stepping up and calling for a capitulation to capitalism when the ADA is under a viscous attack by the conservative courts. Handicapitalists are forging a partnership between wealthy and powerful non-disabled persons with the aspiring-to-be-entrepreneurial disabled middle class ready to jump onboard. This forebodes a political alliance between conservative and liberal disability leaders and government not to push for civil rights but to rely on the handicapitalist strategy for disabled advancement within capitalism.

Let the market rule? Unless disabled people see ourselves as active creators of equality (which means undoing capitalism, which can never be made equitable) we will be doomed to be tools of the owning class, and our people, like other oppressed groups, will remain impoverished.

III.

Disability Incarcerated

CHAPTER 9

Disablement, Prison, and Historical Segregation

Marta Russell and Jean Stewart

The story of disablement and the prison industrial complex must begin with a trail of telling numbers: a disproportionate number of persons incarcerated in US prisons and jails are disabled. Though Census Bureau data suggest that disabled persons represent roughly one-fifth of the total population, prevalence of disability among prisoners is startlingly higher, for reasons we will examine later. While no reliable cross-disability demographics have been compiled nationwide, numerous studies now enable us to make educated estimates regarding the incidence of various disability categories among incarcerated persons. Hearing loss, for example, is estimated to occur in 30 percent of the prison population, while estimates of the prevalence of intellectual disability among prisoners range from 3 to 9.5 percent.

Rates of learning disability are spectacularly high among prisoners; in studies conducted among incarcerated juveniles, learning disabilities have been estimated to occur in up to 55 percent of youth nationwide; in one single-state study, 70 percent of youth qualified for special education. As for mental disabilities, in California anywhere from one-sixth to one-fourth of prisoners are believed to have diagnosable "serious mental disorders." Most stunning of all is a four-state study that examined juveniles imprisoned for capital offenses; virtually 100 percent of those studied were multiply disabled (neurological impairment, psychiatric illness, cognitive deficits), having suffered serious central nervous system injuries resulting from extreme physical and sexual abuse since early childhood.[1]

Why are so many prisoners in the United States disabled? Genetic determinists like to attribute the high prevalence of disability among prisoners to inherited deficiencies. For instance, James Watson of Cold Spring Harbor Laboratory holds that "we perhaps most realistically should see [a person's handicap] as the major origin of a social behavior that has among its many bad consequences the breeding of criminal violence."[2] In opposition to this view, we propose the alternative approach forged by Marx: a material analysis of the economic and social forces of capitalism.

The structure of capitalist America plays a central role in the life of any group, including that of people with disabilities. Given the historic segregation of disabled persons not only from American society but from the accumulation process, disabled people living in the so-called free world have a grim commonality with their disabled compatriots behind bars. Institutions in general, including prisons, have functioned to support the accumulation of capital and the social control of surplus population, including the reserve army of unemployed left adrift by an economic system which dictates that large numbers of workers must be unemployed.

The prison population is not a cross-section of America; prisoners are poorer and considerably less likely to be employed than the rest of the population, and poverty in America is inevitably linked to a higher prevalence of disability. Neither quality health care, nor safe, adequate housing, nor nutritious food has been available to poor people. Environmental racism, the siting of toxic waste dumps and other poison-emitting industries in low-income, mostly non-white neighborhoods has a devastating impact: not only are poor children exposed to lead and other toxins, resulting in high rates of developmental and learning disabilities, they also drink poisoned water and breathe poisoned air, leading to extreme prevalence of asthma and other respiratory illnesses and cancers. Poor people often live in neighborhoods plagued by drug and alcohol abuse, leading to physical and psychological damage, including fetal alcohol syndrome, and marked by violent crime, leading to spinal cord injury, traumatic brain injury, and other disabilities.

As Christian Parenti explains in *Lockdown America*, capitalism, the creator of poverty, simultaneously needs and is threatened by the poor. In order to manage and contain its surplus populations and poorest classes, American capitalism has developed paramilitary forms of segregation, containment, and repression.[3] Not coincidentally, it has created the social condition we are calling "disablement" by excluding disabled persons from full participation in society through segregation, containment, and repression. It is this theory of disablement which we intend to explore here.

Historical Segregation and Social Control

Let us not be lulled into thinking that disabled persons living outside of prisons have autonomous lives. Institutional life, whether in a prison, hospital, mental institution, nursing home, or segregated "school" (and many receive no schooling), has been the forced historical reality, not the exception, for disabled persons.

Unlike race or gender, disablement is not generally thought of as the outcome of capitalist social power relations; rather, it tends to be viewed as a matter for medicine to cure or control. Our medical and social welfare institutions have historically held disablement to be an individual problem (a personal tragedy). They blame a disabled person's inability to participate fully in the economic life of our society on their physiological, anatomical, or mental limitations rather than on economic or social forces.

Disability activists and theorists, however, have laid a materialist groundwork for understanding disability oppression. If we trace how work evolved under capitalism, we can observe its effects on the disabled population. While one cannot claim that working-age disabled persons in pre-capitalist societies had achieved full integration and economic well-being, many occupied a niche in small workshops and family-based production, where they could contribute according to their ability. [. . .]

Early capitalism required a major shift in both the social organization of work and the concept of human labor. As human beings were gathered into the "dark satanic mills" to accomplish the sacred task of capital accumulation, circumstances arose which became barriers to disabled people's survival. [. . .] Disabled workers were increasingly excluded from paid employment on the grounds that they were unable to keep pace with the new, mechanized, factory-based production system.[4]

Industrial capitalism commodified the human body, creating both a class of proletarians and a class of "disabled." [. . .] Over time it became justifiable to remove individuals with impairments from mainstream life and segregate them in a variety of institutions, including workhouses, asylums, prisons, colonies, and special schools.[5]

At the same time as it has marginalized and segregated disabled people in institutions, industrial capitalism, in its grinding push toward productivity at any cost, has caused disabling accidents and conditions to occur at an unprecedented rate. Viewed in this light, black lung, brown lung, asbestosis, and a host of other deadly illnesses are the direct offspring of capitalism, along with a chilling litany of incidents in which factory workers have been paralyzed, burned, blinded, deafened, lost limbs, lost physical or mental function, or have otherwise been rendered disabled. Today, Repetitive Strain Injury debilitates hundreds of thousands of mostly high-tech workers, accounting for 66 percent of all reported work-related illnesses in 1999.

While capitalism shunted disabled persons out of the worker pool and into institutions, the medical industry pathologized traits such as blindness, deafness, and physical and mental impairments that have naturally appeared in the human race throughout history. In the Foucaultian sense, medicalization and institutionalization became means of social control, relegating disabled persons to isolation and exclusion from society; the combination met capitalism's need for discipline and control. Michael Oliver explains:

> [The institution] is repressive in that all those who either cannot or will not conform to the norms and discipline of capitalist society can be removed from it. It is ideological in that it stands as a visible monument for all those who currently conform but may not continue to do so: if you do not behave, the institution awaits you.[6]

Institutions of all descriptions thus became formidable, formalized containment devices. It is now the disability rights movement's primary revolutionary goal to reverse this trend.

The impact on disabled people of this kind of segregation has been profound. They are the least likely to be employed, the most likely to be impoverished and undereducated. [. . .] Disabled persons are twice as likely not to finish high school (22 percent versus 9 percent). A disproportionate number of disabled persons report having inadequate access to health care (28 percent versus 12 percent) or transportation (30 percent versus 10 percent).[7] Of course, one must acknowledge that disabled people live on the economic margins of all societies throughout the world, not merely in capitalist countries. But nowhere else are we witness to the jarring disconnect between a society's vast wealth and its refusal to provide more than the barest means of survival for its most vulnerable citizens. [. . .]

Sentenced to Hard Labor

Social control does not tell the complete story of disabled peoples' segregation and ensuing institutionalization. By placing the focus on "cure," and by segregating "incurables" into the administrative category of "disabled," the medical industry bolstered capitalist business interests and shoved less exploitable workers with impairments, or those who obstructed capital accumulation, out of the workforce. [. . .]

At the same time that US capitalists close their doors to disabled workers, their drive to maximize profits in today's global economy leads them to abandon even their non-disabled employees, relocating factories overseas where wages are as little as twenty cents per hour, child labor is legal, and workers are not provided benefits or health care. They have also rediscovered that they do not have to go so far afield.

If relocation of factories to developing countries has produced lavish profits for the capitalist class, little can compare to the windfall generated in recent years by an even more lucrative worker pool: prison labor. Not only are prisons posited as a primary solution to the country's social problems, but prisons are among the fastest-growing industries in the United States. Workers earn as little as twenty-two cents per hour, and companies avoid the added costs of shipping and infrastructure enhancement required when they operate in poorer countries. Not coincidentally, Occupational Safety and Health Administration laws do not apply to the prison industry, with the result that materials used in prison manufacturing are often toxic and dangerous when handled without adequate protection. For example, urethane foam used in furniture production by California's Prison Industry Authority at Tehachapi Prison is cut to size in unventilated shops, posing a potentially lethal health threat to prisoners. When the foam is cut with power saws, tiny particles are dispersed into the air. Trapped inside human lungs, these particles are carcinogenic, causing a condition similar to asbestosis. Urethane foam also produces a lethal gas if accidentally ignited.

In a grotesque sidebar to this story, state agencies, schools, hospitals, and libraries are forced under California law to buy these prison-made chairs and couches, despite the foam's clearly printed warning. Though the California Furniture Association does not approve the use of this foam in furniture, the Prison Industry Authority ignores the danger.

What we have is a billion-dollar manufacturing industry that legally utilizes slave labor, has little overhead, is unregulated by state and federal workplace safety or labor laws, provides no health insurance or benefits and no sick pay for its employees, includes hazardous materials in the construction of its products, forces customers to buy those products under penalty of law, and prohibits its workers from organizing. "There has not been a larger pool of 'free labor' since the end of the Civil War."[8] [. . .]

The Neoliberal Shift, Deinstitutionalization, and Incarceration

To better understand the relationship between disability and prison, it is instructive to focus on the treatment of those who are mentally ill.[9] In the second half of the twentieth century, the dominance of the mental health institution began to decline as the capitalist economy underwent restructuring. Economic stagnation, low profits, and the fiscal crisis of the seventies were met with Reaganomics, i.e., tax cuts for corporations and the wealthy, an attack on labor, deregulation of health and safety regulations, and cuts in state spending on education, welfare, and social programs, including those institutions housing people with mental illnesses.

Deinstitutionalization, as it related to those who had been labeled mentally ill, was a government policy change driven by cost-cutting motives. Spending by the fifty states on treatment for people with mental illness, for instance, was lower by a third in the nineties than it was in the fifties; fewer than half of Americans diagnosed with schizophrenia receive adequate services today. When the awful snake pits of neglect and abuse we called "mental institutions" were closed, necessary new structures and solutions, including community housing, employment services (a vital component for populations experiencing severe labor market discrimination), and other appropriate programs designed and run by disabled individuals themselves, were never put in place.

Instead, GOP revolutionaries of the 104th Congress, falsely blaming the deficit on the welfare state and entitlements, attacked the social safety net. The 1990's crackdown on federal disability and welfare benefits and state reductions to General Relief and Medicaid further expanded the scope of damage to deinstitutionalized people who had been diagnosed with mental illness, many of whom found themselves destitute the moment they were discharged from the hospitals.

Because the states had abandoned their social contract with deinstitutionalized people labeled mentally ill, many were left stranded on the streets, caught up in the revolving door between homelessness and prison. At present, an overwhelming number of jail inmates with mental illness are homeless. For instance, of the approximately 2,850 mentally ill people in New York City jails on any given day in 1996, 43 percent were homeless. The vast majority were not violent or dangerous; they have been jailed for petty theft, disturbing the peace, and other "crimes" directly related to their illness. Increasingly, the judicial system punishes such people for their "quality of life" misdemeanors by slapping them with jail sentences—six hundred and seventy thousand of them in 1996. At any given moment, 40 percent of all Americans with serious mental illness are estimated to be in jail or prison, comprising from 10 to 30 percent of all inmates. The Center on Crime, Communities and Culture concludes that in many jurisdictions, jails have become the primary "treatment" provider for poor people with mental illnesses.[10]

This "criminalization of mental illness" has its roots in the US capitalist health care system and the growth of the prison industry. The great majority of mentally ill people in New York jails and prisons, for instance, are Medicaid recipients or have no insurance at all. To qualify for Medicaid, low-income individuals must be extremely debilitated and indigent (which many achieve by spending down savings), and they must stay indigent.

Adding insult to injury, mental health parity does not exist in the private US insurance system. For instance, private long-term disability plans, most of them employer-sponsored, provide benefits to eligible recipients with "physical disorders" through age sixty-five, while they impose duration limits of twenty-four months or less on benefits to eligible recipients with "mental disorders." In defending its refusal to provide mental health parity, the insurance industry claims the extra coverage would place a demand on the for-profit system which would cause everyone's premiums to skyrocket. In order to protect its profit margin, the corporate health care industry denies this segment of the population treatment and services.

The rise of managed care, now the dominant paradigm among hospitals and physicians, has also had a debilitating effect. In the name of cost containment, payment mechanisms have shifted; hospitals and doctors are now paid a flat fee, instead of receiving payment for individual services rendered. Because of financial incentives for physicians and hospitals to keep costs low, people who have been hospitalized for "mental illness" are often discharged in three weeks, ready or not, without a discharge plan that would provide them with crucial community support.

People with so-called mental illnesses are generally deemed to have little or no production value. Their unemployment rate is the highest among the disabled population at 80 percent, and disproportionately high within the incarcerated population. Perhaps the term "social junk," as coined by criminologist Steven Spitzer, best describes how society views this cast-off segment of the population. People labeled "mentally ill" experience harsh discrimination in many arenas, among them housing, employment, and health insurance. Increasingly they have become a part of what Christian Parenti calls "a growing stratum of 'surplus people' [who, because they are not] being efficiently used by the economy must instead be controlled and contained and, in a very limited way, rendered economically useful as raw material for a growing corrections complex." Thus, the old "snake pit" mental institution is being replaced with yet another institution, the prison, where incarcerated "social wreckage" contributes to the GDP by supporting thousands of persons associated with expanding and maintaining the prison industry.

Mental health advocacy groups rightly point out that people with mental illness rarely belong in prison. Jail diversion and discharge planning, they say, are key to stopping the "revolving door" of repeated hospitalizations and incarcerations. They recommend ongoing community treatment and support services, all grossly underfunded now, to mend the broken system.

The psychiatric social change movement, comprised of survivors of the mental health industry, is wary of solutions that may lead to forced hospitalization, involuntary psychiatric drugging (psychiatric medicine is not a science and damage is often done by inappropriate drugs), and forced electroshock, all of which have been a part of the corporate psychiatric model. The World Bank now has a "mental health division" to promote corporate psychiatry globally! In thirty-seven states, people living in their own homes can be court-ordered to take psychiatric drugs even though many experience toxic reactions to such treatment. Six states have "at-home" drug deliveries. The shattered mental-health system has largely depended upon one or another form of incarceration and forced treatment, whether in hospitals or prisons. In their efforts to end the involuntary imprisonment of so-called mentally ill persons, grassroots social change groups are concerned that one destructive institution not be replaced with another. The focus must be on human rights (including the right to refuse treatment), empowerment, and alternatives such as community and peer support.

Oppression Behind Bars

We have shown that American capitalism, in its failure to incorporate disabled people into its social fabric, instead shunts them into prisons and other institutions. Not surprisingly, once behind bars, prisoners with disabilities face even greater abuse and discrimination than they had encountered on the outside. For example, throughout the United States, guards are known to confiscate from inmates with disabilities whatever will be most acutely missed: wheelchairs, walkers, crutches, braces, hearing aids, glasses, catheters, egg crates (special mattresses designed to prevent skin breakdown and aid circulation), and medications.[11] Prisoners who require personal care or assistance—for example, quadriplegic inmates who need help with eating, dressing, bathing, etc.—are simply ignored; they go without meals and are forced to urinate on themselves in the absence of bathroom assistance. Because of architectural barriers, physically disabled inmates are unable to access dining halls, libraries, work and recreational areas, and visiting rooms, not to mention the toilets, sinks, and beds in their own cells. Blind prisoners are unable to read their own mail or research their cases in the prison law library because they are not provided with readers or taped/Brailled materials. Deaf prisoners are denied interpreters, making it impossible for them to participate in work programs, counseling, alcohol and substance abuse programs, medical appointments, and their own parole and disciplinary hearings. Disabled prisoners are routinely denied enrollment in work furlough programs, sometimes significantly lengthening their periods of incarceration.

All of the above are violations of the Americans with Disabilities Act which, under the Supreme Court's 1998 ruling in Yeskey (*Pennsylvania Department of Corrections et al. v. Ronald R. Yeskey*), applies to state prisons. In addition, psychological abuse of disabled prisoners by guards—for example, the moving around of furniture in the cell of a blind prisoner, or verbal taunts over a loudspeaker—have been documented in prison after prison throughout the country. Also rampant is medical abuse; across the United States, prisoners with treatable disabling conditions die as a result of medical neglect. Both psychological and medical abuse are clear violations not only of the Eighth Amendment to the Constitution (injunction against cruel and unusual punishment) but of various international human rights statutes.

It is ironic that the institution which most dramatically exemplifies American society's failure to humanize disability not only cranks out furniture and license plates but manufactures disability as well. The harshness of prison life disables people. Inadequate or absent medical care, poor nutrition, violence, and extremes of heat, cold, and noise inside prison, not to mention the lack of sensory, emotional, intellectual, and physical stimuli, all lead directly to acute or chronic physical and psychological disabilities.

Prison overcrowding accelerates the disabling process. Humans who are packed into spaces designed for one-third the numbers of people actually residing in them are bound to find themselves in more frequent, and more disabling, violent confrontations. Guards working in such environments resort to violence more readily. Overcrowded prisons provide an even poorer standard of physical and mental health care, and almost universally produce depression, sometimes acute, as well as a panoply of other immobilizing psychological disorders. Additionally, they provide a ripe environment for the flourishing of gangs and gang violence, resulting in permanent injuries.

Disability is also a byproduct of the correctional system's obsessive infatuation with security and control. Isolation units, sensory deprivation cells, and other instruments of torture such as cattle prods and stun guns generate mental break-downs and exacerbate pre-existing illness.

The prison labor industry, as has been mentioned earlier, is entirely unregulated by workplace safety and health standards, resulting in dangerous work environments. AIDS and Hepatitis C epidemics, unchecked by even the most basic, humane medical intervention, have wrought havoc on the prison population. Finally, as we lock up prisoners for longer and longer periods due to mandatory minimum sentencing laws, the prison population is aging; with age comes disability.

Stopping the Capitalist Juggernaut

In twenty-first century America, the prison industrial complex is a multibillion-dollar capitalist juggernaut, devouring everything in its path. The United States spends far more on corrections than it spends on higher education, locking up more than seven hundred people per hundred thousand, while most "enlightened" countries incarcerate fewer than one hundred citizens per one hundred thousand. In some American inner cities, the rate of incarceration is twenty-five hundred to three thousand per one hundred thousand. In 1995, the prison population topped one million; since then it has grown at a rate of 8.5 percent a year.

Syndicated columnist Anthony Lewis, commenting on proposed legislation that would give the states $10.5 billion to build more prisons, observed: "Once the states have made the investments in such prisons, there will be an inevitable urge to fill them. Sentences will tend to get longer." US District Judge Wilkie Ferguson Jr. continues this line of thought:

> Corrections facilities are being contracted to private corporations for both construction and operation. The private companies are required to operate the prisons at 7 percent below government cost estimates. These firms encourage purchase of their stock by projecting growth in earnings, to be paid mostly from tax dollars. Their rosy projections assume increased incarcerations. Companies that do business with prisons also foresee growth. So, there is already a powerful profit incentive in keeping prisons at maximum occupancy.[12]

With such economic forces as these at work, we should not be surprised that prisons are overcrowded, that mandatory minimum sentences are enjoying unprecedented judicial popularity, and that disabled inmates are dying of abuse and neglect while their complaints fail to register even a blip on the capitalists' Richter scale.

Clearly a well-coordinated, activist, collective, and social change–oriented response is required. Those who are concerned about disability rights, civil rights, prisoners' rights, and human rights must join together and mobilize to put pressure on the prison system. Concomitantly, we must call for a drastic social and economic restructuring of the organization of work. We must create a social order based on equality, an order that does not punish those who cannot work, that does not make "work" the defining measure of our worth, and that offers counter values to the prevailing productionism which only oppresses us all.

CHAPTER 10

Stuck at the Nursing Home Door

Part I

In November [1999—*Ed.*], voters in the liberal city of San Francisco approved a $299 million bond issue to rebuild one of the largest publicly run nursing homes in the nation. "Proposition A," to rebuild the 130-year-old, seismically unsafe Laguna Honda, passed by well over the two-thirds margin needed. It was one of the most expensive bond issues ever approved by the city's voters.

Laguna Honda is the largest nursing home in California. It's also the employer of a thousand members of the Service Employees International Union (SEIU) Local 250.

The campaign to rebuild Laguna Honda began two years ago. Backers of Proposition A spent about $700,000 to influence voters to pass the measure, says the *San Francisco Examiner*, and of that amount, $93,000 came from labor unions.

The political action committee of San Francisco's FDR Democratic Club of seniors and people with disabilities had come out against rebuilding Laguna Honda. The Independent Living Resource Center of San Francisco, the city's independent living center, argued for a commitment of "resources to community living options."

The bond issue exposed a chasm between the goals of the independent living movement and the goals of a union which has only recently gotten involved in in-home services.

Disability activists felt betrayed by the union's drive to rebuild Laguna Honda. The union had "crossed the picket line," as one put it. They charge the SEIU, which represents workers in both private and public nursing homes, with

97

"remaining entrenched in institutional-care models of service delivery"; they say the union has a vested interest in protecting union jobs in the institutions.

According to an article in the *San Francisco Chronicle*, Laguna Honda "is not just a source of jobs to the union. The publicly run center is a model for how unions think workers in this industry ought to be compensated for the unpleasant, often back-breaking chores they perform."[1]

The SEIU represents nursing home and "home healthcare" workers in various settings, both in California and across the nation. Recognizing that low worker wages and lack of healthcare benefits play a major role in both the scarcity of attendants and high turnover in this line of work, the SEIU, the World Institute on Disability and California's independent living centers united in 1992 to force the state to upgrade its In-Home Supportive Services (IHSS), a program based on what the state called the "independent provider" model. The "independent providers" are the attendants themselves; they're considered self-employed and work directly for the disabled person who hires them. Their pay, which is approved by the disabled person they work for, comes from a combination of federal, state, and county funds, and is usually no more than the $5.75 per hour minimum wage. The important thing about California's independent provider legislation, say activists, is that it lets people with disabilities select, direct, and terminate their own attendants.

In the mid-1990s, San Francisco, San Mateo, Alameda, Contra Costa, Los Angeles, and Santa Clara counties opted to set up public authorities to serve as the designated "employer of record" for these independent attendants, for collective bargaining purposes. (Sacramento is currently in the process of setting up a public authority as well.) The SEIU became the union for these workers.

Workers at Laguna Honda—"orderlies," the *Chronicle* calls them—reportedly make $14 to $15 an hour, "and enjoy a full complement of benefits."

"Turnover at Laguna Honda is negligible, compared with rates of 100 percent in some private nursing homes," reported the *Chronicle*.[2]

Laguna Honda's high wages are unusual. Average pay for a nursing home worker is $7 an hour, and few would argue that nursing home aides don't need better pay. The issue is one of pay parity: that $7/hour average is $1.25 more per hour than IHSS workers receive; $14 an hour is well over double what most in-home workers make.

Seniors and people with disabilities in California today find it almost impossible to find or keep attendants. When nursing home aides can systematically get higher wages than in-home workers, it doesn't require much analysis to realize that workers will go for the job that pays better. The bulk of both nursing home aides and IHSS workers come from the ranks of high school dropouts, immigrants, single mothers, and waitresses. Many are working two jobs to make ends meet.

Over the last three years, only one county has significantly raised pay for IHSS workers: San Francisco. Last year SEIU Local 250 and disability activists joined forces to demand a fair wage, and last July Mayor Willie Brown signed a $9/hour wage agreement with sixty-five hundred San Francisco in-home workers, with full medical benefits. But the vast majority of the one hundred and eighty thousand workers across the state—serving approximately two hundred thousand people with disabilities—still earn the minimum wage of $5.75 per hour. They get no benefits, no vacation, and no sick pay. In an interview last summer on Los Angeles' KPFK radio, Democratic Assembly member Gilbert Cedillo, the former general manager of SEIU Local 660, praised the strategic success of unions in getting more money for nursing homes, but failed to mention that IHSS workers had gotten the shaft in the governor's budget.

Local 660 represents more than forty-two thousand Los Angeles County workers, ranging from librarians to healthcare workers to janitors. Yet Cedillo, a member of the Budget Committee and the Appropriations Committee, didn't even mention in-home workers.

Local 250 says it agrees that "non-institutional care" must be expanded, and it has worked to raise attendants' pay in San Francisco. Yet its position paper on the rebuilding of Laguna Honda warned that "we should not make the mistake of assuming that the shift away from institutional long-term care settings to community-based care models will satisfy the dramatically increasing demand for long-term care."

In testimony before the Senate Special Committee on Aging nearly two years ago, the national SEIU, representing nearly a million nursing home workers across the nation, voiced concern about substandard care at nursing homes. "Our members witness first-hand the abuses that hinder their ability to give nursing home residents the care they deserve," said SEIU International President Andrew Stern. "Nursing homes are cutting back on staff and supplies at the same time that the number of older, sicker patients entering these homes is greater than ever before."

Senior groups have in recent years become increasingly vocal about deplorable conditions in nursing homes, yet Stern's singular focus on jobs and staffing seems reactionary. It ignores the central issue: few people ever want to live in a nursing home. Why does the SEIU not go beyond "reform" and push to progressively change the paradigm of long-term care to the "independent provider" model?

If the average cost is $40,000 a year or more to keep someone in a nursing home (or $90,000 in the case of Laguna Honda), then people with disabilities should be allowed to use that money for services at home. With such an amount, workers can certainly get paid a decent wage—with benefits. Such a move would benefit SEIU's workers far more than increasing wages in institutions.

The majority of nursing home and home care corporations operate for profit. To maximize profit, they cut corners in quality of care and keep worker pay low to show their owners and investors as high a return as possible on their money. Home care corporations charge the state $16.50 an hour and pay the worker little more than minimum wage.

Corporate managers and owners reap six-digit salaries and bonuses, while workers, paid below a living wage, are given more tasks than they can physically, emotionally, or safely handle. This is a corporate agenda, one that exploits both labor and disabled peoples' bodies for the benefit of the few at the top.

Disability activist Patrick Connally talks about what he calls "the harvesting of people to fill beds. . . . Pro-institution professionals justify their lockup of people without an involved family, people who need accessibility, people who talk too much, people who are not the beautiful disabled. All can be safely hidden"—and those who hide them can "gain social status."

Under this "money model of disablement," the disabled human being is a commodity, around which social policies are created or rejected based on their market value. [. . .]

Standing strong on principle, Local 250 says it doesn't support for-profit nursing homes. That can be understood in the context of progressive unions' accurate perception that the profit motive takes dollars away from both quality care and worker take-home pay. But progressives' understanding seems to stop at the door of state-run institutions, which are viewed as bastions of liberalist social services and often represent the culmination of long union struggles to organize the state workforce.

Supporters of institutions do so because it's one way to avert a loss of funding that perpetuates the system which both employs and validates them. But fears about job losses have often diverted organized labor from a longer-range understanding of issues. Unions' preservation of jobs in logging, for instance, have rammed up against the goals of the environmental movement. As with the environmental movement, labor must understand that it too will benefit by making personal assistance services the dominant long-term care model in the nation. Union workers themselves become disabled; many will require long-term care as they age. How many workers would really like to *live* in the institutions they now work for?

The same negligence, substandard care, physical and emotional abuse, and rape that unions say occur in for-profit nursing homes also occur in state-run institutions.

Abuse is epidemic in all institutions; and in agency-run home care as well. At least with the independent-provider model, people can select and direct their attendant themselves—and fire an unsatisfactory or abusive one.

Promoting social justice for workers means joining the struggle for living wages and health care. Promoting social justice for people with disabilities means advancing real choice to live where one wants, rather than condoning the current system which commodifies disablement for profits, perpetuating institutions to warehouse undervalued members of our society. [. . .]

Part II

The [. . .] 1999 Olmstead Supreme Court decision declared that "unnecessary institutionalization is discrimination" under the Americans with Disabilities Act and directed states to provide services in the "least restrictive environment." [. . .]

Hand in hand with the implementation of the Olmstead decision I believe that we must simultaneously reject corporate "care" and replace it with a profound and liberating model of in-home services, not a nursing-homes-on-wheels model of services.

The primary goal of the disability movement has been to confront the disablist society in whatever form oppression manifests. The societal practice of institutionalization that segregates disabled persons in liberty-restricting, often dehumanizing and abusive institutions—primarily at this point in history in for-profit nursing home corporations—is one such oppression.

The right to make basic decisions about where and how to live as well as the right to be free from bodily restraints have been recognized as core principles of liberty. States, however, with the power of the purse have historically segregated and institutionalized disabled individuals, extinguishing their fundamental liberties and warehousing them in deplorable public and private facilities.

Not coincidentally, the rise of the institution accompanied the rise of capitalism in Western societies. [. . .] As industrial capitalism demanded a standard worker body which would conform to the needs of production, disabled persons came to be regarded as a social problem and the justification emerged for segregating individuals with impairments out of mainstream life. [. . .]

The widespread theory of eugenics geared towards what scholar Lennard Davis calls "enforcing normalcy" by eliminating "defectives" provided further momentum for segregating disabled persons. According to Davis the term "normal" as "constructing, conforming to, not deviating from, the common type or standard, regular, usual" only enters the English language around 1840.[3]

It is worth taking note that both progressives such as Emma Goldman and conservatives such as John D. Rockefeller and Alexander Graham Bell were all for ridding the world of "cripples," epileptics, deaf and otherwise impaired persons.[4]

Early twentieth century official US reports referred to disabled individuals as "defects . . . [that] wounds our citizenry a thousand times more than any plague," as "by-products of unfinished humanity," and as "a blight on mankind," whose mingling with society was "a most baneful evil."[5] Some laws demanded forced isolation from "normal" society. A 1911 Chicago ordinance, for instance, warned, "No person who is diseased, maimed, mutilated, or in any way deformed so as to be an unsightly or disgusting object or improper person to be allowed in or on the public ways or other public places in this city, shall therein or thereon expose himself to public view."[6]

Although institutionalization reached its peak in the twentieth century, the model persists to this day and continues to restrict disabled persons' democratic participation in society.

Due to pressures from disability activists in the late 1970s the government directed funding to establish independent living centers. Part of the liberation task involved freeing disabled persons not only from confined institutional living but also from dominating social workers and other professionals carrying out policies that disable rather than enable, and from unpaid personal assistance. The disability movement understood that paying one's personal assistant rather than relying on family, friends, or charity meant the autonomy to organize one's life: to arrange one's day, seek employment, attend functions, and keep schedules.

So, setting policies in place that provide funding for disabled persons to live in the community has a significant component: funding programs that allow disabled persons to hire a personal assistant.

Despite some public policy gains such as the Olmstead decision, unfavorable structural and institutional dynamics remain a barrier to user-led and controlled services.

Capitalist commodity relations, for instance, produced the nursing home industrial complex—today a $70 billion industry. Institutionalization as national policy, evolved in part from the realization that financing guaranteed an ongoing source of entrepreneurial revenue. Two thirds of nursing homes are for-profit businesses. Medicaid funds 60 percent, Medicare 15 percent, and private insurance 25 percent.

When a single impaired body generates $30,000–$82,000 in annual revenues,[7] Wall Street brokers count that body as an asset which contributes to a nursing home chain's net worth. Though transfer to nursing homes and similar institutions is almost always involuntary, and though abuse and violation of rights within such facilities is a national scandal, it is a blunt economic fact that, from the point of view of the capitalist "care" industry, disabled people are worth more to the Gross Domestic Product when occupying institutional "beds" than they are in their own homes.

It is also a national scandal that the horrific conditions in nursing homes have been public knowledge for some time. The saga of private nursing home "care" in the US was carefully documented as early as 1980 by B. C. Vladeck. The commercialized nursing home industry of more than seventeen thousand facilities back then had deteriorated to the point where it represented a grave threat to the health and well-being of its "patients." Vladeck blamed the government for this state of affairs asserting that it poorly monitored the industry, but he also blamed the "financial chicanery" of nursing home operators, "whom it seemed were willing to inflict gross indignities on home residents in order to maximize profits."

So even though the infamous state-run institutions such as Willowbrook in New York have been shut down as a result of exposure in the 1960s, little has changed over the past years in terms of respect and dignity under the roofs of private industry–run long-term care institutions. There have been a slew of reports documenting nursing home neglect and abuse. A recent congressional report details thousands of incidents and a range of abuses, including instances of nursing home residents being punched, kicked, or choked by staff members. Some residents also complained of workers groping and sexually assaulting them. Other abuses include untreated bedsores, inadequate medical care, malnutrition, dehydration, and inadequate sanitation and hygiene—all of which can cause death.

One headline from October 13, 2002 from the *St. Louis Post-Dispatch* reads, "Thousands are Being Killed in Nursing Homes Each Year." The mainstream press is far behind the disability movement!

Many disability rights activists certainly have had first-hand experience with the abuse in these euphemistically named "homes," and many do not think that nursing homes can be reformed or that they can ever be a model for good public policy.

There are a host of reasons. Nursing homes are part of an industry that reaps their blood profits from warehousing people who have little or no alternative to institutionalization. Secondly, neither seniors nor younger disabled persons have said that they *want* to live in nursing homes, rather, that is the model thrown at them by the well-endowed nursing home lobby and the Washington politicos in bed with them—and a society that largely accepts this arrangement. But the impetus among disabled and increasingly elderly persons who bear the brunt of our awful system is toward in-home supportive services. Who controls the services, what those services are, and how they are rendered are major issues in disabled people's struggle for self-determination and social membership.

So how might we view a different model of services—one that does not put profits before people—one that we might call an emancipation model?

Workers and disabled persons have a common interest in seeing that in-home services replace the bias towards institutionalization. The vast majority of nursing home corporations operate for profit—according to *US News* some as high as a 20–30 percent margin of profit. [. . .] The profit motive takes dollars away from both quality services and worker take-home pay. [. . .]

Removal of the profit motive is seen by both the National Senior Citizens Law Center and the California Advocates for Nursing Home Reform as an important route to quality care. However, we must also recognize that the same concerns exist when corporations take over the provision of in-home services. [. . .]

A rejection by both disability groups and workers of the corporate "care" paradigm means a rejection of the logic that human labor and disabled people's bodies must be reduced to commodities for sale—in order that someone can make a buck.

A non-commercial model of in-home services could offer a counter paradigm to disablement as a market commodity because there is no profit involved between the worker and the disabled individual. Take away the 20–30 percent nursing home profit margins and put those dollars to worker pay and more hours of service.

The $30,000–$82,000 a year spent to unnecessarily institutionalize must be made available for the individual to opt to use that money for services at home.

Our challenge is to use Olmstead and other means to end the national policy bias toward institutions and create more jobs in the community that have the potential to liberate all persons rather than warehouse and reduce them to raw material for the investors and owners of nursing home or home care corporations.

Changing national long-term care policy to an in-home services model that is based on a contract/partnership between government, personal assistants, and disabled or elderly people has the potential to place democratic participation and human rights above profit. Commercial or entrepreneurial interests that depend upon market structures are antithetical to building social relations based on equality. It seems to me that democratic participation requires community stewardship in recognition of our mutual interdependence. We really don't want a nursing-homes-on-wheels model of services.

IV.

The Social Security Complex

CHAPTER 11

Targeting Disability

In addition to old-age benefits, it is often forgotten that Social Security provides survivor and disability insurance protections as well. The [Bush administration-instigated Social Security—*Ed.*] privatization debate has overlooked the fate of SSDI as a part of the program's family of benefits.

I'll wager that most Americans are unaware of the importance of SSDI, especially young workers who are the target of Bush's campaign to divert funds into private stock market accounts.

I, too, was unaware until the late 1980s, when I found myself unable to work with an eight-year-old child to support. I had worked to put myself through college and made a career in the film industry. Even though I was born with cerebral palsy it never occurred to me that someday I might not be able to continue to work due to complications from my impairment. According to the Social Security Administration three in ten Americans have a chance of becoming impaired before reaching age sixty-seven, able-bodied or not.

I had been paying into SSDI, which today amounts to about one percentage point of the 6.2 percent total payroll tax deducted from one's salary, and had worked sufficiently long so that when faced with a bodily breakdown I could apply for disability benefits. Disability is placed in the same framework established for the old-age program. Like retirement, SSDI is a wage earner social insurance. It is calculated based on wages earned over the number of years worked; it is not a personal investment account. If one becomes unable to engage in "substantial gainful activity" due to impairment, SSDI is there to furnish income in place of wages, as opposed to a 401(K), for instance.

SSDI won't be there in any meaningful form, however, if President Bush dupes the public into believing that Social Security is in "crisis," it is about to become "bankrupt," and the solution is an "ownership society" that promotes privatization—a proposal that could siphon a larger portion of the payroll tax revenue out of the retirement fund into private investment accounts.

The Bush administration could deliver a blow to the Disability Insurance Trust Fund (a separate account in the United States Treasury) just as it plans for the retirement fund. The President's Committee to Strengthen Social Security report titled "Strengthening Social Security and Creating Personal Wealth for All Americans"[1] states that SSDI program outlays are projected to increase as a percent of payroll by 45 percent over the next fifteen years, and SSDI's costs will exceed its tax revenue starting in 2009. In other words, the committee's view is that the disability fund is in "crisis" as is the retirement fund.

Despite Bush's sales-pitch assurances that benefits will not be cut, a leaked private White House memo to conservative allies strongly argues that Social Security benefits paid to future retirees must be significantly reduced to make the plan work.[2]

The committee's blueprint, in fact, cuts disability benefits along with retiree benefits to help pay for the cost of private accounts. The projected $2 trillion shortfall over the first decade alone resulting from the carve-outs from payroll tax revenue to pay for private accounts must either be paid for by cutting benefits or added onto the record deficit if current benefits continue to be paid.

In Bush White House doublespeak, the committee's report cautioned that the disability benefit reductions shouldn't be viewed as a "recommendation," but said, "in the absence of fully developed proposals, the calculations carried out for the commission and included in this report assume that defined benefits will be changed in similar ways for the two programs."[3] If the disability insurance elements of the program were insulated from benefit cuts, then much larger cuts in retirement benefits would be necessary to achieve the same overall level of cost reductions—reductions which are necessary because of the loss of the trust funds' revenue to the individual accounts.

The sums are not insignificant. Already benefits to future retirees could be slashed by as much as 40 percent. According to the Center on Budget and Policy Priorities, one Bush plan being tossed around to "save" Social Security—price indexing—would result in a 46 percent drop in Social Security benefits for the average worker who retired in 2075 as compared to current law.

Currently retirement benefits are matched to changing wage levels but tying Social Security to an inflation index could significantly cut retirement benefits for all working Americans since inflation usually grows at a slower rate than money wages (that is, real wages tend to rise over time). SSDI is run like the retirement program, so it is likely that it too could be switched to an inflation index lowering the already meager disability benefits to levels one cannot survive on. In December 2004, for instance, the average disability benefit was a chintzy $894 per month.

There are more ways SSDI regulations could be manipulated to cut benefits and dismantle the system. The Bush administration could make eligibility rules more restrictive by changing the definition of "disabled" or make formula changes that reduce benefits. It could use Continuing Disability Reviews (CDRs), which determine whether a disabled person can work, to purge disabled people from the rolls, increase the number of work credits required to qualify, and eliminate the annual cost of living adjustments.

Already SSDI can be extremely difficult to obtain owing to denials and the need to appeal one's claim. Too often lawyers must be hired to do battle with the Social Security Administration. The process is rife with undue stress and economic hardship. Some applicants are made to wait one to two years for a final determination. Bush's "ownership society" does not apply to them. After these applicants lose their jobs and while they wait for SSDI, the former workers' homes are often foreclosed on and they lose their cars and savings. Many become homeless and live on the streets due to eligibility process flaws and delays. It is a degrading adversarial process. Some cannot deal with the fear of falling financially and commit suicide. All these chronically ill persons must wait two years to be covered by Medicare.

As Linda Fullerton of the Social Security Disability Coalition explained in her Congressional testimony (September 30, 2004), "The current SSD process seems to be structured in a way to be as difficult as possible in order to suck the life out of applicants in hope that they give up or die in the process, so that Social Security doesn't have to pay them their benefits."[4]

It is well known that in 1981 President Reagan proposed cutting retirement benefits to shore up the retirement fund. Less known is that the Reaganites, hoping to save billions of dollars, arbitrarily sent tens of thousands of disabled people CDR notices that they were no longer "disabled," and cut off their benefits entirely. This paper crackdown on eligibility (without due process) resulted in extreme hardship and in many instances death, sometimes by suicide, since the disability check was the only source of income for impaired people who could not work. The government has done nothing to compensate the victims of its deliberate negligence. It was as if the people whose benefits had been cut off had simply been deemed disposable. When Legal Aid attorneys sought an injunction against the head of the Social Security Administration, a judge in California stopped the Reagan savagery.

In a double whammy to the SSDI program, according to the minority staff of the House Ways and Means Committee, President Bush's committee also recommended that access to disability accounts prior to retirement age be barred. This means not only reduced Social Security benefits, but also no money from the accounts to cushion the loss. Such a change would defeat the purpose of SSDI entirely.

The hard-right conservatives might say that the market, through private disability insurance, can pick up the pieces. But there is no private insurance plan that can compete with a social insurance program such as SSDI in covering disabled workers. For a twenty-seven-year-old worker with a spouse and two children, for instance, Social Security provides the equivalent of a $353,000 disability insurance policy. The vast majority of workers would be unable to obtain similar coverage through private markets.

According to the General Accounting Office (GAO), in 1996, only 26 percent of private-sector employees had long-term disability coverage under employer-sponsored insurance plans. Work-related coverage has been shrinking not expanding since then. It is not unheard of that after forty years of paying into private disability insurance the insurer refuses to recognize impairment as incapacitating and denies a claim.

Last November, for instance, UnumProvident reached a tentative settlement with the insurance regulators of several states, which required UnumProvident and its subsidiaries to reconsider more than two hundred thousand long-term disability claims which had been terminated or denied from January 1, 1997, to the present. The regulators levied a $15 million fine and instructed the insurer to review its claim handling practices. Investigations focused on assertions that UnumProvident had improperly denied claims for benefits under individual and group long-term disability insurance policies. They concluded that UnumProvident had committed numerous violations of its obligation to fairly administer claims.

How about the prospect that private investment accounts could replace lost SSDI benefits? In January 2001, after examining a number of privatization plans, the GAO concluded, "the income [from workers' individual accounts] was not sufficient to compensate for the decline in the insurance benefits that disabled beneficiaries would receive."[5]

This is in part because balances would accumulate over much shorter periods of time than retirement accounts and would, therefore, provide much less income in the event that a worker becomes disabled.

Indeed, it is illusory to believe that the majority of able-bodied or working disabled persons fit the profile of a worker with a lifetime of continuous work (and thus enough gains) to build "savings" accounts. Current labor market realities make staying employed a significant challenge, with workers being forced into many different jobs with long intervals of unemployment.

At the end of 2004, 6,198,000 persons depended on SSDI. Disabled workers and their family members together comprise almost eight million on the program.

The Disability Insurance Trust Fund was created with passage of the Social Security Amendments of 1956 in large measure due to efforts by organized labor—the AFL and CIO—to protect workers, as capitalists used up workers' bodies and cast them aside. Business, especially the insurance industry, was dead set against it. Today business is among the biggest supporters of privatization. The Business Roundtable (a group of blue-chip US companies including Coca-Cola, Exxon Mobil, and IBM), the US Chamber of Commerce, the National Federation of Independent Business, the National Restaurant Association, and the National Association of Manufacturers all contend that individual accounts will stave off a payroll tax hike in the future, and they are anteing up millions of dollars to buy Bush's revamping of the safety net. [...]

Some social analysts describe the disability benefits system as a privilege, because it grants permission to be exempt from the work-based system. Conservatives used to describe the disability system as part of the moral economy. Neither privilege nor morality theories, however, adequately describe the function of the disability benefits system.

This "privileged" or "moral" status does not grant disabled individuals any objective right to a decent standard of living. Retirees' benefits are higher overall than those of disabled persons on SSDI. Disability benefits hover at what is determined an official poverty level. For fiscal year 2004, the federal poverty guideline for one is $9,310. The average monthly benefit that a disabled worker receives from SSDI is $894. Average monthly benefits for disabled women are $274 lower than men's. Income is even less if one is disabled at the bottom of the social strata with no work history or not enough quarters of work to qualify for SSDI. This group of disabled persons must apply for the welfare (needs-based) disability program, Supplemental Security Income (SSI), where the average federal benefit is $417.20 per month.[6] [...]

The conservatives' plan to drain payroll tax revenue from the program through privatization is one way to make the little people pay for Bush's tax cuts for the rich. It will also enrich Wall Street with a guaranteed influx of new clients buying stocks and bonds with their Social Security money—a substantial boon for financial corporations. But it is no less an effort to make workers less secure by undermining the social commitments made with the passage of the Social Security Act in 1935 and the creation of Social Security Disability Insurance, already inadequate when it was instituted in 1956. Private accounts would undermine the guaranteed benefits that are the foundation of Social Security. The Bush-ites want it both ways: to super exploit the workforce and create a you're-on-your-own society that would deprive workers of the security and social compensation owed them. If the privatizers succeed, able-bodied and disabled workers will be made poorer. Under a privatized system, workers may only get out what they put in, unlike the current more progressive Social Security formula that provides guaranteed and proportionally higher benefits to lower earners. Investment accounts that rely upon a shifty stock market can rob workers of every penny saved.

As of this writing there is no final Bush proposal on the table. To squelch criticism and cool dissent Bush has recently stated that he will not cut disability benefit checks. And perhaps he won't directly go after SSDI, not now at least, because the first goal is to start the process of dismantling Social Security by convincing Americans they will be better off with private investment accounts. Building a groundswell for undermining SSDI has been a long-term endeavor, however. Reagan, for instance, aside from severing disabled persons from the rolls, tried to fold SSDI into a social service block grant to the states, which would have effectively eliminated the entitlement. In 1980, President Carter's secretary of Health, Education and Welfare stated, "disability is killing us," as the Carter administration succeeded in putting a cap on disability benefits and changing the way benefits were calculated to lower payments.[7]

Over the years, hard-right critics of SSDI have deemed it rife with fraud. Congresspersons have spoken of the dilemma of disability "dependency" and accused the program's growth of being out of control. One reason that Republicans supported the Americans with Disabilities Act in 1990 was to provide protections against employment discrimination so that disabled persons would get off the dole and into jobs. [. . .]

The current Bush administration's approach is likely to be indirect, by making changes to regulations. For instance, there is already a plan afloat to require that those on SSDI reapply every two years—an arduous task that some may not manage well resulting in their disqualification from the program. In addition, the success of social insurance depends upon the widest pooling of risk. If the privatizers succeed, as money is diverted into private accounts, there will be less in the common pool of funds that comprise retirement and disability benefits. Disability payouts will then appear to be taking a larger piece of the pie, making the SSDI program an easy target for the hard right.

Economics, however, is not the prime motive behind the push to privatize our public commonwealth. Bush has admitted that privatization will not make Social Security solvent. The reasons are political and ideological. The White House memo mentioned earlier stated, "For the first time in six decades, the Social Security battle is one we can win—and in doing so, we can help transform the political and philosophical landscape of the country."[8]

Hard-right conservatives have been working since the New Deal's inception to kill off Roosevelt's vision—no matter that it has been a success story. In the early 1980s, free-market conservatives such as the Cato Institute and the Heritage Foundation began to hammer out the free-market manifestos that laid the groundwork for the current campaign. Now, the Bush administration is forcing us to defend the Social Security system that conservatives despise so much, rather than fighting to improve it. It is an all-out assault. Newt Gingrich called one strategy "starve the beast"—drive up the deficit then use that as justification to cut the safety net. Privatization is the next step of a calculated, long-term campaign to end Social Security. We must do all we can to see this doesn't happen to our children.

CHAPTER 12

Between Dependence and Independence: Rethinking a Policy Wasteland

My friend David just went through a noxious and unproductive bout with the Social Security Administration (SSA). David, one of the autistic individuals Dustin Hoffman spent time with while developing his "Rainman" character, works for a large chain electronics retail corporation. He remains qualified for Supplemental Security Income (SSI) even though he has a job, both because he is disabled and because he earns so little money. When David wanted a computer, he saved for six long years before he was able to have the funds to buy one.

The story is a simple one. After the Los Angeles earthquake, David and his mother had to move out of their apartment for earthquake repairs. David went to stay in a board-and-care facility while his mother made other arrangements for herself for the months it took to do the repairs. Prior to this move, David had been sending the SSA the required reports of his earnings so SSA could calculate deductions. But due to the disruption of the earthquake, David's routine was upset and he did not send the required copies of his paychecks to SSA during the months he was not living at home. So SSA put a stop on David's SSI check.

David and his mother got a hearing before an administrative law judge; David's mother presented the judge with proof of his earnings. As caretaker of his SSA account, she pled that although she is ultimately responsible for sending in the copies of his paychecks, she has given David any and every possible means of being self-sufficient and independent in keeping with independent living philosophy—and has allowed him to make and send his reports himself. David was very capable of doing this, and had done it without failure prior to moving into the group home. As it turned out, David thought that he did not have to send the paycheck copies, because he was living at the group home, not at his home. "David is not capable of lying, he doesn't know what that is," his mother told the judge.

David's mother told the judge she had explained to each of the three workers at the board-and-care facility that David needed to send SSA the copies of his paychecks each month, but that they had failed to see that he did it.

The judge made no allowances for any of this, and ruled that not sending the reports was enough reason to discontinue David's SSI payments for the period in question.

Later, SSA reinstated David's SSI payments—but made no back payments for those months during which David had failed to send his paycheck copies.

David had his mother to fall back on for financial support in the interim—but what about others who do not have such support, who innocently make mistakes and get penalized? A loss of a few hundred dollars to some may mean losing one's apartment and winding up on the streets. It may create conditions where one can no longer hold a job.

It can even end in death. Some may recall Lynn Thomson's story. She tried to earn some extra money by stuffing envelopes at home.

Unbeknownst to Thomson, the work she did was in violation of SSA regulations. When she reported her income to SSA, they responded with a letter stating that she had received an overpayment and that her benefits would be terminated until it was paid back. SSA claimed that her Medi-Cal and attendant benefits would also be cut off. Losing one's attendant is a ticket for a nursing home, but loss of Medi-Cal is a death sentence to a quadriplegic.

SSA was wrong about this part; she would not have lost her Medi-Cal. But she was never told this, and after a protracted and demeaning contest with SSA, Thomson killed herself, leaving a recorded message saying that the reason for her suicide was that SSA had put her through hell and she could no longer live with the anxiety.

Laura Hershey, who often writes about SSA and the pitfalls of work, quotes a colleague: "A co-worker of my sister killed himself last week. He had been working part-time while receiving disability benefits due to his visual impairment. He had gotten a letter from Social Security saying he should never have gotten disability benefits, and that he would need to pay back all that he had received."[1]

Sporadic or Part-Time Work Has Many Pitfalls

In order to comply with the rules, individuals who rely on sporadic work need to have their personal assistance services, SSI/SSDI, and Medicaid share of cost recalculated every month that they earn income, something these systems are not efficient enough to do without delays and shortfalls for the recipient. It would be "highly inadvisable for any disabled individual to work at part-time or sporadic employment," warns Los Angeles disability activist Nancy Becker Kennedy; it risks "throwing these very sluggish benefit systems into confusion."

Experience shows that this often results in losing one's healthcare, living allowance, and money to pay the personal assistant—for months or even years—while SSA and other agencies sort it out (and hopefully get it right when they do).

Disability organizations have been working to incrementally reform Social Security's work rules for these very reasons. The Ticket to Work and Work Incentives Improvement Act of 1999 is one such reform; SSI Plan 1619, which allowed more deductions, was an earlier one. The Social Security Administration has now proposed to make automatic adjustments each year to the current "substantial gainful activity" (or SGA) level, which is currently at $700 a month for individuals with impairments other than blindness; this figure would now increase along with increases in the average wage index.

Even tied to the wage index, a SGA amount of $700 per month "is still out of step with today's marketplace," says Bryon MacDonald, Social Security analyst for the World Institute on Disability.

Who can support themselves on $700 a month? The $700 SGA cut-off is an at-poverty level subsistence. The Federal poverty guideline sets the poverty level for an individual at $8,350/year; a SGA of $700 a month works out to $8,400 a year—assuming one would be consistently working for a full year, which is often unlikely.

What is "poverty"—and who defines it? The current system of measuring poverty dates back to the 1960s; there has been no recognition of changes that have occurred over the last 30 years. At that time, Department of Agriculture research showed the average family spent a third of its income on food; therefore a "poverty income" was determined to be three times what experts thought the minimum food budget should be. Even so, that economy food plan was "for temporary or emergency use when funds are low" and was only 75 to 80 percent of a Department of Agriculture "low cost food plan" (which, "if strictly followed," could "provide an acceptable and adequate diet," wrote Mollie Orshansky in 1965).[2]

Nonetheless, the government has never adjusted the equation to take into account the sharp rise in housing, medical care, and child care costs of the following four decades which have altered the average household's economic picture. A 1990 study by Patricia Ruggles of the Urban Institute concluded that, in order to be comparable to the original threshold, the poverty level would have to be at least 50 percent higher than the current official standard.[3] [. . .]

Cutting disabled persons off from disability benefits when they earn just $700 a month does not lift one out of poverty, much less give one a chance to achieve a decent standard of living before shoving one off what the National Council on Independent Living calls "the earnings cliff." The proposed raising of the SGA level will make no real difference to SSI recipients.

However, two meaningful reforms would be to end earnings limitations entirely and to raise the SSI resource limit from $2,000—and raise it substantially.

Others have made suggestions for SSA reform. Pointing out that the disability rolls have grown since passage of the ADA and employment expectations have not been met, leaving too many dependent on government benefits, Andy Imparato, head of the American Association of People with Disabilities, locates part of the problem in how "disability" is defined by SSA. To be disabled under Social Security regulations, one must pledge that one can't do any work at all.

Imparato calls for a redefinition of disability. "We need to reform disability benefits laws and systems so that people get the supports and services they need, have maximum choices and opportunities regarding employment, place to live, transportation, health care, long-term services and supports—and never, ever, have to swear to the government that they cannot work in order to establish eligibility for long-term supports and services," says Imparato.

Yet even if we change the view of Congress "from 'disability means dependent and unemployable' to the view that 'all people with disabilities can and should work,' it will not change the view of society," says scholar David Pfeiffer of the University of Hawaii. "People with disabilities will still be seen as dependent and unemployable."

In large part, unemployment and poverty are the by-products of our economic system. Unemployment is not an aberration of capitalism; rather, it is a built-in component of a market economy that requires many people be unemployed and impoverished. [. . .]

Disabled persons routinely get conceptualized as non-productive "dependent" freeloader members of society. Some disability policy makers, conceding that this is the prevailing view and that not much can be done to change it, have bought the line that, in order to be seen as having any value in this society, disabled people must be gotten off the benefits rolls.

A reality-based understanding, however, would acknowledge that, short of a revolution, unemployment is simply going to be the condition for millions in our market economy—and that disabled people will continue to be disproportionately affected by monetary policy. This view challenges the notion that the problem is one of economic "dependency," and the solution "independence."

The political right uses "dependency" as a way to pathologize and degrade populations that rely on government supports. Should we follow their lead? Most Americans benefit from government supports, whether they are CEOs of corporations or homeowners. Some of the wealthiest people in this country are "dependent" upon corporate subsidies. Middle-class homeowners are "dependent" upon mortgage interest rates being tax-deductible. Why not view disability supports as part of the same largess, rather than framing them negatively as leading to dependency, paternalism, or "welfare"?

Labor market discrimination is a steady reality for most significantly disabled persons. [. . .] The unemployment rate for disabled people, at 65 percent to 71 percent, depending on what source one uses, remains much higher than for the population as a whole. A recent Rutgers University study shows that most working disabled persons are twice as likely to be self-employed or in part-time or temp jobs. That means that income may be sporadic. [. . .]

To achieve a decent quality of life, significantly disabled persons who face labor market discrimination will need ongoing support from government, regardless of how SSA defines disability.

MacDonald says, "I would argue that all persons with disabilities should be able to move in and out of public disability programs the way mainstream America goes to an ATM machine."

There is a case to be made for never-ending disability benefits, once one qualifies for them. Last year President Clinton signed the Social Security Earnings Test Elimination Act which permits seniors to earn as much as they want—seniors can earn $100,000 or more a year and continue to receive their Social Security retirement benefits in full, without any deductions.

The same should be done for disabled people. Disabled persons are nearly three times as likely to live below the current poverty line—29 percent of disabled people live in poverty compared to 10 percent of non-disabled persons, according to a recent National Organization on Disability/Harris poll.[4] During 1999, nearly 600,000 households filed for bankruptcy in the aftermath of a serious accident or illness. Those who manage to successfully become employed will not likely make up for the financial losses suffered during years of lost employment.

Historically those groups of persons who experience high labor market discrimination and cannot as readily get jobs in the market remain compulsorily unemployed and require more support from government. Framing the issue as one of "independence" versus "dependency" seems to miss the mark. Until we address the matter of full employment and the right to a job or a guaranteed livable income in its place for all citizens, disabled or non-disabled, disability policy will remain in SSA's "incremental-reform" policy wasteland. People like David, Lynn Thomson, and those battling SSA who too often go unknown and unnamed, will continue to pay a terribly high price.

V.

Beyond Ramps

CHAPTER 13

"Crips Against War"

In a truly "developed" world where diplomacy reigned over brute force and the wealth of a nation was used to better the lives of its citizenry, the US military would be stripped of the billions of the people's tax dollars it wastes. Militarism would be sidelined, if not outlawed.

I got arrested at the March 19 [2003,—*Ed.*] LA antiwar protest near the Westwood Federal Building. There were several hundred of us who gathered at noon before the military dropped Bush's "Shock and Awe" bombs onto the people of Iraq. We were marching to make a last-ditch effort to raise American voices against the oncoming so-called preemptive strike that would initiate an illegal act of aggression and stop a manufactured war for the sake of geopolitical dominance.

The four earsplitting helicopters hovering overhead gave me pause. US military flying objects now in Iraq [harbor] what the military casually calls a "daisy cutter" or a "cluster bomb."

The chain of command for use of a cluster bomb goes like this. Bush, the born-again Christian self-anointed "by God"[1] thumbs his nose at the United Nations' attempts to maintain the peace and insists upon bloodshed. He has a vast murderous arsenal and generals at his disposal, unlike any in history. His general directs the air force plane to fly in and drop the bomb at just the right angle. It breaks up into "bomblets" separating in mid-air and then seconds later a huge wave of fire and shrapnel shoots along a straight line obliterating everything in its path.

Now envision this. The "compassionately conservative" and pious Bush bean counters have a shrapnel agenda at home. It, too, is to alter the domestic policy landscape. The Bush machine, reminiscent of the Gingrich Congress of the mid-nineties, is out to dismantle social entitlement programs. Former secretary of the treasury Paul O'Neill said as much before he was fired. The planes flying in are loaded with numbers in a budget that Congress is to approve.

Already across the nation, teachers are being laid off, schools closed, health care pared down, and college aid slashed to pay for tax cuts for President Bush's upper-class friends.

A single tomahawk missile costs about one million dollars. The military has dropped hundreds in Iraq.

After telling the broke governors last Christmas that the federal government had no money to help bail their states out of debt and help them avoid deep cuts to domestic programs, this spring the Bush-Cheney-Rove-Rumsfeld-Wolfowitz-Perle machine got $80 billion from Congress for the Iraq war. Already the military gets over half of annual federal revenues. It just got more.

The Bush machine proposed and the House passed a Y2004 budget bill that would cut $94 billion from Medicaid (over ten years), $18.5 million from SSI, $14 billion from veterans' programs, $13 billion in food stamps, and $1.2 billion in child care programs. These are all poor people's programs.

The war at home against entitlements, upstaged by the Iraq occupation (and future invasions?), is off the radar screen. Make no mistake. It has reignited.

The "nonexistent" American class system has a class warrior in the oval office who very well knows what class war is all about. The Bush machine gave the rich $1.6 trillion in tax cuts through 2010 and promised more—nearly $2 trillion through 2013 (including added interest on the national debt, according to the Center on Budget and Policy Priorities).

The President's "growth package" would cost the treasury $726 billion (over ten years according to the Tax Policy Center) and result in tax reductions averaging $90,000 each (Y2003) for Americans who have annual incomes of more than $1 million! Does it get any clearer than that?

As I watched an American soldier who occupied one of the palaces in Basra on TV condemn the Hussein version of the Ba'ath party government for such great wealth disparity that would allow lavish palaces to co-exist beside poverty-ridden neighborhoods, I wondered why the low-paid soldier could not see the same in his own native land. What is so different about the Bush version of the Republican Party aiding and abetting the owners of the giant American estates—or the fact that Bush just gave the wealthy who don't need it a huge tax cut, spitting on the working stiffs? Most of the benefits of Bush's tax plan go to those making incomes over $300,000 per year. Does the soldier fit in that class? Hardly.

This disconnect cannot be understated or overemphasized. The polls are full of figures citing Americans who think they are in the top 1 percent who aren't and those who expect to get rich but won't.

Wealth disparity in the US, both in assets owned and the income gap, is greater than at any time since the Great Depression. According to the Gini Index, a measure of income inequality from 1913, income distribution has been getting more unequal for over thirty uninterrupted years. The top 1 percent has nearly 40 percent of the nation's wealth, up from 20 percent in 1976!

The reasons disabled persons organizations have come out against the Bush war are in sync with many others—moral, realpolitik, and geopolitical. We, however, add another dimension.

Whirlwind Wheelchair International (WWI), for instance, is a group against the war that promotes the design and production of sturdy low-cost wheelchairs around the world. Pointing out that already more than 20 million people in the world are still in need of a good wheelchair, WWI works in more than 40 countries, some of which are post-conflict nations, seeing to it that every person who needs a wheelchair can obtain one.

The collateral damage and human rights abuses fomented by the warmongers have just made their job harder.

WWI says that it "feels a great responsibility to help people with disabilities in Iraq."

Crips Against War, formed out of Chicago, says the Bush administration's agenda promises "to rob us of the self-determination for which we have fought for so long."

The Bush machine, including John Ashcroft, has had no use for anyone's civil rights, but the budget will ensure that the civil rights divisions of the federal agencies assigned to enforce the Americans with Disabilities Act won't have the resources either.

Further, under capitalist medicine—dominated by for-profit insurance corporations and the ongoing institutional discrimination in education, welfare, the built environment, and employment practices that exclude disabled people in large measure—self-determination often includes the ability to access Medicaid, Medicare, or Social Security. Entitlement, however, is a word the "compassionate conservatives" intend to eliminate from government's dictionary and erase from the collective memory.

"The war is a perfect smokescreen to accomplish this. Disabled people will be sacrificed at the altar of war," warns Crips Against War.

With estimates approaching a trillion-dollar deficit each year for the next five years, the predicament is dire.

The broke states facing unprecedented deficits are already cutting or slapping co-payments onto the "optional" benefits. Those are medical services the federal government does not mandate the states to provide. People are losing Medicaid "optionals" such as prescription drugs, rehabilitative services, dental services, physical therapy, prosthetic devices, and eyeglasses, to name but a few.

Some states are halting progress on home- and community-based services or personal care services that allow disabled persons an alternative to being warehoused in institutions.

Further there are "optionally eligible persons" under Medicaid. These are populations that (amongst others) include working disabled individuals whose incomes are above the SSI limit or who have high medical expenses that allow them to qualify. With the states in debt and looking to reduce expenditures these people's health care is on the line.

By the end of this fiscal year forty-nine states will have cut Medicaid and thirty-two states will have cut Medicaid twice.

That was before the beginning of the "endless war" Dick Cheney, speaking on behalf of the machine, promised after September 11. It doesn't take a genius to know that one cannot cut taxes for the wealthy and wage a war that will cost endless dollars—especially not during a recession—without curtailing spending somewhere.

"Collateral damage" is the euphemistic term that describes what happens to civilians caught in the crossfire of war.

What about collateral damage at home? With counties in debt and looking to cut costs, health care, and social support services, poor people's lives or those least likely to weather the cutbacks, will change for the worse. Can we extend the term "collateral damage" to encompass people who die prematurely from lack of appropriate health care or go without vital social services?

At a rally to prevent the closure of Rancho Los Amigos Rehabilitation Hospital in Downey, California, due to LA County budget deficits, Janelle Rouse shared her story with me. Rouse came to Rancho as the result of a significant brain injury that regressed her function to the level of an infant. With the knowledge of the rehab expertise at Rancho she had relearned most everything—from the seemingly smallest things like how to dress to the more complicated like continuing to live in her community.

Rouse, who lives with short-term memory loss, contributes her time as a volunteer at Rancho.

Faced with Rancho's closure, however, Rouse is uncertain of her future. Where will she go for the non-replaceable support services she receives from Rancho? Can she continue to live in the community? Will she find a doctor who will take Medi-Cal? Where will she wind up—on the streets with so many others?

Other people who rely on Rancho will surely get displaced. People who use ventilators, for instance, are faced with no other LA hospital that will take them (stated by the county's own consulting firm).

The present Congress, swayed by the right-wing Zionist lobby, the right-wing Christians, and the military industrial complex with defense companies lobbying for military contracts all over the nation, is likely to accomplish what Gingrich could not. Clinton vetoed his contract on America. Bush-Cheney-Rove-Rumsfeld-Wolfowitz-Perle will not. This budget has the devout blessing of the evangelicals-on-a-mission and the hawks beside them.

The organization Disabled Peoples' International took a stand appropriately called "Peace is a Disability Issue." DPI declared, "Let us call for all nations' economies to be transformed from war economies to peace economies. Let us insist that the $600 billion now spent on armaments is diverted to socially useful projects."[2]

Socially useful would not include pouring money into bigger and better killing devices, such as "daisy cutter" bombs, or training our young people to become troops who kill other human beings.

While the popular culture often has interpreted impairment/disability as a metaphor for evil and menace, the real Dr. Strangeloves are people like able-bodied Donald Rumsfeld, a clinically "normal" person. Let's call this the Cheney-Rumsfeld-Wolfowitz-Perle "perfect body" complex? The born-again President who says God told him to start this war would be considered delusional in a psychology textbook or suffering from "grandiosity" at an AA meeting or a violent fundamentalist at the very least. Then again, those who use the banner of religion as a cover for their deeds are seldom questioned for lack of coherence.

As I was being arrested I tried to talk two decent cops out of working for the LAPD. Why support that, I asked? I felt that they deserved more. How does one not harden into a tool of the state when protecting the interests of people who care nothing for one's class? When it came down to it they had more in common with the working people, women, and children that day on the streets, not the Bush machine's strategy for world domination nor his friends' money-making agendas at Halliburton, Bechtel, Trireme (Perle is a managing partner), and Fluor corporations.

Americans live in an imperialist state with a passive, depoliticized population. The soldier in Iraq and the cops who arrested me do not make the connections. How could it be much different given the central values upon which capitalism rests: individualism, competitive "free enterprise," and consumerism?

Still we built a vigorous antiwar movement and we must keep opposing this war plan, militarism, and imperialism generally. Damage control is needed now to stop the cluster of bombs dropping on the home front and to get these self-serving criminals out of office.

CHAPTER 14

Disability and the War Economy

2003: The Iraq War Begins

I happen to be one of those movement people who do not believe disability civil rights or "equal opportunity" will equate with a reduction of government outlay. To my way of thinking, equity and inclusion for disabled persons under capitalism will mean ongoing government supports, not ending them via welfare reform for some mythological libertarian "independence" in a free-market storybook. Entitlements and rights must go hand in hand to advance disabled people's liberation.

We need to be damned concerned about what [President George—*Ed*.] Bush's cronies are doing inside the administration and beyond it. Under the cloak of words like "human rights," "free markets," and "democracy," current US foreign policy makers have embarked on a long-planned military imperialist aggression that will cost billions of taxpayer dollars.

At the same time, the Bush administration demands more tax cuts for the richest Americans during times of recession. That has left massive deficits—and will leave them for years to come. This portends a further narrowing of social programs—read restriction of civil rights and a rollback of expenditures on public healthcare, education, and social services.

Across the nation the official unemployment rate is over 6 percent (double that to include those who have given up finding a job). Teachers are being laid off, schools closed, healthcare pared down, in-home support services curbed, college aid slashed.

How can that happen in the richest nation in the world?

Since 1973 the reigning economic ideology has been neoliberalism. Under neoliberalism, the elites moved to protect the rates of investment profit by appropriating an increased share of the treasury's surplus in light of the steadily-slowing growth of the global economy as a whole. If the elites and corporations get more, and the pie doesn't get that much bigger (like now), the people get less.

At a time when inequality is at a seventy-year high, Bush has given the rich $1.6 trillion in tax cuts. [...]

The predicament is dire. Sources estimate up to a trillion-dollar deficit each year for the next five years. A Brookings Institution study shows that Bush's militarism will require a 40 percent cut in spending on discretionary programs—items like IDEA [Individuals with Disabilities Education Act—*Ed.*], housing, assistive technology—over the next decade.

"More extreme Republicans," reported London's *Financial Times*, actually want what *New York Times* economic columnist Paul Krugman called a "fiscal train wreck": "Proposing to slash federal spending, particularly on social programs, is a tricky electoral proposition," *FT* said, "but a fiscal crisis offers the tantalizing prospect of forcing such cuts through the back door."[1] [...]

Bush funding-formula changes meant nearly 3.9 million children, over 1.2 million disabled people, almost six hundred and ninety thousand seniors, and approximately 1.7 million other adults stood to lose health coverage, according to Families USA. [...]

Current policy can be dropped at the feet of the neoconservatives—"neocons"—running US foreign policy.

Remember when US Army Brigadier General Vincent Brooks unveiled pictures of fifty-five "wanted" men from Saddam's administration at a briefing at Central Command in Qatar? These were pictures of those whom the US wanted chased, caught, or killed.

The Trade Regulation Organization—a spoof on the World Trade Organization run by the Yes Men, a loose-knit group of online hoaxers—then issued a "55 most wanted" playing-card deck similar to the one the Pentagon issued in Iraq. The heads here, though, are the neocons and American Enterprise Institute think-tank fellows who have moved national policy to that of "preventative" war and opened the door to unilateral attacks on any nation deemed a threat to US interests.

In this deck, Bush factors in only as a four of clubs (but the head shot of Bush in front of the Great Seal of Office makes him seem to be sporting a halo). Secretary of Defense Donald Rumsfeld is the ace of diamonds, and Bush senior advisor Karl Rove is the ace of clubs.

The ace of spades in the deck is Dick Cheney. Iraq War I was good to Cheney financially. While Cheney was CEO of Halliburton, its subsidiary Kellogg Brown & Root got a lucrative contract to reconstruct the demolished oil fields. Halliburton is reportedly setting aside even more sums of money for Cheney when he leaves public office.

Norman Podhoretz, editor of *Commentary*, and Irving Kristol, editor of the *Public Interest*, two of the most influential leaders of the neocon community, are missing from the deck—a major oversight since they have buoyed the neocon line for the American public. But publishing magnate Rupert Murdock is the King of Hearts. Irving's son William Kristol edits Murdock's magazine the *Weekly Standard*. Podhoretz once claimed that the neocons "shook the position of leftists and liberals in the world of ideas and by doing so cleared the way to the presidency of Ronald Reagan."

The neocons—William Bennett is also amongst them—diagnosed the 1960s student unrest, countercultural movements, concern for poverty and racial justice, and the women's liberation movement as "cultural problems," a "moral breakdown in society." They attacked social welfare programs because these programs, they claim, cause dependency on government rather than the corporation. Ending "dependency" was part of the economic rationale for passing the ADA—crips will get jobs and they'll quit taking government handouts.

The American Enterprise Institute (AEI) is a well-funded right-wing think-tank that for years has been making the case for getting rid of entitlements. Bush has appointed some 20 AEI fellows to his administration. Richard Perle, who resigned his chairmanship of Bush's Defense Policy Board over a business conflict of interest, is a fellow at AEI.

AEI sees "entitlement spending" as consuming too much of the budget and doomed to programmatic failure. The neocon directive is toward increasing the military budget and "national security." "Freedom" at home means fewer entitlements (fewer jobs as well). "Freedom" abroad means military might to impose rule that will carry out the interests of the US corporations.

Michael Ledeen, holder of the Freedom Chair at AEI, says, "Every ten years or so, the US needs to pick up some small crappy little country and throw it against the wall, just to show the world we mean business," reports the *National Review's* Jonah Goldberg.[2]

It's actually better planned than that. If Americans had looked deeply enough they would have found the rationale for war in the Middle East laid out in The

Project for the New American Century's 1997 "Statement of Principles." The group is not a secret cabal nor are its goals any conspiracy theory. It was run out of Kristol's *Weekly Standard* office and is available online.[3]

The statement, signed by Rumsfeld, Podhoretz, Cheney, Bennett, and Enron's Ken Lay, plus a few others like the president's brother, Jeb Bush, asserted that conservatives had not fought for a big enough military budget and vowed to "maintain American security and advance American interests in the new century."

The language is clearly imperialist: the US "stands as the world's preeminent power"; we must "increase defense spending significantly" and "promote the cause of political and economic freedom abroad"; the US needs "the resolve to shape a new century favorable to American principles and interests." The neocons have never made any secret of their imperialist intent.

The founding document of neocon policy is the Defense Planning Guidance drafted for Cheney in 1992 during his stint as defense secretary. Written by Paul Wolfowitz, now Bush's deputy secretary of defense, and "Scooter" Lewis Libby, then Cheney's chief of staff and another AEI fellow, with input from Rumsfeld and four of diamonds Jeb Bush, this document raised the idea of "pre-emptive" attacks and called on America to increase military spending to a level that would make the US virtually unchallenged in the world.

The neocons and crony capitalists have come together in one big giddy-on-power Dubya cocktail government—making him a most dangerous president.

In Eugene, Oregon, parents and teachers and friends of the public school are selling their blood plasma to raise money for next year's school budget. What is this kind of pressure going to add to the budget woes of inclusive education?

The House gutted the Individuals with Disabilities Education Act on April 30.[4] Every disabled kid receiving any kind of education services is affected. "Right of appeal? Gone," a parent wrote me in frustration. "Yearly reviews? Let's make those optional, every three years. Legal fees? Limit what families can hope to retrieve in fighting mistreatment from the school district (the school districts have no such limits)."

The American Association of Retired Persons reported that one-third of disabled people over fifty have postponed healthcare because of cost. This is an increase over previous surveys—yet a lot more state health spending cuts and private health insurance out-of-pocket expense increases are on the way. The future portends worse as insurance companies hike premiums more than 10 percent in one year.

Meanwhile Senate Majority Leader Bill Frist (R-Tenn.), the under-rated seven of diamonds, told the *Tennessean* in May that Medicare is an "antiquated system" that cannot sustain itself in the current healthcare market. Frist is part owner of Columbia/HCA, the healthcare corporation nabbed by the government for tens of thousands of dollars of fraudulent Medicare billing.

Domestic programs, crony capitalism, and the national bent towards militarism are connected. Militarism is diverting money from state and local governments. While AEI complains, "entitlement programs are crowding out the rest of government," the US spends more [on its military] than the defense budgets of countries with the next 14 biggest militaries combined, and is accelerating production of state-of-the-art weapons of mass destruction—initiating another costly arms race.

Bush, in his Memorial Day speech, referred to the "battles of Afghanistan and Iraq" as mere moments in Cheney's fifty-year war. As Michael Hardt, author of *Empire*, said on WBAI radio recently, war used to be considered an exception; now the exception has become the norm. [. . .]

2005: Two Years On

Defending the success of the Iraq War a defiant Bush bragged, "[there are] more cell phones in the hands of Iraqis than before."[5] And guess what, some sod has been laid in a Najaf soccer field.

That is no consolation to Maggie Dee, a significantly disabled woman living in northern California who worked through most of her adulthood as a disabled woman and has fought for disability rights for years. Now, unable to work, she survives only on her Social Security disability check, a meager $812 per month.

Economic insecurity has gotten worse for the average American as earnings fail to keep up with inflation or jobs get shipped overseas. The exception, of course, is the richest, upon whom the Bush administration has bestowed unbridled wealth. Before the Congress is a $70 billion package that would include an extension of Bush's 2001 tax cut for stock dividends and capital gains.

But for disabled people economic insecurity has gotten really bad.

"All the things we have to cope with," says Maggie Dee, "take so much out of people. They cannot keep chipping away at people."

"One can only take so much oppression without wanting to just give up," she added.

A fellow advocate in Marin County had recently committed suicide because he just found his life overwhelming with the lack of support as a quadriplegic. He had lost several attendants who had come in each day to assist him with daily tasks and was having a hard time finding and keeping a stable situation. He wrote in a note to his family that he loved them so much and he knew it would hurt them but he just could not stand the stress of being so poor and the lack of a sufficient support system to keep him afloat. And he is not alone. Reports have come in from Tennessee where [Democratic Governor Phil—*Ed.*] Bredesen severed about 191,000 poor people from TennCare—the state's version of Medicaid.

Journalist John Spragens reported from Tennessee on the TennCare cuts. One story he told was about a forty-eight-year-old man who had a bipolar condition and thought he would be cut from TennCare and unable to get his meds.

"Bob wrote a note to his family and a poem for his sister. 'I know what a burden I'm going to be, and I don't want to put you all through it,' he wrote. He went to the local cemetery, called 911 and told the dispatcher that they could find him on his mother's tombstone. Then, he pulled out a gun and shot himself," wrote Spragens.[6]

If I traveled the country and visited states where Medicaid has been cut back like Missouri, Mississippi, and Minnesota I certainly would find more stories of similar life and death distress.

Maggie's benefit amount would have been increased by $48 starting January 1, 2006 were it not for Republican Governor Schwarzenegger and the Democrat-dominated California legislature that made a budget compromise in which disabled people who rely upon Supplemental Security Income would be denied both their federal and state cost of living increases for 2006.

SSI cost of living increases are small but greatly needed. This year the increase due is 4.1 percent. Twenty-four dollars are due to those on SSI from the state and twenty-four from the federal government, but they won't see that forty-eight dollars at all. They may get twenty-four dollars in April if the state keeps its word. So, in April, Maggie may have $836 to survive on each month while the state pockets the federal twenty-four dollars pretty much for good.

Meanwhile, the California legislators who are the highest paid in the country will see a 12 percent increase in their salaries bringing their salaries up to a whopping $110,880 per year. That is their cost of living increase! (California lawmakers also receive $153 a day in expense money when they are in session.)

Says Maggie, "they are taking our SSI money and giving it to themselves."

There is no deficit in California this year. Is that any consolation to anyone with any sense of social or economic justice? Look at how the state has done it. The disparity is so great that there are no words for these wrongful acts.

What is happening to poor disabled persons at the state level is happening at the federal.

The squeeze on poor disabled people goes deeper. Section 8 [low-income rental assistance—*Ed.*] voucher formulas have changed. Once, disabled people paid one-third of their income for rent while the federal government paid the rest (up to the established federal rent rate for the area). Now Public Housing Authorities are taking a greater share of people's income. In one case an individual's share went from $246 to $330 per month. On an income of $812 that leaves $482 to pay for food, utilities, transportation, postage, clothing, and other necessities.

Add to this the fact that many of these individuals are on both Medicare and Medicaid and *must* sign onto a Medicare Part D drug plan by January 1. They will go from having no co-pays to paying $2–5 per prescription. While that may not sound like much, think about what $40 might do to one's food budget when there is too little to begin with.

It is a humiliating, debasing, demeaning life this nation condemns on poor disabled persons.

There is more to come. House and Senate Republican leaders have edged closer (at the time of this writing) toward an agreement to cut as much as $45 billion over the next five years from domestic programs like Medicaid, food stamps, student loans, and child-support enforcement.

Big money in control of government cuts taxes for the wealthy and corporations at the expense of the rest of us.

So, neoliberalism continues to worm its way through our social fabric, wreaking havoc while the neocons advance their death march to "democracy" in the Middle East at a cost of $225,076,331,348 to this minute, 2:46 p.m. PST on December 8, 2005.[7]

They say the neocons don't have a domestic agenda.

While the Bush administration is killing Americans abroad in an illegal war largely financed by the Chinese continuing to buy US bonds, the neocon foreign agenda is killing Americans at home by starving the nation of funds for taking care of our own.

Disabled people are going first. That is how it always happens.

None call it cleansing. The euphemism is benign neglect or balancing the budget—but it is criminal neglect and just as murderous as the state-sponsored death penalty.

While Bush is pushing cell phones in Iraq we must recognize and stop this gross infraction of human rights under our noses.

CHAPTER 15

Un-Natural Disasters: Reflections on Hurricane Katrina

If you are disabled and rich, or somewhat well-off, and lived in New Orleans [during the 2005 catastrophe of Hurricane Katrina—*Ed.*], you probably got out of the city before the levees broke and flooded some 60 percent of the parishes. If you are rich and use a wheelchair you probably had a van with a ramp or car of your own with gas money to get you to safety. If you are blind (and rich) you likely had a driver with a car to take you to the high lands. If you are deaf, use a cane, walker, crutches, service animal, or have mental health needs and you have money, you also got yourself out perhaps with the help of family. But if you are disabled and poor in New Orleans you likely had none of these options.

A 911 caller told the operator, "I am handicapped and have an eight-month-old baby. We are lying on the bed—the water is coming up fast. We need help." But no help came. No help came because there was no planned evacuation for poor disabled residents. Being disabled and poor meant one's chances for survival were less than one's non-disabled counterparts. While many of the least fortunate were waiting and hoping for the absent cavalry to arrive on those rooftops, at least one quadriplegic could not be pulled up on the roof to semi-safety. He drowned instead. There were others. We know that in New Orleans 23.2 percent of residents were disabled persons out of a city of about 484,000 people. There were

102,122 disabled people 5 years of age and older who lived in New Orleans at the time of the flood.

At least half of the disabled persons in New Orleans who are of working age were not employed.

To be disabled and poor in New Orleans and much of the US meant to rely on a variety of government programs such as Supplemental Security Income and Medicaid to help one meet one's daily service and support needs.

Being disabled and poor in one group home for the blind meant staff abandoned one to sink or swim. Being disabled and poor meant being separated from any type of accessible public transportation before the flood and there was no accessible transportation afterwards.

Being disabled and poor for blind people meant being unable to even get around in one's own flooded neighborhood because one could no longer navigate the environmental landscape.

Being disabled and poor for people with physical disabilities who are over 65 years of age meant being unable to leave one's home, group home, nursing home, or hospital without significant assistance.

Being disabled and poor meant to have lost or become separated from the drugs one relies on daily for diabetes, high blood pressure, and other chronic conditions and have little means to access pharmacies when it became apparent the cavalry was permanently absent.

Being disabled and poor for those driven by flood waters from institutions, group homes, or nursing homes meant being housed in less than satisfactory conditions, with considerably less than the necessary range of services and supports needed, for an unknown stretch of time.

Being disabled and poor meant that one stood a good chance of dying from the insufferable heat; at least one hundred and fifty-four patients died this way, suggesting that vulnerable people plummeted to the bottom of priority lists if they were on lists at all.

Being disabled and poor for those who have service animals meant not being able to rely on those animals outside of the house or group home because these animals could not navigate safely in the flooded streets.

Being disabled and poor for deaf persons meant being unable to access emergency information through television, TTY, or other communications for the deaf because public communications systems were compromised, and those available through the federal government were holed up outside the city awaiting orders to move into New Orleans.

Being disabled and poor meant being unable to secure life-saving food and water as many were trapped within the confines of inadequately supplied shelters, the convention center, or the Superdome with all the other evacuees.

Being disabled and poor meant that when you died sitting in your wheelchair some respectful survivor might cover you with a sheet or some plastic.

Being disabled and poor meant that when the first responders at long, long last got to the Superdome, disabled persons were forced to leave their wheelchairs, walkers, crutches, and service animals behind, as these were not allowed on the buses.

Being disabled and poor means that one will have to wait months and months—if not years—to replace the wheelchairs and service animals that were taken from them in New Orleans.

Being disabled and poor often meant being evacuated to some nursing home in a strange town where one will have to fight hard to ever acquire the support services to live in the community again.

Being disabled and poor means needing Medicaid yet being relocated to another state where state governors have cut Medicaid to the extent that it is not serving those already enrolled; it is to find out that people are being dropped off the roles by the thousands—not added—when you desperately need your medications.

Being disabled and poor in need of accessible housing means depending upon the Department of Housing and Urban Development (HUD) which has allowed its funding to be cut so thin by the Bush administration that it is pitting the evacuees against the already poor and homeless in need of low-income housing. At the time of writing, HUD has refused to offer any emergency funding to the nation's housing authorities that are providing housing assistance to Katrina's victims.

Being disabled and poor meant that if one managed to get to a Red Cross shelter with their wheelchair, that the Red Cross would deny one entrance into their shelters because the shelters were not accessible. When the National Organization on Disability advocates went down there to see what was going on, they too were denied access.[1]

We don't have and may never have the data to tell us how many disabled people lost their lives when the waters rose above their heads. We do know that disabled people were disproportionately affected. I'm sure the government does not want the public to know how many disabled persons drowned—their bodies bloated, floating in the toxic sewer that was once a street—or dehydrated or starved in this preventable catastrophe and its aftermath.

But the tremendous loss of life and ongoing devastation was not at root caused by Hurricane Katrina. It was caused by a corrupt government run by people who saw more profit for themselves and their friends in diverting taxpayer dollars to multibillion-dollar corporate contracts in a senseless and lawless war, and doling tax cuts out to the richest people in this nation, rather than in buttressing the faulty levee system protecting New Orleans from Lake Pontchartrain.

When Bush said, "I don't think anybody anticipated the breach of the levees," he lied.[2] The Corps of Engineers, the Federal Emergency Management Agency, and other scientific experts alerted the nation it needed to devote resources and taxpayer dollars to fix this "accident" waiting to happen. The *Times-Picayune*, the daily newspaper of New Orleans, published numerous articles during the last two years citing the danger caused by the loss of hurricane protection funds to the war in Iraq.[3]

The Bush administration slashed funds for flood control operations in New Orleans. Bush's war left the Corps of Engineers only 20 percent of the needed funding to protect New Orleans.

Bush played golf and turned away as hundreds of people—including disabled persons—drowned and starved.

What happened to disabled poor people in New Orleans is nothing less than criminally negligent homicide. Bush says he is responsible; but the question is will the nation hold the man accountable for murder?

CHAPTER 16

The Affordable, Accessible Housing Crisis

Affordable housing was already at a crisis point pre-S11 [September 11, 2001—*Ed.*], during the economic "boom." Now in the recession, people are being pink-slipped and losing their jobs by the tens of thousands. The Bush economic stimulus bailout plan does nothing for laid-off workers; rather, it is a giveaway of taxpayer dollars to the richest corporations and people in this country. Meanwhile, thanks to neoliberal policies that have hacked away at the social safety net since the Reagan years, unemployment benefits are at historic lows. The state of public housing isn't much better.

Over time displaced workers will be threatened with a loss of housing and will be joining the ranks of those who the private sector has already failed—the working poor (disabled or not) and disabled persons on fixed incomes from pensions or disability checks.

Working people in low paid jobs who cannot pay the rents ushered in by the economic expansion have found themselves sharing one-bedroom apartments with several persons or facing homelessness. Lack of affordable and accessible housing is a barrier to the full inclusion of disabled persons in the community and in the workplace. Disabled persons face extreme discrimination in the private housing market and also encounter a lack of accessible housing options even with Section 8 housing vouchers. Both groups have been struggling to survive on the remnants of a never adequate public plan for housing and have been failed by the Department of Housing and Urban Development (HUD).

The strength of America's economy has not brought down homelessness. In Massachusetts, for instance, home costs increased 45 percent over the past five years. According to a study by Harvard University, low income families—even those earning 30 percent more than the minimum wage—cannot afford the rent of a two-bedroom apartment in any state in the country. The US Conference of Mayors' sixteenth survey (2000) on "Hunger and Homelessness in America's Cities" found increased levels of hunger and that the average demand for emergency shelter increased by 15 percent—the highest one-year increase of the decade.[1] Causes of homelessness included the lack of affordable housing, low paying jobs, and changes in public assistance, amongst other findings.

There are no reliable figures on the numbers of homeless who have disabilities. We do know, however, that one of the greatest challenges facing the disability community today is the lack of affordable, accessible housing, either private or public. For instance, Washington, DC, housing statistics show that of ten thousand four hundred and sixty public housing apartments only one hundred and ninety-one or 1.7 percent are classified as accessible for disabled persons. (Section 504 of the Rehabilitation Act requires these owners to make 5 percent of their rental units fully accessible.) Further, for every public housing unit now occupied, there is approximately one person or family waiting for it. For every accessible unit, nine people are waiting.

Federal fair housing laws require that larger private apartment buildings built after 1990 have minimum accessibility features, including at least one accessible entrance. As a practical matter, however, these laws have been of limited utility in increasing the supply of affordable, accessible housing. One reason is that most affordable housing was built prior to 1991 and is not subject to accessibility requirements. Another is that although federal laws require landlords to allow disabled tenants to make and pay for access modifications, tenants with disabilities are disproportionately low-income and lack sufficient funds to pay for expensive modifications such as exterior ramps, which in difficult architectural situations can cost as much as twenty thousand dollars. There are virtually no sources of funds available to tenants to pay for such ramps.

Even builders and landlords who have used federal funds to build or rebuild apartment complexes do not always comply with state or federal laws that require accessible accommodations for disabled persons.

Local government agencies in charge of enforcing both private and public building disabled access are not getting the job done. In Sacramento County, for example, an undercover survey by the Human Rights/Fair Housing commission found that as many as 51 percent of the apartment complexes in Sacramento County don't meet legal requirements for serving mobility impaired persons.

In Washington, after years of waiting for better results, a suit was filed on behalf of disabled persons against the DC Housing Authority for violating the Rehabilitation Act. There, children with disabilities are crawling up stairs to reach bathrooms and young men are forced into nursing homes because the District of Columbia has failed to comply with access regulations.

As people find it more and more difficult to get another job during a recession, history shows that applications increase for disability benefits and for public assistance. Some of those fired workers may eventually have to rely on a greatly scaled back safety net to survive. They will find that coming by a federal Section 8 housing voucher takes years. The average Section 8 wait nationally is three years; in Los Angeles it is five to eight years. How many people will be able to stay off the streets for that long a time?

Here in Los Angeles I know of several disabled persons facing issues with landlords. One has been holed up in a cheap motel for months after being hospitalized (his roommate/landlord took that opportunity to ditch his things on the street). He found that no landlord he has approached wants to rent to him. He is certain that part of the problem is that he uses a wheelchair and that landlords don't want to rent to him because of that. Unless they say "no crips" outright, however, he doesn't have a lawsuit. Meanwhile there are not any slots available for him in HUD buildings either.

In yet another instance, a mother of a disabled child who is the primary support person for her son is facing eviction because of her Section 8 voucher. Her landlord is taking advantage of a new law which allows property owners to opt out of the Section 8 program if they give the tenant ninety days termination notice before their contract expires.

She said that although Legal Aid was representing her, they "want to settle" and are encouraging her to move. This woman is a tough advocate and she has doubts whether the Legal Aid attorney knows the law as it applies to the disabled population. She finds her resources to fight the landlord severely limited by her circumstances. This is how empowered people can be defeated—when there is not real access to legal protection.

Then, there is the woman who wrote me that due to her chronic illness she was becoming less able to fight the landlord when he attempted to oust her from her apartment. During this ordeal she has found herself conflicted over the issue of assisted suicide. She doesn't want to support it because she feels that chronically ill and disabled persons would become its victims. Yet the reality that so many people face as the world gets harsher and less hospitable to vulnerable populations make her less certain. Wouldn't it just be easier to get a physician to give her a lethal injection and save her from being homeless, she asks?

Where the hell are HUD and the local Public Housing Authorities? Held hostage to the private landlords by their failure to develop abundant alternatives? Why do they not have a strong department devoted to protect tenants? A new report from the National Council on Disability (NCD) established to make policy recommendations to the president and Congress informs: "HUD has lost control of its own enforcement process. The promises of the fair housing laws have been empty for many Americans, with and without disabilities."[2]

According to NCD, HUD ruled out discrimination in all but 2.4 percent of more than 12,000 complaints between 1988 and 2000. NCD found that by 2000, HUD was taking an average of nearly fourteen months—more than four times the one hundred days prescribed by law—to complete its investigations. The seventy-four-day average achieved in 1989 was the only time HUD met the requirement. NCD concluded that HUD's performance has dramatically deteriorated since.[3]

Our public housing has increasingly become driven by the "free" market system. Landlords have been freed by tenants' lack of meaningful legal recourse, the underfunding of legal services, HUD's failings, and the grinding poverty of those who would protest. These stories are but a few of the consequences. Clintonism's "less government" and the Democratic Party's support of privatization of public housing which allows the profit motive to take over public responsibilities—have resulted in less democratic equality, less "equal opportunity," and less security.

As the economy recedes and coalitions form for economic survival under the self-serving Bush clan and associates, the housing needs of disabled persons must be on the radar screen and be included on the agenda.

CHAPTER 17

The United States versus the World

The Bush administration continues to set itself apart from world opinion, this time by not actively supporting a UN effort to create a disability-sensitive human rights treaty. Fortunately, more than a hundred other nations do not share the US's position.

The administration's views became known at "The Second Ad Hoc Committee Meeting of the United Nations on a Comprehensive and Integral International Convention to Promote and Protect the Rights and Dignity of Persons with Disabilities," held in New York June 16 to 27 [in 2003—*Ed.*].[1] The General Assembly charged the panel with deciding whether the United Nations should develop a disability-themed human rights treaty.

Almost immediately, Ralph Boyd, the US Assistant Attorney General for Civil Rights said a global treaty on disability and human rights was not necessary. Instead, he said countries should follow the US model and adopt non-discrimination laws. The United States would help craft such model laws, he said, but "not with the expectation that we will become party to any resulting legal instrument."[2]

For disabled people's organizations (DPOs), this assertion was especially galling, because, if anything, the recent record of the US court system, Congress, and many state legislatures is one that has consistently undermined these very rights. The administration's perception that the United States has laws that "seamlessly integrate" disabled people into American society belies reality.

141

For many years now, disability activists have watched the business-friendly Supreme Court shrink the legal definition of disability to accommodate employers, instead of employees with disabilities. Increasingly, deserving Americans who seek redress in court face summary judgments, instead of jury trials. Meanwhile, enforcement of key laws, such as the ADA, the Rehabilitation Act of 1973, and the Individuals with Disabilities Education Act has fallen short. Yet the administration now asserts that our laws are a model for the world.

It is also important to understand the inherent limitations of adopting "non-discrimination" laws. While these laws have moved public policy from a medical notion of disability to the wider recognition that disabled persons are a grouping within society that faces rampant social and economic discrimination, non-discrimination laws are not enough to address the entirety of disability rights.

Under principles of non-discrimination, for instance, there is no broader right to be free from hunger or right to have shelter. With 82 percent of the six hundred million disabled persons worldwide living in "developing" nations, the lack of access to food kills thousands of disabled children yearly. Thirteen percent of over two million recorded instances of human rights breaches since 1990 have resulted in the deaths of disabled individuals.

In addition, many policies pushed by the International Monetary Fund and the World Bank have widened socio-economic inequalities in developing countries, not narrowed them. Thus, increasing global poverty has compounded the isolated, degrading, and dehumanizing conditions in which disabled persons live.

For DPOs, a comprehensive treaty would include a guarantee of social and economic rights—along with non-discrimination measures. It would embrace affirmative action to ensure that disabled persons have access to community living, in-home support services, jobs, affordable health care, accessible housing and other societal supports in non-segregated settings. Even in a wealthy society such as the United States, disabled people too often go homeless because of a lack of rights and social policies within our borders.

There are twenty-eight rights in the UN Declaration of Human Rights. A few rights tailored to disability would include:

The right to be free from torture and cruel, inhuman and degrading treatment or punishment, including violent and harmful medical practices (such as putting developmentally disabled persons in cages or performing involuntary psychiatric procedures)

The right to personal integrity, freedom from degrading, dehumanizing treatment (not to be institutionalized or abused by caregivers)

The right to marry and have a family

The right to life (as opposed to being chained in a public square and starved to death)

The right to be free from forced sterilization

The right to access the justice system (i.e., to sign language interpreters in court).

Additionally, it is necessary to include disabled peoples' right to bodily and psychic integrity including autonomy in decision-making.

In sum, disabled peoples' movements seek to overturn the assertion that disability is pathological in health terms and a social problem in welfare terms. Disabled persons want to be citizens with human rights. This was the agenda promoted at the United Nations, by groups including the World Federation of the Deaf, the World Blind Union, Disabled Peoples' International, the World Federation of the Deafblind, the World Network of Users and Survivors of Psychiatry, and Inclusion International.

Fortunately, the administration's efforts to derail progress on global disability rights were largely ignored by the international community participating in the UN session. Delegates agreed not only to proceed with drafting a treaty but also to include disabled persons selected by DPOs in the drafting group.

While it is likely a treaty will be drafted, whether the outcome will be a strong treaty and whether it will be ratified and implemented are yet other matters.

The United States has failed to ratify the Convention on the Rights of the Child, the Convention on the Elimination of All Forms of Discrimination against Women, the Land Mine Ban Treaty and to sign on to the International Criminal Court or the Kyoto Accord.[3] And it has failed to enforce numerous domestic laws that would work toward the goals expressed by the international community in these treaties.

Regardless, the United Nations has a role to set a globally recognized set of standards, whether or not countries sign onto them. The significance here is historic—disabled people are at long last gaining the power to secure a place for legally binding disability law at the human rights table.

VI.

Body Politics:
The Missing Link

CHAPTER 18

Dollars and Death: The Question of Physician-Assisted Suicide

Part I

Living in a neoliberal era—where the interests of business dominate government and public policy, and in a climate that more and more measures one's worth by economic efficacy—demands that we scrutinize the "right" to die beyond a liberal expansion of individual rights. We must look at the timing of these proposals.

Why assisted suicide now, with the increase of mysterious viruses and incurable illnesses like chronic fatigue, AIDS and fibromyalgia, which require costly drugs and long-term care? Why now, with managed care corporations rationing health care, and with public health care under the budget ax?

In his latest book, *Freedom to Die: People, Politics, and the Right to Die Movement*, Derek Humphry, cofounder of the Hemlock Society, the oldest and largest pro-euthanasia/assisted suicide group, says it will be the unspoken argument for assisted suicide—cost containment—that will ensure the eventual passage of laws legalizing assisted suicide and euthanasia.[1]

Humphry argues it will be the drive to save health care dollars that will push public policy in their direction, not the drive for increased autonomy (as the Death with Dignity slogans assure the public). Humphry is right to make the connection. But some have unabashedly been speaking the unspoken for years now.

The convicted murderer Kevorkian exposed his real agenda in a Written Statement to Court (August 17, 1990): "The voluntary self-elimination of individuals and mortally diseased or crippled lives taken collectively can only enhance preservation of public health and welfare."[2]

Courts are listening to this line of reasoning. When the Ninth Circuit Court in San Francisco ruled that individuals have a constitutional right to physician-assisted suicide, it specifically targeted the handicapped as "beneficiaries," stating that it may be acceptable for "competent, terminally ill adults to take the economic welfare of their families and loved ones into consideration" when deciding whether to live or die, and defended the use of assisted suicide to control medical costs.

An editorial in the *Weekly Standard*, the voice of the GOP majority, concluded in 1995, "Sick people are expensive. The dead are a burden to no one. Fifty years ago there was whooping cough and diphtheria. 'The child either lived or died, and, for the most part, did so quickly and cheaply,' noted [Columbia Professor Willard—*Ed.*] Gaylin. Now that child 'will grow up to be a very expensive old man or woman.' . . . Ultimately, the only answer is some kind of rationing, under whatever guise."[3]

This gives cause to ask what is really happening when Kevorkian and others talk about voluntary self-elimination. Are people who seek assisted suicide choosing death or being cornered into it by inadequate national disability policy, a lack of quality long-term and palliative care that, in their absence, makes life so unbearable that death seems preferable to life?

Oregon, which legalized assisted suicide [in 1997,—*Ed.*] made changes to its Medicaid policy so that the state will prioritize payment for physician-assisted suicide since federal laws prohibit funding. Physicians there reported that the state also restricted funding for a key pain medicine, Oxycontin, making this needed treatment virtually unavailable to many chronically or terminally ill patients; effective doses were not available to patients with conditions like amyotrophic lateral sclerosis (Lou Gehrig's disease), diabetic neuropathy, multiple sclerosis, reflex sympathetic dystrophy, and a host of painful, disabling, or fatal disorders. Disability advocates have reported that there are difficulties in obtaining the hours of attendant services needed to remain at home in Oregon.

Surveys have consistently found that most people would rather continue to live at home than in a nursing home. What has not been known until recently is that the aversion to nursing homes is so strong that a new study of seriously ill people in hospitals found that 30 percent would rather die than live forevermore in a nursing home.

Research on those who elected to die under the Oregon law reveals that people did so over concerns about loss of autonomy or loss of control of bodily functions—

fears which are not being addressed by uniform public policy like quality in-home care and psychological support services to ease the transition to disablement.

Instead, Humphry's answer, and increasingly that of more assisted suicide advocates, is to give elderly and disabled people the "freedom" to kill themselves rather than to demand a national attendant service (PAS) program be put in place that would enable elderly and disabled people to remain in their homes rather than being warehoused in institutions.

In the Managed Care Era it is essential to ask, will people choosing death be the victims of a health care system which is more oriented towards reaping Wall Street dividends rather than relieving pain and depression, providing comfort at the end of life—care which is costly to health corporation and state budget bottom lines?

With the advent of managed care, there has been a payment paradigm shift. In the name of containing costs, HMO hospitals and doctors no longer get paid for individual services rendered; they get paid a flat fee. This shift means that those needing the most health care are no longer perceived as an asset (bringing more money in) they are seen as a liability (draining the profits).

Furthermore, managed care corporations manipulate fees to control gate-keeper physicians' approval of expenditures on patients; doctors are given bonuses for keeping costs low and often find their contracts revoked when they do not conform to HMO administrators' directives.

Dr. Linda Peeno, a physician who found herself in such a predicament, testified before the House Commerce Committee (May 30, 1996):

> I wish to begin by making a public confession. In the spring of 1987, as a physician, I caused the death of a man. . . . Although this was known to many people, I have not been taken before any court of law or called to account for this in any professional or public forum. In fact, just the opposite occurred: I was "rewarded" for this. It brought me an improved reputation in my job, and contributed to my advancement afterwards. Not only did I demonstrate I could do what was expected of me, I exemplified the "good" company doctor: I saved a half million dollars![4]

Is all this not sufficient evidence to conclude that there is a direct link between physician-assisted suicide and efforts to reduce health-care spending on poor, sick, and disabled people? The issue of physician-assisted suicide must be viewed within the context of an economic order which is eviscerating the social contract by encouraging government to retreat from its responsibilities to the public's welfare. Will the public now in support of assisted suicide hear the "unspoken"?

Part II

Being a veteran of the war for truth during the Kevorkian era of the assisted suicide debates, it astounds me when I see that some companions battling for social
justice are still entangled in the Kevorkian-as-humanist illusion web. Someone
emailed me recently that before Kevorkian was jailed they saw an all-smiles Tom
Cruise go over to Kevorkian at a Hollywood party and pat him on the back. Vonnegut fantasizes about being guided into and back from death by Jack and his
death machine in "God Bless You, Dr. Kevorkian."[5] Of course, Kevorkian is the
number one martyr for the Hemlock Society which recently aired the video version of "Final Exit" on Oregon public access TV.

Not Dead Yet, which has taken the lead in opposing Kevorkian, calls the
Hemlockers "the 4 W's: White, Well-off, Worried, and Well." Organizer Diane
Coleman explains, "They [Hemlockers] don't care how many of our people are
encouraged—even pressured—to die, so long as they themselves can have the security of a clean, neat, sanitized suicide at the hands of a medical professional."[6]

Despite the fact that Jack has been stripped of his doctorhood in several states
and, most recently, jailed for murder, some believers hold onto the image of Kevorkian as a symbol of humanism.

It follows that my question must be: Does Kevorkian have the humanists
fooled or what? Or maybe I misunderstand what humanism is. Is it humanistic,
for instance, to be willing to step in and help a disabled person die rather than provide the means to live? Is it humanistic (or even defensible) to assist an obviously
depressed forty-three-year-old woman to her death who was diagnosed with a non-
terminal but impairing condition and then abandoned by a husband who also took
her children away from her? That is what Kevorkian did to the vulnerable Sherry
Miller who needed antidepressants and a good lawyer, not a visit with Dr. Death.

Is it humanistic to assist a quadriplegic to his death, do a botched job taking
out his kidneys, and then dump him at a hospital doorstep? That is what Kevorkian did to Joseph Tushkowski. The Oakland County Medical Examiner, L.
J. Dragovic, called Tushkowski's body a scene from a slaughterhouse.[7] For the
uninformed, Kevorkian's self-stated goal (prescription medicide) is to establish a
"new specialty" of obitiatry (that is, medical killing), and to carry out human ex-
perimentation and transplantations in death centers he planned to set up all over
the country. Harvesting Joseph's organs must have been practice for this scheme.

Is it humanistic to assist in the suicide of a disabled man who has been waiting
for nine agonizing months for a wheelchair from his horrible HMO? That is what
Kevorkian did to Matt Johnson. Matt's wheelchair came the day after Kevorkian's

visit—one day too late to free him from his seemingly permanent bed-ridden state and the actually permanent state of death.

Is it humanistic for a doctor to fatally inject a man with whom the doctor has only had two meetings within the 48 hours before he kills him? When asked later by the *Oakland Press* what Thomas Youk's last words had been, Kevorkian responded, "I don't know. I never understood a thing he said."[8] That was Youk's "dignified" death at the hands of this "understanding" and "compassionate" administrator of death.

Is it humanistic to aid in the death of a man whose greatest fear is that he will be forced to live in a rat-infested nursing home? That was a reason Wallace Spolar gave when he called on Kevorkian and engaged his services.

Published reports and court records indicate that sixty-six of Kevorkian's ninety-three "patients" did not fall within the generally described category of terminally ill (life expectancy of six months or less). Janet Adkins, who had recently been diagnosed with Alzheimer's, was reported to have played tennis the week before her appointment with Kevorkian. Judith Curren had chronic fatigue, was depressed and had filed domestic abuse charges against her husband two weeks before her killing. Yet another was a depressed battered wife who did not have Multiple Sclerosis as claimed. Kevorkian, who defines terminal illness as "any disease that curtails life even for a day," aided all these people into the irreversible state of death.

Is it humanistic to assist people to a premature death when they suffer ugly economic circumstances and social conditions and need help from society to get through a difficult time? Isn't it humanistic, rather, to fight for resources and social justice and to avoid death as the social "solution"?

Why is it that some people are so quick to join the death-is-the-answer position when it comes to disablement and don't seem to be able to see disability as a neutral factor in life? Why is disability so charged for them? I can only surmise that these non-disabled people fear disablement so much that they automatically assume that they are doing us a favor by supporting our right to die. But, in a social justice context, if the right to die was an equal opportunity matter and not specifically directed at those with chronic conditions, then the advocates would give healthy twenty-year olds the same right to die too, wouldn't they?

Well-informed individuals on other social justice issues have come up to me on more than one occasion and said, "I just don't see how you do it. I couldn't do it"—meaning, get on with my life "in spite of" my disability. These people seem to think that they could not accept life with a disability and make projections about what they could or would not do if they were in my shoes, but this is often just a first take on a complex continuum of experience. For instance, I have quadriplegic friends who did contemplate suicide their first weeks of disablement but are glad that the option of physician-assisted death wasn't available because they got over their depressions, adjusted to the disability, and are living out their lives being a comedian, a spouse, and/or a parent. A good friend of mine has lived with multiple sclerosis for about a decade now. Her son just finished college.

Further, ableist and individualist projections about the experience of disablement are a complete avoidance of the headier collective issues at stake. Why don't these same people ask me, "are disabled people getting the health care and services that they need?" Don't they know money is being valued over people in the health care system? Don't they know people are still forced into nursing homes against their will? Don't they also know about the role of race and poverty discrimination in the health care system? How about acknowledging that ableism plays a role similar to race and class?

What well-intentioned humanists miss, it seems, is that economics are in the background of the "right to die" movement. [. . .]

Who are the stake holders? The Oregon assisted suicide bill was authored by an HMO executive. Vice President Barbara Coombs Lee of Ethix Corp., was chief petitioner of the measure which created Oregon's law legalizing physician-assisted death. But media reports concerning Coombs Lee failed to make much of her professional occupation within a health insurance group. She was portrayed as a passionate ideologue who cared only for things like "patient autonomy," an end to "intolerable pain," and offering "death with dignity." Coombs Lee's role as a financially motivated health industry hatchet woman was carefully buried throughout the 1994 campaign. Ethix Corp. embraced the new "treatment," stating that they "welcome broad coverage for assisted suicide in a medical economic system already burdened." A lethal dose in Oregon costs only $35 to $50; compare that to one day's stay in a hospital at about $1,000. [. . .]

If Kevorkian's actions accurately describe humanism, then humanism is aligned with the bourgeois eugenicists, Social Darwinists, corporate bean counters, and Malthusian population control zealots who target disabled lives as lives not worth living and label us a burden on society and their bottom lines.

Could liberal court decisions be used for their purposes? Of course! The issue of physician-assisted suicide must be viewed within the context of an economic order which is overriding public welfare and a health care system which is entrenched in profit making. Millions of Americans are uninsured or under-insured and in need of quality health care. Some insured have already found themselves denied life-giving treatments because HMO health care rationing is a real, not an imaginary, thing. Some may have found themselves without the cash to pay for the treatment or to pay a lawyer to intervene. Most anyone can become depressed because they do not want to be a burden on the family. One may not be ready to die, yet see no other way out.

Or perhaps the family might decide such a member is too burdensome and join the Hemlock society. The Hemlock Society issued a widely ignored press release which asked that family members and other "agents" be able to procure court orders to kill "a demented parent, a suffering severely disabled spouse, or a child" if their lives are "too burdensome to continue."[9] That's involuntary euthanasia. According to the National Elder Abuse Incidence Study conducted by the Administration on Aging, several hundred thousand elderly Americans are abused by family members each year in this country. The FBI reports that 21.2 percent of homicides of individuals age 50 and over are committed by family members. [Hemlock Society cofounder Derek—*Ed.*] Humphry's new video provides detailed information on how to disguise murders of disabled and elderly people as suicides.[10]

Would Kevorkian at your doorstep, then, look like a savior or a guy who was furthering his future at the expense of yours?

The genuine humanists, it seems, are not the ones joining the death culture. Rather, they are the ones fighting for a disability sensitive universal health care system, a national in-home care program like MICASSA (Medicaid Community Attendant Services and Supports Act), living wages, and an income floor beneath which no one falls. They are the ones calling for enforcement of civil and human rights and for imposing serious penalties on those who commit domestic violence. They are the ones searching for the means to build an economy which supports people's needs over capitalist accumulation.

•

Life is better than death, I believe, if only because it is less boring, and because it has fresh peaches in it.

—Alice Walker

CHAPTER 19

Eugenics and the
"Sole Possible Economic Order"

Part I

Wisdom comes by disillusionment.

—George Santayana

Most people, excluding the neo-Nazis, accept that there was a holocaust in Germany, but how many know that disabled people were the first to be systematically exterminated by physicians?

Disabled people know that quality-of-life judgments made about us by non-disabled people can prove not only inaccurate but deadly. To combat oppression, we must understand its historical roots, particularly the institutional support that makes it possible.

"Lives Not Worth Living" and "Useless Eaters"

The phrase "lives not worth living" came from the title of a book published in 1920, *Release and Destruction of Lives Not Worth Living*, by two German Social Darwinists, Alfred Hoche, a professor of medicine, and Rudolf Binding, a professor of law. The book defended the right to suicide, and called for the killing of not only incurably sick people but also the mentally ill, the feeble-minded, the intellectually disabled, and deformed children. Arguing that such people led "ballast lives" and were only "empty human husks," these professors medicalized the concept of killing disabled people by making it seem therapeutic; they upheld that it would be "healing work" and humane to destroy such lives which, in their view, were "not worthy of life."[1] These were not uniquely German ideas; support for eugenics also existed in the United States and in England, where euthanasia was viewed as a way to "economize" into a more "efficient" society.

Not long after the publication of this book, hundreds of thousands of disabled people were systematically killed in German gas chambers set up in the very institutions where people went for treatment. How can a society be maneuvered into a regimen of murder? The answer is found in the ideas that led to a "science" of eugenics, the economics that made the practice attractive, and the history of the agents applying euthanasia.

The Roots: Racism, Physicalism, and Classism

With the publication of *Origin of Species*, Charles Darwin introduced his theory that man evolved by way of a gradual adaptation of varied life-forms to the environment by the process of "natural selection, or the preservation of *favoured races* in the struggle for life," (italics mine). "Favoured races," translated, meant his race, the Caucasians.

The English philosopher Herbert Spencer substituted the phrase "survival of the fittest" for "natural selection" and is credited with the development of Social Darwinism, the application of Darwin's ideas to sociology.[2]

In 1871, with *The Descent of Man*, Darwin clarified his thoughts on artificial selection:

> We civilized men, on the other hand, do our utmost to check the process of elimination; we build asylums for the imbecile, the maimed, and the sick; we institute poor-laws; and our medical men exert their utmost to save the life of everyone to the last moment. . . . Thus the weak members of society propagate their kind. No one who has attended to the breeding of domestic animals will doubt that this must be highly injurious to the race of man.[3]

If this undesired situation were to be "corrected," then selective breeding of humans would follow as the next logical step, to rid civilization of disabled, sick, and poor people and to limit the propagation of unfavored races.

In 1883 a cousin of Darwin's, biologist/geneticist Francis Galton, coined the term "eugenics," furthering the march towards selective breeding. Drawn from Darwin's ideas, eugenics upheld that biological groups could be strengthened (cleansed) by eliminating the "unfit" through genetic and hereditary screening. Sickness, indigence, dependence, immorality, and race were factors in the determination of fitness.[4] Darwin himself suggested that people ought to refrain from marriage if they "are in any marked degree inferior in body and mind."[5] Galton's solution was widely accepted in scientific circles all over the world.

Spencer, a staunch supporter of the eugenics movement, became a guru in the US on the subject, presenting seminars and lectures on the benefits of eliminating the "unfit," largely those in need of public services.

The pre-Nazi "scientific" theory of racial hygiene (originally coined in 1903), in keeping with the work of Darwin, Spencer, and Galton, held that the German race could and must be kept pure and not allowed to "degenerate." Social Darwinists such as Alfred Ploetz feared that the misfits and the poor were multiplying at a faster rate than the fit (bourgeoisie) and that elimination was necessary to preserve the German plasm. They professed that those "weak" who were surviving with the assistance of medicine were interfering with the natural selection process and should die in order to keep the German gene strain strong. Racism, physicalism, and classism formed a cultural triad that permitted eugenic theory to turn into a full-blown societal frenzy of murder.

The Nazi/American Physician Connection

The Nazi Party relied on scientists and physicians to give eugenics and racial hygiene scientific credibility and to win the support of the German people.

In 1933 the Nazi government passed the Law for the Prevention of Genetically Diseased Offspring, or the Sterilization Law, as it came to be known. It designated people for sterilization who "suffered" from "genetic illness," including feeble-mindedness, schizophrenia, manic-depressive insanity, genetic epilepsy, Huntington's chorea, genetic blindness or deafness, or severe alcoholism. Physicians became the genetic police, with genetic courts to back up their findings.

An influential manual of Rudolf Ramm of the medical faculty of the University of Berlin proposed that each doctor was to be no longer merely a caretaker of the sick but was to become a "cultivator of the genes," a "physician to the Volk," and a "biological soldier." To carry out these programs properly, the individual physician must become a "genetics doctor" (Erbarzt). He could then become a "caretaker of the race" and a "politician of population."[6]

The eugenic purge was widespread. Targeted for sterilization were 200,000 congenitally feebleminded; 80,000 schizophrenics; 20,000 manic-depressives; 60,000 epileptics; 600 people with Huntington's chorea; 4,000 blind; 16,000 deaf; 20,000 gravely bodily deformed; and 10,000 alcoholics. Reich interior minister Wilhelm Frick, forming the Expert Committee on Questions of Population and Racial Policy, estimated the number of genetic "defectives" in Germany to be 500,000, noting that "some experts consider the true figure to be as high as 20 percent of the German population."[7]

Sterilization practices eventually expanded to encompass race, especially to control what became known as the "black scourge," and were widely and cruelly practiced on Jewish people in the death camps.

In the US, eugenics policy focused on the incarcerated population, developing into an entire "science" of criminal anthropology. Physical characteristics were linked to criminal behavior and disabled people were said to be predisposed to commit crimes. A 1911 textbook on treating disabled people stated, "A failure in the moral training of a cripple means the evolution of an individual detestable in character, a menace and burden to the community, who is only too apt to graduate into the mendicant and criminal classes." American physicians were performing vasectomies on the penal population as early as the turn of the century. By 1920, sterilization was compulsory for criminals considered genetically inferior in twenty-five states. And by 1950, according to the Human Betterment Foundation, 50,707 Americans had been sterilized, many against their will.[8]

Eugenic propaganda institutions existed in England and the US such as the one at Cold Spring Harbor in New York led by Charles B. Davenport and funded by the Carnegie Institution and Mary Harriman. The Rockefeller Foundation funded the Kaiser Wilhelm Institute for Anthropology, Human Heredity, and Eugenics which was headed by Ernst Rüdin, who also headed the Racial Hygiene Society under the Nazis. Fritz Lenz, the physician-geneticist and propagator of racial hygiene theory in Germany, complained that the Germans were being held back, in comparison to their US counterparts, by the socialist Weimar Constitution (which prohibited alterations of a person's body).[9]

German sterilization did not stop until the end of the war. Even so, the physicians performing sterilization were immune from prosecution because "allied authorities were unable to classify the sterilizations as war crimes, because similar laws had only recently been upheld in the United States."[10]

Due to mounting evidence that not enough was known about heredity to draw the conclusion that sterilization did in fact eliminate the "defectives" from the gene pool, eugenic practices were eventually quelled. In the US and England, continual legal pressure was applied to halt sterilization, under the banner of individual rights (interestingly now an argument for physician-assisted suicide). "Rational" science proved not to be immune from physicalist and racist tendencies that resulted in the unnecessary destruction of the reproductive rights of thousands of innocent people.

Useless Eaters and Economics

What happened to disabled people in Germany must be understood in the context of the broader socio-economic issues. German philosopher Friedrich Nietzsche had proclaimed that "the sick person is a parasite of society."[11] The phrase "useless eaters" became popular descriptive speech during the deep recession after World War I. Such ideas served to turn the German people into supporters of the euthanasia program, by branding disabled people as deplorable consumers of state funds at a time when the German people were experiencing economic hardships. It became openly shameful to be disabled. No longer just an "aberration" of nature, the "disabled parasite" was a social cost not to be tolerated.

But the social funds "saved" by eliminating the useless eaters were to be devoted to beefing up the Reich's military for an attempt at Aryan world domination. Since "defectives" were unproductive to the war effort (not soldier material), even seen as taking away from it by consuming social funds, we became highly disposable.

In 1930s Germany, biomedical scientists combined eugenics with Social Darwinism to produce a biological ideology that not only called for man-made selection but began the mechanisms to socially engineer it. The German state took these actions:

> In 1933, the first year of Nazi government, expenditures for the handicapped and invalid were drastically cut. In 1933 German medical insurance companies paid 41.5 million RM for invalids—ten million less than in 1932, in the depths of the recession. . . . For the Nazi medical philosopher, support for the mentally ill was simply not worth the cost.[12]

Reich propagandists took every opportunity to inculcate resentment toward "defective" Germans. Schoolchildren were a primary propaganda target. Adolf Domer's 1935–36 high school mathematics textbook included the following problems:

Problem 94

In one region of the German Reich there are 4,400 mentally ill in state institutions, 4,500 receiving state support, 1,600 in local hospitals, 200 in homes for the epileptic, and 1,500 in welfare homes. The state pays a minimum of 10 million RM/year for these institutions.

I. What is the average cost to the state per inhabitant per year?

II. Using the result calculated from I, how much does it cost the state if:

A. 868 patients stay longer than ten years?

B. 260 patients stay longer than twenty years?

C. 112 patients stay longer than twenty-five years?

Problem 95

The construction of an insane asylum requires 6 million RM. How many housing units at 15,000 RM could be built for the amount spent on insane asylums?[13]

So, it is not surprising that 1939 was designated by Hitler as the year of "the duty to be healthy." The state shifted the public focus away from social welfare onto the "culprits" using all the public resources. Those who could not be "cured" must be killed.

The Needle Belongs in the Hand of the Doctor

Physicians were among the most numerous and strongest supporters of state-sanctioned killing. When Hitler ascended to power he congealed racial hygiene into a political biology which became the mold for Nazi social policy. Large numbers of German physicians joined the Nazi Party. Robert Proctor, author of *Racial Hygiene: Medicine Under the Nazis* writes:

> In 1937 doctors were represented in the SS seven times more often than was the average for the employed male population. Membership records for the Nazi Physicians' League indicate that nearly forty thousand physicians joined the league in 1942; Georg Lilienthal has discovered archival evidence that by the beginning of 1943, some forty-six thousand physicians had joined. If ninety thousand physicians were active from 1931 to 1945, then roughly half of all physicians joined the Nazi Party.[14]

The German physicians were charged with the duty to determine who was worth health care costs and who was not. They became the gatekeepers marshaling the "health" of the state. There were four categories for extermination:

1. Patients suffering from specified diseases who are not employable or those with schizophrenia, epilepsy, senile diseases, therapy-resistant paralysis and

other syphilitic sequelae, feeblemindedness from any cause, encephalitis, Huntington's chorea and other neurological conditions of a terminal nature.

2. Patients who have been continually institutionalized for at least five years.

3. Patients who are in custody as criminally insane.

4. Patients who are not German citizens, or are not of German or kindred blood, giving race and nationality.[15]

Disability was the primary qualifier for death in the eyes of the physician and the state. It is most important to understand that disability persecution was all-encompassing. If one was of pure Aryan blood and disabled, one was slated for extermination for contaminating the race. If one had a job but was disabled, one could still be determined as genetically "unfit" based on the disability and murdered. And euthanasia was not limited to "sick" people, it was imposed upon intellectually disabled people even though they were "healthy." Without question, *all* disabled people were considered to be not worthy of life and all were given the unsubstantiated diagnosis of "terminal" illness with one exception: Nazi Germany did not euthanize its disabled veterans.

Disabled children became the first victims of the euthanasia program. Baby Knauer was the first official victim. Born blind, without part of one arm and a leg, Baby Knauer, according to Dr. Karl Brandt, a leading physician in the euthanasia program, "*seemed* to be an idiot" (italics mine). Her father, a full-blooded German, asked Hitler to grant a "mercy" death. Hitler granted the request for death; from this point on physicians were guaranteed immunity from prosecution for infanticide by proclamation. The results were monstrous.

Soon thereafter, the Committee for the Scientific Treatment of Severe, Genetically Determined Illness required that all children born with congenital deformities be registered with the health authorities. These included "idiocy or Mongolism (especially if associated with blindness of deafness); microcephaly or hydrocephaly of a severe or progressive nature; deformities of any kind, especially missing limbs, malformation of the head, or spina bifida; or crippling deformities such as spastics [Littleschen Erkrankung]."[16] The list was expanded to include epilepsy, paralysis, and any disfigurement of the body.

Officials estimated that by 1945 some five thousand children of all ages had been systematically killed by their physicians. The physicians' choice of methods included lethal injection, starvation, withholding of treatment, exposure to the elements, and the use of cyanide gas or other chemical warfare weapons. Some twenty-eight institutions were fitted with extermination facilities, "including some of Germany's oldest and most highly respected hospitals (Eglfing-Haar; Brandenburg-Gorden; Hamburg Rotherburg and Uchtspringe; Meseria-Obrawalde, among others)."[17]

The adult phase began in 1939, with a plan to exterminate all of Germany's mental patients. The operation was given the code name T-4, shortened from Tiergartenstrasse 4, the address of the nonprofit Patient Transport Corporation that rounded up the economically unfeasible culprits slated for disposal and took them to the nursing homes, mental institutions, and hospitals which housed the killing chambers. In fact, the prototype for the gas chambers that exterminated the Jews in Poland was created in a hospital in Brandenburg to kill the disabled. It was a shower-like room with benches around the walls, equipped with small holes from which the carbon monoxide gas would be piped into the chamber:

> The first gassing was administered personally by Dr. Widmann. He operated the controls and regulated the flow of gas. He also instructed the hospital physicians Dr. Eberl and Dr. Baumhardt, who later took over the exterminations in Grafeneck and Hadamar . . . At this first gassing, approximately eighteen to twenty people were led into the "showers" by the nursing staff. These people were required to undress in another room until they were completely naked. The doors were closed behind them. They entered the room quietly and showed no signs of anxiety. Dr. Widmann operated the gassing apparatus; I could observe through the peephole that, after a minute, the people either fell down or lay on the benches. There was no great disturbance or commotion. After another five minutes, the room was cleared of gas. SS men specially designated for this purpose placed the dead onto stretchers and brought them to the ovens . . . At the end of the experiment Viktor Brack (who was of course also present and whom I'd previously forgotten), addressed those in attendance. He appeared satisfied by the results of the experiment, and repeated once again that this operation should be carried out only by physicians, according to the motto: "The needle belongs in the hand of the doctor." Karl Brandt spoke after Brack, and stressed again that gassings should only be done by physicians. That is how things began in Brandenburg.[18]

The word got out that killing was taking place, so disabled people often had to be dragged onto the T-4 buses forcefully. Those who resisted were beaten into submission. Entire wards of epileptics were killed and the families told that they died of flu, inflammation of the lungs, or apoplexy. Some living in institutions knew beforehand that they were scheduled for disposal and would write their parents that their death was imminent. Elderly people feared they were next and refused to go into institutions for the aged.[19]

It is estimated that two hundred and seventy-five thousand (one estimate puts it at over one million) disabled people were exterminated before the church, which had the power to stop it all along, belatedly brought an end to the official euthanasia program in 1941. A small group of pastors and some incensed citizens motivated Bishop von Galen of the Roman Catholic Church to stand up to Hitler and these physicians in a sermon, in which he said:

> Broadly speaking, there is near certainty that none of the unexpected deaths of these mental cases have been due to natural causes, but were artificially induced, in accordance with the "unworthy lives" and, consequently, the killing of innocent people, if their existence is no longer held to be productive for the nation or for the state. It is a frightful concept that seeks to justify the murder of innocents and allows the killing of invalids incapable of work or the infirm, or incurable, and of old men and women afflicted by senility. Confronted with this doctrine the German bishops declare: No man has the right to kill an innocent person, no matter what the reason, except in case of war or in legitimate self-defense.[20]

Hitler called off the T-4 euthanasia program in August 1941. He recognized that killing the Bishop would be political suicide and he was deeply involved in the Russian front fighting, which was not going well. The gas chambers were dismantled and moved to Poland, where extermination was horrifically escalated.

But the official end to the euthanasia program did not stop the killing of disabled people. Physicians were encouraged to continue with methods of killing that were less noticeable and that fit better into normal hospital routine. They switched from "active" to "passive" killing of disabled children by simply withholding treatment or food. The children died slowly and in agonizing pain. The killing of "defective" adults continued, too, but it was contrived in a less visible manner, performed quietly by doctors who gave their "patients" lethal injections or doses of medication, withheld treatment, or starved them within their own tightly controlled institutions.

Off the Hook at Nuremberg

At the Nuremberg trial Dr. Brandt defended his actions, saying that euthanasia was "out of pity for the victim and out of a desire to free the family and loved ones from a lifetime of needless sacrifice." He emphasized that Hitler's proclamation was not an "order to kill" children but gave physicians the right to do so if the patient was "incurably sick."[21]

Baby Knauer was not "incurably sick." She had multiple disabilities; with prosthetic devices and training in Braille, her ability to function in the world would only have been limited by what the world would allow. Disabled people who were employed and thus no "burden" to their families were also indiscriminately slaughtered.

The Nuremberg court avoided the euthanasia of the disabled by shifting the debate. The court said, "The evidence is conclusive that almost at the outset of the program *non-German nationals* were selected for euthanasia and extermination . . . We find that Karl Brandt was responsible for, aided and abetted, took a consenting part in, and was connected with plans and enterprises . . . in the course of which murders, brutalities, cruelties, tortures and other inhumane acts were committed [against non-German nationals]. To the extent that these criminal acts did not constitute war crimes they constituted crimes against humanity"[22] (italics mine).

The original victims of Nazi cleansing were not non-German individuals but the German disabled. Some interpret the killings of disabled people as the beginning of the Jewish holocaust, but the murders of thousands of disabled people represented a holocaust of its own. The logic for killing disabled people was distinct from the rationale for killing other identity groups.

The Nuremberg court did not view disabled people as equal citizens against whom it would be illegal to commit a crime. The treatment of disabled people by the court was discriminatory; no reparations were ever made to the families of those killed, no one was punished for their murders.

Social Darwinism marked the beginning of the need for the disabled to justify our very existence. If medicine could be viewed as an inhibitor to biological cleansing, even seen as reversing some "natural selection" process where the disabled and sick should die, then who would be safe? Disabled people's struggle for survival took on a new dimension. It was not Darwin's "natural" world that we would be pitted against; it was man's "civilized" world of dominant physicalist notions and the growing culture of wealth accumulation that would become our biggest adversary.

Part II

There has never existed a truly free and democratic nation in the world. . . .
I have entered the fight . . . against the economic system under which I live.

—Helen Keller, socialist, addressing the Woman's Peace Party
and the Labor Forum in New York City, 1916

The *American Heritage Dictionary* defines capitalism as "an economic system characterized by freedom of the market with increasing concentration of private and corporate ownership of production and distribution means, proportionate to increasing accumulation and reinvestment of profits." If democracy is the practice of promoting social equality where more people participate in governance, then capitalism with its economic tendency to concentrate wealth works against that equality, because wealth and ownership reside in fewer and fewer hands. This glaring contradiction is at the heart of modern-day inequities, and this is what Helen Keller meant above when she addressed the Woman's Peace Party and the Labor Forum at Carnegie Hall. There can be no democracy without economic democracy.

The godfather of capitalism, Adam Smith, in *An Inquiry into the Nature and Causes of the Wealth of Nations*, recognized that class-based policy was not beneficial to the democratic masses. He pointed out two centuries ago that "the vile maxim of the masters" was, "all for ourselves and nothing for other people." In Smith's day the "masters" were the rich mercantile class who manipulated government and public policy to their advantage. In Nazi Germany, the "masters" were the Aryan militarists and entrepreneurial class that dismantled the democratic Weimar Republic health care system, the most respected and comprehensive social services program in the world, to shift public funds to the fascist goal of world domination.

Smith advocated for a capitalism that would advance economic equality—something that has never materialized. And he opposed the concentration of wealth—something the US government defends by protecting the rich against the poor. Since Smith's day, capitalism has worked its will upon the people to produce an enormous gap between rich and poor. Author Michael Parenti explains:

> Income and wealth disparities are greater today than at any time since such information was first collected in 1947. As one economist put it: "If we made an income pyramid out of a child's blocks, with each layer portraying $1,000 of income the peak would be far higher than the Eiffel Tower, but almost all of us would be within a yard of the ground."[23]

Today we have the "masters" of the market—the corporations, speculators, banks, and global capitalists—maintaining the inequality and widening the income disparity.

The Social Darwinists were masters at keeping societal resources in the hands of the wealthy by marginalizing lives perceived to be of no use to the economic order, but, as this chapter will explore, capitalism's production dynamics adversely affected disabled people's ability to participate in the sole economic order.

The Sole Economic Order

It is an obscure fact that industrialization and entrepreneurialism were prominent in both the US and the Nazi National Socialist government of Germany. Although the Nazis called themselves National Socialists, Nazis were pro-profiteering industrialists like the Rockefellers, Du Ponts, and Mellons. Hitler made this clear when he wrote, "We stand for the maintenance of private property.... We shall protect free enterprise as the most expedient, or rather the sole possible economic order."[24]

Walter Russell Mead writes that "major US corporations collaborated with Hitler throughout the '30s and into WWII." For example, Rockefeller's Standard Oil was partnered with the German corporation IG Farben, which patented and made gasoline from coal with the help of concentration camp slave labor. Mead points out that Hitler had repeatedly offered to send the Jews to the US instead of to death camps, but the US refused to take them. Historian Howard Zinn explains that the US did not get involved in the war over the persecution of the Jews, nor over Hitler's invasion of Poland, Czechoslovakia, or Austria, nor over Italy's attack on Ethiopia; rather it "was the Japanese attack on a link in the American Pacific Empire that did it;" it was the attack on US business interests that determined our "vital" interest in World War II.[25] This is to say that economic interests rose above democratic and humane principles; even delayed our involvement in World War II because businesses in the US and Nazi Germany had a common hatred of egalitarian economic ideals. The US saw fascists like Hitler (and Mussolini) as infinitely preferable to communism because he fostered the sole economic order, capitalism.

Body Politics and Capitalist Disadvantages

Capitalism is characterized by certain disadvantages. One byproduct is that large numbers of people remain unemployed and in poverty. While capitalism held the promise of expanding the base of people benefiting from it, it is inherently exclusionary. Some segments would fall harder to the bottom of the market-driven society, like the disabled and the elderly. [...]

While the accumulation of wealth remained of paramount import, the fact that large segments of the population were excluded from benefiting from the sole economic order did not rate concern. The expendable were squeezed out while the Social Darwinists who were profiting from the status quo justified this state of affairs as the "natural" order of things.

Nazi Germany viewed disabled people as a burden on the state and a drag on the economy, and exterminated us. The desire to solve the "defect" problem in

America was inextricably mixed with matters of money; masters of efficiency in the US were bean-counting like their Nazi counterparts. Economics factored into the widespread support for eugenics and euthanasia. In 1935 Dr. J. N. Baker, a health officer in Alabama, stated, "With bated breath, the entire civilized world is watching the bold experiment in mass sterilization recently launched by Germany. It is estimated that some 400,000 of the population will come within the scope of this law, the larger portion of whom fall into that group classed as inborn feebleminded.... It is estimated that, after several decades, hundreds of millions of marks will be saved each year as a result of the diminution of expenditures for patients with hereditary diseases." Dr. Baker included as targets for compulsory medical intervention any "sexual pervert . . . or any prisoner who has been twice convicted of rape" or imprisoned three times for any offense, as well as those "habitually and constantly dependent on public relief or support by charity."[26]

Other Americans followed suit:

> Many American advocates also argued that euthanasia might be a good way to save on medical costs. Dr. W. A. Gould, for example, in the *Journal of the American Institute of Homeopathy*, defended euthanasia as one way of resolving economic difficulties; he asked his reader to recall in this context the "elimination of the unfit" in ancient Sparta. Some offered more radical suggestions: in 1935 the French-American Nobel Prize winner Alexis Carrel (inventor of the iron lung) suggested in his book *Man the Unknown* that the criminal and insane should be "humanely and economically disposed of in small euthanasia institutions supplied with proper gases." W. G. Lennox, in a 1938 speech to Harvard's Phi Beta Kappa chapter, claimed that saving lives "adds a load to the back of society"; he wanted physicians to recognize "the privilege of death for the congenitally mindless and for the incurable sick who wish to die; the boon of not being born for the unfit."[27]

The "unfit" unquestionably meant those of no use to the market economy, the non-working members of the society. The connection between eugenics, euthanasia, and the economic order is clear; those of no use to the economic order were marginalized. What was not clear was that the development of the market economy itself—the sole economic order—was to construct barriers that precluded segments of society from reaping any reward from it. It directly affected disabled people's ability to be productive members of the community.

The Vile Maxim and the Social Darwinists

Philosopher Herbert Spencer's proclamation—that capitalism's "natural selection" process of individualism and competition weeded out the "unfit" by leaving the inferior in poverty to die—fit in perfectly with laissez-faire capitalism, which from the very start would never be economically egalitarian and needed some credible public justification to explain why some prospered and larger numbers of "others" did not. If society viewed non-prosperity as the fault of the individual's shortcomings and not inherent in the design of capitalism, then capitalists were off the hook from admitting that class differences were a result of capitalism's economic structure and inherently exploitative nature.

Robert Proctor explains that:

> When phrases such as "the struggle for existence" and "the survival of the fittest" became catchwords for the new Social Darwinism, this reflected the broader social and economic structure of the times: this is what is meant when we hear that Darwin's theory cannot be understood apart from the Manchester economics of Ricardo and Smith and the dog-eat-dog world of mid-nineteenth-century British capitalism.[28]

Social Darwinists used the science of biology to support their undemocratic politics by upholding that heredity—race and genes—prevailed over the class and economic issues raised by Karl Marx. Just as the "inferior" were not meant to survive in nature, nor were they meant to economically survive in society.

The Social Darwinists elevated individual competition to the status of a "natural law." If the entrepreneurial business process, as explained by John D. Rockefeller, was "merely the working out of a law of nature and a law of God," then the rich capitalists were free to accumulate vast hordes of wealth and claim they were the "fittest." Free enterprise magnate Andrew Carnegie, a follower of Spencerian philosophy, expressed a sigh of relief when he said, "All is well since all grows better," getting off the moral hook with capitalism's "natural" law.[29]

While Hitler dismantled the democratic socialist Weimar Republic, the American Social Darwinists did their best to prevent the formation of any social contract that would compensate for the injuries, occupational illnesses, high unemployment, and deaths propagated by industrial capitalism. Refusing to redistribute societal wealth and meet the pre-Nazi German democratic standard, the industrial class sought to prevail over the greater public's interests by using science as a political weapon. Laissez-faire sociologists and anthropologists used biological determinism to argue against implementing reforms that would better the living conditions of the poor, claiming that biology conferred a non-correctable individual condition that could not be solved by social reform. By erecting these "logical" barriers against humane social policy, Social Darwinists could make the case for a bare-bones government, and use futility as a reason to curtail the role of government in society, to oppose socialized medicine, and to make public expenditures unpopular.

The elite Social Darwinist's solution was to weed out the "unfit": the non-Caucasian races (particularly immigrants), the poor, the deaf, and the disabled. But clearly class rose above Spencerian "natural laws"; disabled offspring of the "fittest" (prosperous) class inherited the means to survive and did not starve to death, making it clear that "natural law" had little to do with survival, but man-made selection had everything to do with it.

Dissenters of the Spencerian view, such as sociologist Lester Frank Ward, spoke out against the Social Darwinists' invocations by branding Social Darwinist doctrine as:

> the most complete example of the oligocentric world view which is coming to prevail in the higher classes of society and would center the entire attention of the whole world upon an almost infinitesimal fraction of the human race and ignore the rest . . . I want a field that shall be broad enough to embrace the whole human race [not a select class], and I would take no interest in sociology if I did not regard it as constituting such a field.[30]

In the Social Darwinist tradition, Charles Murray, coauthor of *The Bell Curve*, made the class link when he wrote, "Some people are better than others. They deserve more of society's rewards."[31] It is the "fit" bourgeoisie busily concentrating their wealth and control over the means of production who deserve and get capitalism's rewards. The privileged who "deserve" more do get more under government policies (subsidies) that amount to a socialism for the rich, while the underprivileged struggle on Darwin's terms—capitalism for the poor.

Social Darwinism proved to be a convenient self-serving veneer for the masters of Smith's vile maxim—the Rothschilds, the Carnegies, the Harrimans—who benefitted from the sole possible economic order and did not want to see a more equitable system evolve. Social Darwinism provided the business class who controlled the means of production with the justification to leave the surplus population in poverty to die, rather than design an economic system that would accommodate all of society.

Missing the Link: Blur in the Eugenic Political Lines

It must be noted that the "defect question" did not fall neatly into "left" or "right" camps of political thought either in the US or in Germany. Alarmingly, elements on both sides supported euthanasia and eugenics. For instance, in the US, turn of the century Progressive reformists viewed eugenics and euthanasia as positive social change:

> Eugenicists were an integral part of the progressive movement in the United States. Their policies were jumbled in with such other progressive issues of the day as electoral reform, government regulation of commerce, international disarmament, women's rights and suffrage, prohibition and birth control.[32]

The democratic movement saw eugenics as a secular, rational means to control what it perceived as meandering nature that interfered with the march of progress. It entirely missed the link to market capitalism, which de-valued disabled people's non-exploitable bodies. It missed the link to Social Darwinism, where the "unproductive," of no use to building more wealth, were disposable.

Unwittingly, the labor movement contributed to the ethics that propelled anti-humanistic eugenics. If work defines human worth and work is the central criterion for human validation, then the worker has their pride and the capitalist has their labor to exploit, two sides of the same paradigm. If work was to be the end-all of existence, then disabled people (who could not work) inevitably would be marginalized, and relegated to a corner of society.

In Germany, eugenics was seen as progressive in socialist circles:

> Many socialists identified eugenics with state planning and the rationalization of the means of production; many thus found the idea of a "planned genetic future" an attractive one. . . . Alfred Grotjahn, for example, today considered the father of German social medicine and one of the leading architects of Weimar Germany's progressive health reforms, saw racial hygiene as a legitimate concern of medicine. He was one of those who defended the use of the term eugenics (rather than racial hygiene) in order to avoid confusion with racist notions of the political-anthropological variety.[33]

The vast majority of German physicians were not critical of euthanasia practices other than out of their concern not to do something illegal. A small group of doctors who were treating disabling diseases caused by economic, industrial, or environmental conditions heroically opposed the increasing power that Nazi biology and the insurance companies were exercising in the health care fields. The Marxist physicians, concerned that the poor, disabled, and unhealthy were getting the short end of the stick, stuck to humane principles that put care above profit and life above economizing and efficiency. Holding that capitalism was the greatest malady afflicting industrial society, Dr. Ernst Simmel said that capitalism forces wage earners "to squander and waste the only thing they possess—their labor power and their health."[34] Forced into exile when the Nazi revolution took full root, their organization, the Association of Socialist Physicians, continued criticism from afar:

The association marveled at the willingness of Nazi physicians to dismantle public medical services—services that had taken decades to construct, and for which Germany was world renowned. It ridiculed suggestions that such measures were designed to serve "the whole, rather than the individual" and deplored the Nazi contempt for the handicapped and the elderly—individuals who, in Nazi medical jargon, were nothing but useless "ballast lives," lives not worth living.[35]

But the majoritarian political spectrum simply missed the fact that social power relations control the nature of work and by having political power oppress those perceived to be of little use to their ends.

Beyond "Adapt or Perish"

"To aid the bad in multiplying is, in effect," wrote Herbert Spencer in *The Study of Sociology*, "the same as maliciously providing for our descendants a multitude of enemies." Allowing society to "foster good for nothings," Spencer claimed, is "injurious," for that "puts a stop to that natural process of elimination by which society continually purifies itself."[36]

Spencer held capitalism in regard for providing such a service, but one has only to look at Roy Cohn or J. Edgar Hoover, Michael Milken or Charles Keating, to see how individualism and competition have failed at weeding out "the bad."[37] One could even say it has produced an unprecedented opportunity for the most "injurious" to prosper, through adaptation to obsessive capital accumulation. Take Robert Allen, CEO of AT&T, for instance, who became the poster boy for corporate greed by firing forty thousand workers and getting an accumulative $16 million in perks and bonuses for his dastardly deeds.[38]

Feudalism was toppled by capitalism, yet, as under feudalism, the world's billionaires—all 358 of them—own more assets than the annual combined incomes of 45 percent or 2.5 billion of the world's people.[39] The sole economic order, set upon increasing the concentration of wealth and ownership of production, has done just that; the billionaires are the new feudal lords, the new masters keeping the hierarchy of wealth in place.

Adam Smith's "vile maxim" is the mantra of the twentieth century business class. Our society is plagued with stock and securities fraud, medical billing fraud, telemarketing fraud, racketeering, price fixing, and unlawful labor practices. Political bribery is commonplace. Corporations like Nike, Disney, Wal-Mart, Reebok, and Kathi Lee Gifford Clothing take their manufacturing to Indonesia, Honduras, and Haiti where they can pay subhuman wages to young girls who work a grueling ten- to twelve-hour day for 28 or 40 cents an hour. The market society that glorifies efficiency and profit above principles of cooperation and equality has brought our "civilization" to an inhumane abyss.

Most dangerously, Social Darwinist conditioning has paved the way for decision-making classes to successfully put the spin on welfare that it is the failure of the individual—not the economic system that benefits the few at the expense of the many. The critical link is that the capitalist market economy produces a negative social outcome: by fixating on the accumulation of money it produces social casualties.

In 1940, economist Karl Polanyi warned of the dangers when markets dominate the affairs of society. He wrote:

> [C]ontrol of the economic system by the market is of overwhelming consequence to the whole organization of society: it means no less than the running of society as an adjunct to the market. Instead of economy being embedded in social relations, social relations are embedded in the economic system. The vital importance of the economic factor to the existence of society precludes any other result. For once the economic system is organized in separate institutions, based on specific motives and conferring a special status, society must be shaped in such a manner as to allow that system to function according to its own laws.[40]

Its own laws would produce a "market society" where human concerns and social orders get subsumed by a kind of economic tyranny; the inversion of what Polanyi believed was needed to foster a cooperative and healthy society. [. . .]

The basic law of evolution is not about adaptation, it is about self-transcending creativity. Moving beyond "Adapt or Perish," that is, beyond simply accepting one's environment as permanent and then adapting to it, is to move into a realm where one seeks to transform the inequalities. Our freedom lies in the fact that we are not at the mercy of some "natural law" but are part of a social order which is by no means fixed, but needs democratizing to offer a counterforce to the dominant market "society."

Acknowledgments

Introduction originally published as Marta Russell and Ravi Malhotra, "Capitalism and Disability," *Socialist Register* 38 (2002): 211–228.

Chapter 1 originally published as Marta Russell, "Disablement, Oppression, and the Political Economy," *Journal of Disability Policy Studies* 12, no. 2 (September 2001): 87–95.

Chapter 2 originally published as Marta Russell, "The New Reserve Army of Labor?" *Review of Radical Political Economics* 33, no. 2 (Spring 2001): 223–34.

Chapter 3 originally published as Marta Russell, "Capital Destroying Jobs," *Z Commentaries* March 4, 2004, ZComm.org.

Chapter 4 originally published as Marta Russell, "A Brief History of Wal-Mart and Disability Discrimination," *ZNet* February 15, 2004, ZComm.org.

Chapter 5 originally published as Marta Russell, "Backlash, the Political Economy, and Structural Exclusion," *Berkeley Journal of Employment and Labor Law* 21, no. 1 (2000): 335–66.

Chapter 6 originally published as Marta Russell, "What Disability Civil Rights Cannot Do: Employment and Political Economy," *Disability & Society* 17, no. 2 (2002): 117–35.

Chapter 7 originally published as Marta Russell, "Supremes Continue to Disable Disabled: Part One of Two," *Z Commentaries* August 2, 2002, ZComm.org; and Marta Russell, "Supremes Continue to Disable Disabled: Part Two of Two," *Z Commentaries* August 22, 2002, ZComm.org.

Chapter 8 originally published as Marta Russell, "Handicapitalism Makes Its Debut," *Z Commentaries* April 20, 2000, ZComm.org.

Chapter 9 originally published as Marta Russell and Jean Stewart, "Disablement, Prison, and Historical Segregation," *Monthly Review* 53, no. 3 (July–August 2001): 61–75.

Chapter 10 originally published as Marta Russell, "Stuck at the Nursing Home Door: Organized Labor Can't Seem to Get Beyond the Institutional Model," *Ragged Edge Online* 21, no. 1 (January–February 2000); and Marta Russell, "No Nursing Homes on Wheels," *ZNet* November 5, 2002, ZComm.org.

Chapter 11 originally published as Marta Russell, "Targeting Disability," *Monthly Review* 56, no. 11 (April 2005): 45–53.

Chapter 12 originally published as Marta Russell, "Rethinking the Social Security Policy Wasteland," *Ragged Edge Online* 22, no. 1 (January 2001).

Chapter 13 originally published as Marta Russell, "Clusters of Bombs," *Z Commentaries* May 1, 2003, ZComm.org.

Chapter 14 originally published as Marta Russell, "A Most Dangerous President," *Ragged Edge Online* 24, no. 4 (July–August 2003); and Marta Russell, "None Call It Cleansing," *Z Commentaries* December 15, 2005, ZComm.org.

Chapter 15 originally published as Marta Russell, "Being Disabled and Poor in New Orleans," *Z Commentaries* September 25, 2005, ZComm.org.

Chapter 16 originally published as Marta Russell, "Affordable Accessible Housing Needs to Be on Housing Radar Screen," *ZNet* May 18, 2002, ZComm.org.

Chapter 17 originally published as Marta Russell, "Too Many Human Rights," *Feminist International Radio Endeavour* (2003).

Chapter 18 originally published as Marta Russell, "Dollars and Death," *ZNet* May 11, 1999, ZComm.org; and Marta Russell, "Humanists: Momentarily Dazed and Confused, or What?," *California Disability Alliance* January 26, 2000, DisWeb.org.

Chapter 19 originally published as Marta Russell, "Nazi and American Eugenics, Euthanasia, and Economics," in *Beyond Ramps: Disability at the End of the Social Contract* (Monroe, ME: Common Courage Press, 1998), 18–28; and Marta Russell, "A Missing Link: Body Politics and the Sole Economic Order," in *Beyond Ramps*, 57–68.

APPENDIX

Current Disability Statistics

Overall

Number of disabled people in the US: 64 million or 20 percent of the total population; 32 million or 10 percent have a "severe" disability

Percentage of women with disabilities: 25 percent

Percentage of Black people with disabilities: 30 percent

Percentage of Native Americans with disabilities: 24 percent

Percentage of lesbian, gay, and bisexual adults with disabilities: 33 percent

Percentage of transgender people with disabilities: 39 percent

Percentage of all non-disabled Americans who will acquire a disability before reaching retirement age: 25 percent

Most common types of disability: mobility and cognition

Leading cause of disability in the US: neuropsychiatric disorders

Education

Number of children receiving special education services in public schools: 6 million or 13 percent of total public-school enrollment

Most common form of disability among special education students: learning disability (35 percent of total)

Percentage of public-school students receiving special education services who graduate with a high school diploma, by race: white, 73 percent; Black, 57 percent (compared to 88 percent and 75 percent respectively, for non-disabled students)

Percentage of disabled people with a bachelor's degree or higher: 14.4 percent (compared to 33.8 percent for those without a disability)

Living Conditions

Poverty rate for disabled people: 28 percent

Annual median income of households that include any working-age people with disabilities as a percentage of the annual median income of households without any disabilities: 63 percent ($43,300 compared to $68,700)

Average annual earnings wage gap between a full-time disabled employee and a full-time non-disabled employee: $5,100

Percentage of households with an annual income of less than $15,000 in which a disability is present: 50 percent

Percentage of total homeless population that has a disability: 40 percent

Rate of homelessness for people with schizophrenia: 20 percent (compared to 1 percent for the general population)

Percentage of disabled people living in US Department of Housing and Urban Development (HUD)–assisted public housing that were provided with disability-accessible units: 3 percent

Percentage of disabled people living in HUD–assisted public housing that are denied subsequent requests for disability-accessible features: 70 percent

Labor

Employment–population ratio for people with disabilities: 19.2 percent

Percentage of disabled people who self-identify as preferring to have a job: 68.4 percent

Percentage of jobs in businesses with over 50 employees which must be set aside for disabled people under employment quota systems that cover a majority of European countries: 2–5 percent

Percentage of quota-covered jobs for the disabled in the US: 0 percent (nor does the US mandate affirmative action for disabled people)

Number of disabled people nationwide working in subminimum wage "sheltered workshops," legally being paid as little as 25–50 percent of the federal minimum wage: 420,000

Annual pay of the CEO of Goodwill Industries, the largest national employer of disabled people at subminimum wages (some as low $2 an hour): $712,000

Working Conditions

Number of annual nonfatal occupational injury and illness cases that lead to days away from work across the US: 1 million

Percentage of disabled people whose impairment resulted from a work-related injury or illness: 36 percent

Total number of Occupational Safety and Health Administration inspectors nationwide, responsible for the health and safety of 130 million workers employed at more than 8 million worksites: 2,100

Annual federal budget of the Occupational Safety and Health Administration: $550 million

Annual federal military budget: $600 billion

Social Security

Number of people receiving Supplemental Security Income (SSI, the federal assistance program for low-income disabled people, based on need): 8.2 million

Number of people receiving Social Security Disability Insurance (SSDI, the federal assistance program for disabled people, based on work history): 10 million

Federal poverty level: $12,140 per year (individual)

Average annual SSI payment: $6,600 per year

Average annual SSDI payment: $12,700 per year

Percentage of initial SSDI claim applications that are denied: 65 percent

Percentage of initially-denied SSDI claims that are approved after an appeal hearing: 60 percent

Average number of days the Social Security Administration (SSA) takes to process an initial disability claim: 105

Average number of days it takes for the SSA to grant an appeal hearing to an initially-denied disability claimant: 660

War

Percentage of veterans of the US wars in Iraq and Afghanistan reporting service-related disabilities: 45 percent

Estimated number of Afghans currently disabled as a result of forty years of war and invasion (Russia, 1979–89; US, 2001–present): Between 800,000 and 2 million

Percentage of Afghans affected by mental disorders or illnesses: 67 percent

Percentage of all childhood disabling injuries in Iraq resulting from military violence: 15 percent (compared to a worldwide rate of 2 percent)

Percentage of children in Iraq suffering psychological and trauma-related disorders: 46.8 percent

Crime and Policing

Disabled individuals are more than twice as likely as non-disabled individuals to be the victim of violence (and those with cognitive disabilities in particular are more than four times as likely as those without disabilities)

Disabled individuals are three times as likely as non-disabled individuals to be the victim of rape or sexual assault (and those with multiple disabilities are five times as likely as those without disabilities)

Percentage of disabled victims of violence who are familiar with the perpetrator of violence (acquaintance, intimate partner, relative): 96 percent

Percentage of women with disabilities who experience domestic violence: 40 percent (compared to 25 percent of all women)

Percentage of people killed by police annually that have a disability or mental disorder: 50 percent and 25 percent, respectively

Percentage of the over 2 million Americans incarcerated in prison or jail that have a disability, by gender: male, 35 percent; female, 44.5 percent

Percentage of those incarcerated in state prisons who have a mental health disorder, by gender: male, 55 percent; female, 73 percent

Nursing Homes

Number of people (of all ages) residing in the nation's 16,000 nursing homes: 1.4 million

Number of disabled people currently residing in nursing homes who report that they would prefer to live in a community-integrated assisted living setting: Over 250,000

Percentage of nursing homes that have been federally cited for at least one serious violation (neglect, abuse, or death) between 2013 and 17: 40 percent

Percentage of nursing homes that are for-profit institutions: 69.8 percent

Percentage of nursing home residents that rely on Medicaid to cover the $83,000 average annual per-person cost: 70 percent

Average annual profits of the nursing home industry: $18 billion

Median annual pay for a nursing home attendant worker ("orderly"): $26,000 per year

Sources:
Bronson, Jennifer and Laura M. Maruschak. "Disabilities Among Prison and Jail Inmates, 2011–12." Bureau of Justice Statistics. NCJ 249151. US Department of Justice. December 2015.

Bureau of Labor Statistics. *Census of Fatal Occupational Injuries Summary, 2016.* (US Department of Labor. December 19, 2017.)

"Commonly Used Statistics." Occupational Safety and Health Administration. 2018. OSHA.gov.

"Data on behavioral health in the United States." American Psychological Association. apa.org

Dawkins, Casey and Mark Miller. *A Picture of Disability and Designated Housing.* (Washington, DC). US Department of Housing and Urban Development. March 6, 2015.

———. "The Characteristics and Unmet Housing Program Needs of Disabled
HUD-Assisted Households." *Housing Policy Debate* 27, no. 4 (July 2017): 499–518.

"Disability Characteristics." *2012–2016 American Community Survey 5-Year Estimates.*
US Census Bureau. December 7, 2017.

"Disability Impacts All of Us." Centers for Disease Control and Prevention. July 18,
2017, cdc.gov.

"Disability Statistics." Council for Disability Awareness. July 3, 2013, disabilitycanhappen.org.

"Disability, Employment & Homelessness 2011 Policy Statement." National Health
Care for the Homeless Council. September 2011, nhchc.org.

"Education, Health & Human Services: Disabilities." National Congress of American
Indians. NCAI.org.

Ellis, Justin. "Media Missing the Story: Half of All Recent High-Profile Police-Related
Killings Are People with Disabilities." Ruderman Family Foundation. March 8, 2016,
rudermanfoundation.org.

Erickson, W. et al. *2016 Disability Status Report: United States* (Ithaca, NY: Cornell
University Yang-Tan Institute on Employment and Disability, 2018).

Frederiksen-Goldsen, Karen et al. "Disability Among Lesbian, Gay, and Bisexual Adults:
Disparities in Prevalence and Risk." *American Journal of Public Health* 102, no. 1
(January 2012).

Goode, Erica. "For Police, a Playbook for Conflicts Involving Mental Illness." *New York
Times.* April 25, 2016.

Greve, Bent. *The labour market situation of disabled people in European countries and implementation of employment policies: A summary of evidence from country reports and
research studies* (report prepared for the Academic Network of European Disability
experts. April 2009).

Harris-Kojetin, L. et al. "Long-Term Care Providers and Services Users in the United
States: Data from the National Study of Long-Term Care Providers, 2013-2014." National Center for Health Statistics. *Vital Health Statistics* 3, no. 38 (February 2016).

"Housing Access Across America." ADAPT. ADAPT.org.

Houtenville, Andrew J. et al. *Kessler Foundation 2015 National Employment and
Disability Survey: Report of Main Findings* (West Orange, NJ: Kessler Foundation,
2015).

James, S. E. et al. *The Report of the 2015 US Transgender Survey* (Washington, DC:
National Center for Transgender Equality, 2016).

Kennedy, Madeline. "Iraqi Children Face High Rates of Death and Disability." *Reuters.*
May 13, 2016.

Kentane, Bie. "The Children of Iraq: 'Was the Price Worth It?'" *Global Research.* February 19, 2013.

Marchione, Marilynn. "Almost Half of New Veterans Seek Disability Benefits." *Boston
Globe.* May 28, 2012.

Masoud, Ahmed. "Most of 800,000 People with Disabilities in Afghanistan are Uneducated and Unemployed." *Khaama Press.* February 6, 2013.

McFarland, J. et al. *The Condition of Education 2017.* NCES 2017-144 (Washington, DC: US Department of Education, 2017).

"Monthly Statistical Snapshot, February 2018." US Social Security Administration. February 2018. ssa.gov.

Noor, Ayan Ahmed et al. *National Disability Survey in Afghanistan, 2005* (Lyon, France: Handicap International, 2006).

Occupational Employment and Wages, May 2016: 31-1015 Orderlies. (Washington, DC: US Bureau of Labor Statistics. March 31, 2017).

Office of Justice Programs. "2017 NCVRW Resource Guide: Crimes against People with Disabilities Fact Sheet." US Department of Justice. 2017. ovc.ncjrs.gov.

Oliver, Kelsey. "Nursing Care Facilities in the US." *IBISWorld Industry Report* 62311 (August 2017).

Rau, Jordan. "Trump Administration Eases Nursing Home Fines in Victory for Industry." *New York Times.* December 24, 2017.

Report on the Rights of Persons with Disabilities in Iraq: December 2016 (UN Assistance Mission for Iraq & UN Office of the High Commissioner for Human Rights, 2016).

Reville, Robert T. and Schoeni, Robert F. "The Fraction of Disability Caused at Work." *Social Security Bulletin* 65, no. 4 (2003/2004).

"Social Security Administration (SSA) Data for Title XVI Blind/Disabled Average Processing Time." Social Security Administration. March 12, 2018. ssa.gov.

Social Security Administration. *Annual Statistical Report on the Social Security Disability Insurance Program, 2016.* SSA Publication No. 13-11826. October 2017.

"SSI Federal Payment Amounts for 2018." Social Security Administration. ssa.gov.

"Subminimum Wage and Supported Employment." National Council on Disability. August 23, 2012. ncd.gov.

"The High Cost of Nursing Home Care." *Face the Facts USA.* George Washington University. December 20, 2012.

"US Federal Poverty Guidelines Used to Determine Financial Eligibility for Certain Federal Programs." US Department of Health and Human Services. January 2018. aspe.hhs.gov.

"US Leading Categories of Diseases/Disorders." National Institute of Mental Health. 2013. nimh.nih.gov.

"US: Number of Mentally Ill in Prisons Qaudrupled." Human Rights Watch. September 5, 2006. hrw.org.

"What is Social Security Disability?" Disability Benefits Center. DisabilityBenefitsCenter.org.

ENDNOTES

1   Vic Finkelstein, "A Personal Journey into Disability Politics," presented at Leeds University Centre for Disability Studies, 2001, www.independentliving.org/docs3/finkelstein01a.html; Michael Oliver and Colin Barnes, *The New Politics of Disablement* (New York: Palgrave Macmillan, 2012).

2   See Samuel R. Bagenstos, "Foreword: Thoughts on responding to the Left Critique of Disability Rights Law," in *Disability Politics in a Global Economy: Essays in Honour of Marta Russell*, ed. Ravi Malhotra (New York: Routledge, 2017).

3   See for example, Alex B. Long, "Introducing the New and Improved Americans with Disabilities Act: Assessing the ADA Amendments Act of 2008," *Northwestern University Law Review Colloquy* 103 (2008): 217–29.

Introduction: Capitalism and the Disability Rights Movement

1   UPIAS, *Fundamental Principles of Disability* (London: Union of the Physically Impaired Against Segregation, 1976), 3.

2   Michael Oliver coined the phrase. See his *Politics of Disablement* (New York: St. Martin's Press, 1990).

3   *International Classification of Impairments, Disabilities and Handicaps: A Manual of Classification Relating to the Consequences of Disease* (Geneva: World Health Organization, 1980), 29.

4   Colin Barnes, Geof Mercer, and Tom Shakespeare, *Exploring Disability: A Sociological Introduction* (Cambridge: Polity Press, 1999), 25.

5   Harlan Hahn, "An Agenda for Citizens with Disabilities: Pursuing Identity and Empowerment," *Journal of Vocational Rehabilitation* 9 (1997): 34, (explaining the minority model); Nirmala Erevelles, "Disability and the Dialectics of Difference," *Disability & Society* 11, no. 4 (1996): 522, (explaining limitations of liberal concept).

6   Marta Russell, "Disablement, Oppression, and the Political Economy," *Journal of Disability Policy Studies* 12, no. 2 (September 2001): 87–95.

7   Edward Yelin and Patricia Katz, "Making Work More Central to Work Disability Policy," *Milbank Quarterly* 72 (1994); R. L. Bennefield and John M. McNeil, "Labor Force Status and Other Characteristics of Persons with a Work Disability: 1981 to 1988," *Current Population Reports*, Series P-23, no. 160 (Washington, DC: US Bureau of the Census, 1989).

8 L. Harris & Associates and National Organization on Disability, *Americans with Disabilities Still Face Sharp Gaps in Securing Jobs, Education, Transportation, and in Many Areas of Daily Life*" (New York: Louis Harris & Associates/National Organization on Disability, 1998).

9 "United States Current Population Survey," US Census Bureau, Current Population Survey, March 1998.

10 Louis Harris, *The 2000 National Organization on Disabilities/Harris Survey of Americans with Disabilities* (New York: Louis Harris & Associates, 2000).

11 Ibid.

12 James I. Charlton, *Nothing About Us Without Us: Disability Oppression and Empowerment* (Berkeley: University of California Press, 1998), 45.

13 Victor Finkelstein, *Attitudes and Disabled People* (New York: World Rehabilitation Fund, 1980), 8.

14 The focus here is necessarily on European feudal societies. A discussion of precapitalist Asian societies and the politics of disablement is beyond the scope of this article.

15 Finkelstein, *Attitudes*, 8.

16 Pauline Morris, *Put Away: Institutions for the Mentally Retarded* (London: Routledge & Kegan Paul, 1969), 9.

17 Russell, "Disablement, Oppression, and the Political Economy."

18 Finkelstein, *Attitudes*, 10; Oliver, *Politics*, 28.

19 J. Harris, B. Sapey, and J. Stewart, "Blairface: Third-Way Disability and Dependency in Britain," *Disability Studies Quarterly* 19, no. 4 (1999): 365; Oliver, *Politics*, 104–5.

20 Andre Gorz, *Reclaiming Work: Beyond the Wage-Based Society* (Cambridge: Polity Press, 1999), 4.

21 Deborah Stone, *The Disabled State* (Philadelphia: Temple University Press, 1984), 179.

22 Marta Russell, "The Political Economy of Disablement," in *Real World Micro*, 9th edition, ed. Marc Breslow, Ellen Frank, Cynthia Peters, and the Dollars & Sense Collective (Cambridge, MA: Economic Affairs Bureau, Inc., 2000), 94–97.

23 Russell, "Disablement, Oppression, and the Political Economy."

24 Marta Russell, "Backlash, the Political Economy, and Structural Exclusion," *Berkeley Journal of Employment and Labor Law* 21, no. 1 (2000): 349.

25 Russell, "Backlash," 349.

26 John McNeil, *Americans with Disabilities: 1994–95* (Washington, DC: Bureau of the Census, 1997).

27 Russell, "Disablement, Oppression, and the Political Economy."

28 The US federal poverty guideline for one is $8,350 (FY2000). Since $759 is the average per month benefit that a disabled worker receives from SSDI, and $373 is the average federal income for the needs-based Supplemental Security Income (SSI), the annual income of more than 10 million disabled persons on these programs is between $4,000 and $10,000. The extremely low SSI benefit was set up for those with no work history or not enough quarter-years of work to qualify for SSDI: the

least valued disabled members of society.

29 Marta Russell, *Beyond Ramps: Disability at the End of the Social Contract* (Monroe, ME: Common Courage Press, 1998), 81–83.

30 Gary Albrecht, *The Disability Business: Rehabilitation in the United States* (London: Sage, 1992).

31 Russell, *Beyond Ramps*, 96–108.

32 Charlton, *Nothing About Us*, 46.

33 H. Radice, "Taking Globalisation Seriously," *Socialist Register* (1999): 1–28.

34 Karl Polanyi, *The Great Transformation: The Political and Economic Origins of Our Time* (Boston: Beacon Press, 1944), 70–71.

35 B. Epstein, "The Marginality of the American Left: The Legacy of the 1960s," *Socialist Register* (1997): 146–53.

36 There are various and distinct social movements struggling around disablement politics including the physical disability rights movement, the psychiatric rights movement, the blind people's movement, and others.

37 T. Fagan and P. Lee, "'New' Social Movements and Social Policy: A Case Study of the Disability Movement," in *Social Policy: A Conceptual and Theoretical Introduction*, ed. M. Lavalette and A. Pratt (London: Sage Publications, 1997), 140–60; H. Meekosha and A. Jakubowicz, "Disability, Political Activism, and Identity Making: A Critical Feminist Perspective on the Rise of Disability Movements in Australia, the USA and the UK," *Disability Studies Quarterly* 19, no. 4 (1999): 393.

38 Oliver, *Politics*, 114–15.

39 Tom Shakespeare, "Disabled People's Self-Organisation: A New Social Movement?" *Disability, Handicap and Society* 8, no. 3 (1993): 260.

40 Charlton, *Nothing About Us*, 138.

41 Fagan and Lee, "New Social Movements."

42 Joseph Shapiro, *No Pity: People with Disabilities Forging a New Civil Rights Movement* (New York: Random House, 1993), 63–64; Paul Longmore and David Goldberger, "Political Movements of People with Disabilities: The League of the Physically Handicapped, 1935–1938," *Disability Studies Quarterly* 17, no. 2 (1997): 94–98.

43 Shapiro, *No Pity*, 58.

44 Ibid., 64–70.

45 Ibid., 127–39.

46 Charlton, *Nothing About Us*, 122.

Chapter 1: Marxism and Disability

1 Michael Oliver, *The Politics of Disablement* (New York: St. Martin's Press, 1990).

2 Karl Marx, *Critique of the Gotha Programme* (1895; reprint, New York: International Publishers, 1938), 3.

3 Frederick Engels, *The Origin of the Family, Private Property and the State* (1884; reprint, Moscow: Progress Publishers, 1969).

4 S.J. Rose, *Social Stratification in the United States* (New York: New Press, 2000);

E. Wolff, *Top Heavy: The Increasing Inequality of Wealth in America* (New York: Twentieth Century Fund Press, 1995).

5   M. Harrington, *Socialism: Past and Future* (New York: Penguin Books, 1989), 4.

6   Karl Marx, *Capital: A Critical Analysis of Capitalist Production*, 3 vols. (1867; reprint, New York: International Publishers, 1967), 167.

7   Ibid.

8   Ibid.

9   Ibid., 534–37.

10 J. Ryan and F. Thomas, *The Politics of Mental Handicap* (London: Harmondsworth Penguin, 1980).

11 Richard Epstein, *Forbidden Grounds: The Case Against Employment Discrimination Law* (Cambridge, MA: Harvard University Press, 1992), 485.

12 Russell, "Backlash."

13 Ibid.

14 John McNeil, *Americans with Disabilities: 1994–95* (Washington, DC: Bureau of the Census, 1997); National Institute on Disability and Rehabilitation Research (NIDRR), *Chartbook on Work and Disability in the United States* (Washington, DC: US Government Printing Office, 1998).

15 McNeil, *Americans with Disabilities*.

16 United States Commission on Civil Rights, *Helping Employers Comply with the ADA: An Assessment of How the United States Equal Employment Opportunity Commission is Enforcing Title I of the Americans with Disabilities Act* (Washington, DC: US Government Printing Office, 1998), 212.

17 National Council on Disability, *Promises to Keep: A Decade of Federal Enforcement of the Americans with Disabilities Act*, Section 3.3.5.2 (Washington, DC: National Council on Disability, 2000).

18 W. Branigin, "Legally Blind, Legally Underpaid," *Washington Post*, C08, December 12, 1999.

19 Marx, *Capital*, 819.

20 Deborah Stone, *The Disabled State* (Philadelphia: Temple University Press, 1984).

21 E. D. Berkowitz, *Disabled Policy: America's Programs for the Handicapped* (Cambridge: Cambridge University Press, 1987).

22 Ibid.

23 C. Barnes, G. Mercer, and T. Shakespeare, *Exploring Disability: A Sociological Introduction* (Cambridge: Polity Press, 1999); Oliver, *Politics*.

24 H. Hahn, "Public Support for Rehabilitation Programs," *Disability, Handicap and Society* 2, no. 1 (1986): 121–38.

25 Oliver, *Politics*.

26 Stone, *Disabled State*, 28.

27 Ibid., 143.

28 Ibid.

29 P. Ruggles, *Drawing the Line: Alternative Poverty Measures and Their Implications for Public Policy* (Washington, DC: Urban Institute Press, 1990).

30 Marta Russell, *Beyond Ramps: Disability at the End of the Social Contract* (Monroe, ME: Common Courage Press, 1998), 81–83.

31 H. Boushey, "The Political Economy of Employment Inequality: Job Access and Pay Differentials," in *Political Economy and Contemporary Capitalism*, ed. R. Baiman, H. Boushey and D. Saunders (New York: M. E. Sharp, 2000).

32 Erich Fromm, *On Being Human* (New York: Continuum Publishing, 1994), 139.

33 Marx, *Critique of the Gotha Programme*, 10; [dis], author's addition.

Chapter 2: The New Reserve Army of Labor?

1 "Willing and Able: Americans with Disabilities in the New Workforce," *Business Week*, October 1991.

2 Louis Harris, *The 1998 National Organization on Disabilities/Harris Survey of Americans with Disabilities* (New York: Louis Harris & Associates, 1998).

3 Karl Marx, *Capital: A Critical Analysis of Capitalist Production*, 3 vols. (1867; reprint, New York: International Publishers, 1967).

4 Adam Smith, *An Inquiry into the Nature and Wealth of Nations* (1776; reprint, Oxford: Oxford University Press, 1993).

5 David Blanchflower and Andrew Oswald, *The Wage Curve* (Cambridge, MA: MIT Press, 1994).

6 James Galbraith, *Created Unequal: The Crisis in American Pay* (New York: Simon and Schuster, 1998), 266.

7 Alan Greenspan, testimony before US Senate Banking Committee, February 26, 1997.

8 J. A. Meyer and P. J. Zeller, *Profiles of the Disabled: Employment and Health Coverage* (Washington, DC: Kaiser Commission on Medicaid and the Uninsured, 1999).

9 L. Trupin, et al., "Trends in Labor Force Participation among Persons with Disabilities," 1997, http://dsc.ucsf.edu/reps/rends/index.html#trends.

10 Harris, *Survey*.

11 E. Yelin and P. Katz, "Making Work More Central to Work Disability Policy," *Milbank Quarterly* 72 (1994).

12 L. Mishel, J. Bernstein, and J. Schmitt, *The State of Working America, 1998–1999* (Ithaca, NY: Cornell University Press, 1999).

13 Edward Wolff, *Top Heavy: The Increasing Inequality of Wealth in America* (New York, NY: Twentieth Century Fund Press, 1995).

14 Marta Russell, "Backlash, the Political Economy, and Structural Exclusion," *Berkeley Journal of Employment and Labor Law* 21, no. 1 (2000).

15 Richard Epstein, *Forbidden Grounds: The Case Against Employment Discrimination Law* (Cambridge, MA: Harvard University Press, 1992).

16 Marta Russell, *Beyond Ramps: Disability at the End of the Social Contract* (Monroe, ME: Common Courage Press, 1998); Russell, "Backlash."

17 Thomas Snyder, *Digest of Education Statistics, 1996*, NCES 96-133 (Washington, DC: US Department of Education, 1996).

18 L. Mishel and J. Schmitt, *Cutting Wages by Cutting Welfare: The Impact of Reform*

on the Low-Wage Labor Market (Armonk, NY: M. E. Sharpe, 1995).

19   National Urban League, *The State of Black America* (New York: National Urban League, 1999).

20   J. DeParle, "Flaws Emerge in Wisconsin's Welfare-To-Work Program," *New York Times*, October 17, 1998.

21   Children's Defense Fund and the National Coalition for the Homeless, *Welfare to What? Early Findings on Family Hardship and Well-Being* (Washington, DC: Children's Defense Fund, 1998).

22   Marx, *Capital*, 592.

Chapter 3: Disability and Capitalist Globalization

1   [Kevin Hopkins, "The New Competitive Advantage: Expanding the Participation of People with Disabilities in the American Workforce," *Business Week*, May 30, 1994.—*Ed.*]

2   [Council of Economic Advisors, *Economic Report of the President*, 108th Congress, 2nd Session (Washington, DC: United States Government Printing Office, 2004), 229.—*Ed.*]

3   See Doug Henwood, *Left Business Observer* 106 (January 2004).

Chapter 4: A Brief History of Wal-Mart and Disability Discrimination

1   ["EEOC Files Contempt Motion Against Wal-Mart for Violating Consent Decree in Disability Bias Case," News Release, *US Equal Employment Opportunity Commission*, May 10, 2001.—*Ed.*]

2   "Suits Say Wal-Mart Forces Workers to Toil off the Clock," *New York Times*, June 25, 2002.

Chapter 5: Backlash and Structural Inequality

1   "[T]he Nation's proper goals regarding individuals with disabilities are to assure ... economic self-sufficiency[.] Discrimination ... costs the United States billions of dollars in unnecessary expenses resulting from dependency and nonproductivity." Americans with Disabilities Act, 42 USC. § 12101(a)(8)-(9) (1994).

2   See "Read 'Em and Weep," *Disability Rag* (July–August 1992): 28.

3   Rick Kahler, "ADA Regulations Black Hole," *Rapid City Journal*, April 2, 1995. Kahler later published a retraction to this piece.

4   Trevor Armbrister, "A Good Law Gone Bad," *Reader's Digest* (May 1998): 145, 155.

5   Edward L. Hudgins, "Handicapping Freedom: The Americans with Disabilities Act," *Regulation: The Cato Review of Business and Government* 18, no. 2 (1995).

6   See Howard Botwinick, *Persistent Inequalities: Wage Disparity Under Capitalist Competition* (Princeton: Princeton University Press, 1993). See generally Michael Perelman, *The Natural Instability of Markets: Expectations, Increasing Returns, and the Collapse of Capitalism* (New York: St. Martin's. Press, 1999); Paul Baran and Paul M. Sweezy, *Monopoly Capital: An Essay on the American Economic and Social Order* (New York: Monthly Review Press, 1966).

7   See, e.g., Americans with Disabilities Act (delineating, in introducing the purpose
     of the Americans with Disabilities Act, Congressional findings regarding the his-
     torical isolation and segregation of people with disabilities).

8   Louis Harris, *The 1998 National Organization on Disabilities/Harris Survey of
     Americans with Disabilities* (New York: Louis Harris & Associates, 1998).

9   The wage gap is a statistical indicator often used as an index of the status of women's
     earnings relative to men's. It is also used to compare the earnings of people of
     color to those of white men. Wage gap statistics can be found in US Bureau of the
     Census' study, *Money Income in the United States: 1997*; or from Census Bureau
     Current Population Reports, Series P-60, US Commerce Department.

10   Harris, *Survey*.

11   Census data confirms that there has been no improvement in the economic well
     being of disabled people. In 1989, for instance, 28.9 percent of working-age adults
     with disabilities lived in poverty; in 1994, the figure climbed slightly to 30.0
     percent. H. Stephen Kaye, "Is the Status of People with Disabilities Improving?,"
     Disability Statistics Abstract (May 1998), 2.

12   Six million, two hundred and twelve thousand persons receive Supplemental
     Security Income and 4 million receive Social Security Disability Insurance. "Social
     Security Administration Basic Facts About Social Security," Social Security Ad-
     ministration, http://ssa.gov/pubs/10080.html; "1998 SSI Annual Report," Social
     Security Administration, May 1998, ssa.gov.

13   Title VII of the Civil Rights Act of 1964 prohibits wage and employment discrim-
     ination on the basis of race, color, sex, religion, or national origin. 42 USC. § 2000e-
     2 (1994).

14   Pay equity demands that the criteria used by employers to set wages must be sex and
     race neutral. The Equal Pay Act of 1963 prohibits unequal pay for equal or "substan-
     tially equal" work performed by men and women. 29 USC. § 206(d) (1994). Title
     VII of the Civil Rights Act of 1964 prohibits wage and employment discrimination
     on the basis of race, color, sex, religion, national origin. 42 USC. § 2000e-2 (1994).
     In 1981, the Supreme Court made it clear that Title VII is broader than the Equal
     Pay Act and prohibits wage discrimination even when jobs are not identical. See
     County of Washington v. Gunther, 452 US 161, 177-81 (1981).

15   Title I of the Americans with Disabilities Act prohibits disability discrimination in
     employment. 42 USC. § 12101-12117 (1994).

16   US Census Bureau, "Current Population Survey," March 1998, census.gov; US
     Census Bureau, "Historical Income Tables—Families, Table F-5, Race and Hispan-
     ic Origin of Householder—Families by Mean and Median Income, 1947–1998"
     March 1998, census.gov. For a discussion of empirical evidence on earnings gaps
     and discrimination for Hispanics, see Gregory DeFreitas, *Inequality at Work: His-
     panics in the US Labor Force* (Oxford: Oxford University Press, 1991).

17   US Census Bureau, "Current Population Survey"; US Census Bureau, "Historical
     Income Tables."

18   For a time-series discussion of Black/white earnings ratios, see John Donohue and

James Heckman, "Continuous Versus Episodic Change: The Impact of Civil Rights Policy on the Economic Status of Blacks," *Journal of Economic Literature* 29 (1991): 1603; Peter Gottschalk, "Inequality, Income Growth, and Mobility: The Basic Facts," *Journal of Economic Perspectives* 11 (Spring 1997): 21, 28–29. Gottschalk demonstrates that the earnings gap between Blacks and non-Blacks narrowed between the early 1960s and 1975, but progress ceased after this point.

19   William A. Darity Jr. and Patrick L. Mason, "Evidence on Discrimination in Employment: Codes of Color, Codes of Gender," *Journal of Economic Perspectives* 12 (Spring 1998): 63, 76.

20   See *Labor Force Statistics from the Current Population Survey* (Washington, DC: US Bureau of Labor Statistics, 1999). The Census does not count the prison population as unemployed. 70 percent of the prison population is Black. Adding in the incarcerated population as unemployed—almost 8 percent of all Black adult males—changes the unemployment rate for Black men from the reported 6.7 percent in December 1998 to 16.5 percent. Angela Davis, speech at California State University, Fullerton, March 23, 1999. *Cf.*, Robert Cherry, "Black Men Still Jobless," *Dollars and Sense* 43 (November–December 1998): 43.

21   See US Bureau of Labor, *Labor Force Statistics*.

22   See US Census Bureau, "Historical Income Tables—People, Table P-4: Race and Hispanic Origin of People (Both Sexes Combined) by Median and Mean Income: 1947 to 1998," 1999, census.gov.

23   See *Facts on Working Women: Earnings Differences between Women and Men* (Washington, DC: Women's Bureau, US Department of Labor)

24   Ibid. Between 1980 and 1990 the ratio of hourly earnings climbed by 13.1 percentage points; between 1990 and 1997 it climbed by only 2.9 points. Between 1980 and 1990 the annual ratio climbed by 11.4 points, but between 1990 and 1996 the ratio climbed by only 2.2 percentage points. "Between 1980 and 1990 the *weekly earnings ratio* climbed by 7.5 percentage points; between 1990 and 1997 the ratio climbed 2.5 percentage points." (emphasis added).

25   Electronic mail from Heather Boushey, N.Y.C. Housing Authority, to Marta Russell (April 22, 1999).

26   See *Facts on Working Women*.

27   Kaye, "Status," 2.

28   Ibid.

29   Harris, *Survey*. See generally Laura Trupin et al., "Trends in Labor Force Participation Among Persons with Disabilities, 1983–1994," *Disability Statistics Report* (June 1997).

30   President's Committee on Employment of People with Disabilities, "Employment Rate of People with Disabilities Increases under the American with Disabilities Act" (Washington, DC: US Department of Labor, 1996).

31   Employment rates are 11 percent for those with a very severe disability, 14 percent for those who are very or somewhat severely disabled, and 29 percent for those with any disability. See L. Harris & Associates and National Organization on Disabil-

ity, *Americans with Disabilities Still Face Sharp Gaps in Securing Jobs, Education, Transportation, and in Many Areas of Daily Life* (Harris & Associates and National Organization on Disability, 1998).

32   Ibid.

33   See Jonathan S. Leonard, "The Impact of Affirmative Action Regulation and Equal Employment Law on Black Employment," *Journal of Economic Perspectives* 4, no. 4 (Fall 1990): 47–63; John Donohue III and James Heckman, "Continuous Versus Episodic Change: The Impact of Federal Civil Rights Policy on the Economic Status of Blacks," *Journal of Economic Literature* 29 (1991): 1603.

34   See, e.g., Cornell West, *Race Matters* (Boston: Beacon Press, 1993), 95.

35   For conservative opposition to government regulation, see R. P. O'Quinn, "The Americans with Disabilities Act: Time for Amendments," *Cato Institute Policy Analysis* 158 (August 9, 1991); Brian Doherty, "Unreasonable Accommodation," *Reason Magazine* (August–September 1995): 18.

36   Marta Russell, *Beyond Ramps: Disability at the End of the Social Contract* (Monroe, ME: Common Courage Press, 1998), 109–116.

37   See Nicholas Lemann, *The Promised Land* (New York: Alfred A. Knopf, 1992), 218; Michael Parenti, *Democracy for the Few*, 6th ed. (Boston: St. Martin's Press, 1995), 99–119, 271.

38   These objectives were accomplished, in part, through the promotion of policies such as the North Atlantic Free Trade Agreement (NAFTA) and General Agreement on Tariffs and Trade (GATT). See Parenti, *Democracy*, 67-75, 80; see generally Jeff McMahan, *Reagan and the World: Imperial Policy in the New Cold War* (New York: Monthly Review Press, 1984).

39   See generally Lawrence Mishel et al., *The State of Working America 1998–1999* (Economic Policy Institute, 1999); William Wolman and Anne Colamosca, *The Judas Economy: The Triumph Of Capital And The Betrayal Of Work* (Reading, MA: Addison-Wesley Publishing, 1997).

40   See generally Parenti, *Democracy*; Hudgins, "Handicapping Freedom."

41   Mishel et al., *Working America*, 25.

42   Russell, *Beyond Ramps*, 113–21.

43   For an analysis on the impact of state and federal civil rights legislation on the employment and wages of disabled people, see Nancy Mudrick, "Employment Discrimination Laws for Disability: Utilization and Outcome," *The ANNALS of the American Academy of Political and Social Science* 549, no. 3 (January 1997): 53–70.

44   Harris, *Survey*; Laura Turpin, *Trends in Labor Force Participation Among Persons with Disabilities, 1983–1994* (Washington, DC: National Institute on Disability and Rehabilitation Research, 1997).

45   An important study revealing the near unanimous opinion among economists of the positive impact of government anti-discrimination programs on income of African Americans can be found in Donohue III and Heckman, "Continuous Versus Episodic Change," 1603–43. Richard B. Freeman's paper, "Changes in the Labor Market for Black Americans, 1948–72," *Brookings Papers on Economic Activity* 1

(1973): 67–120, was among the first to identify government anti-discrimination programs as a source of progress.

46   See Ruth Colker, "The Americans with Disabilities Act: A Windfall for Defendants," *Harvard Civil Rights-Civil Liberties Law Review* 34, no. 1 (Winter 1999): 99, 100.

47   Ibid.

48   See Gregory Mantsios, "Class in America: Myths and Realities," in Paula S. Rothenberg, *Race, Class, and Gender in the United States*, 6th ed. (Boston: St. Martin's Press, 1998), 210–13.

49   See Donald Tomaskovic-Devey, "Race, Ethnic, and Gender Earnings Inequality: The Sources and Consequences of Employment Segregation," Report to the Glass Ceiling Commission, US Department of Labor, 1994.

50   Scholars such as Robert J. Samuelson, William E. Becker, Donald A. Hicks, and William J. Baumol are representative of this point of view.

51   See Robert Topel, "Factor Proportions and Relative Wages: The Supply-Side Determinants of Wage Inequality," *Journal of Economic Perspectives* 11, no. 2 (Spring 1997): 55, 69. Topel states that: "Wage inequality has risen in modern economics because rising demands for skills have made talented people more scarce. As in other market situations, this 'problem' of a demand-driven rise in price contains the seeds of its own solution. Supply is more elastic in the long run than in the short run. Rising returns to skill encourage people to invest in human capital, which in the long run will increase the proportion of skilled workers in the labor force." See also Robert Z. Lawrence, *Single World, Divided Nations?: International Trade And OECD Labor Markets* (Paris: Organization for Economic Cooperation and Development, 1996), 129.

52   See, e.g., Darity and Mason, "Evidence on Discrimination in Employment," 2; James K. Galbraith, *Created Unequal: The Crisis in American Pay* (New York: The Free Press, 1998). See generally Jared Bernstein, *Where's the Payoff? The Gap Between Black Academic Progress and Economic Gains* (Washington, DC: Economic Policy Institute, 1995). For an economist's explanation of why Blacks have narrowed the human capital gap between Blacks and whites, yet slid further behind in average earnings, see Martin Carnoy, *Faded Dreams: The Politics of Economics and Race in America* (New York: Cambridge University Press, 1994).

53   Mishel et al., *Working America*, 162.

54   Ibid., 30.

55   Ibid., 26–27, 198.

56   Galbraith, *Created Unequal*, 50–88. There was no systematic change in skill premiums within industries during the period 1920 to 1947, despite a large increase in the supply of educated labor during this time. See Claudia Goldin and Lawrence Katz, "The Decline of Non-Competing Groups: Changes in the Premium to Education, 1890 to 1940," *National Bureau of Economic Research* 5202 (August 1995); Claudia Goldin and Lawrence Katz, "The Origins of Technology-Skill Complementarity," *National Bureau of Economic Research* 5657 (July 1996).

57 See Gottschalk, "Inequality." Gottschalk shows that the earnings gap between Blacks and non-Blacks narrowed between the early 1960s and 1975, but progress ceased after this point; see also Carnoy, *Faded Dreams*. Carnoy shows that three dominant views of economic differences between Blacks and whites—that Blacks are individually responsible for not taking advantage of market opportunities, that the world economy has changed in ways that puts Blacks at a tremendous disadvantage compared to whites, and that pervasive racism is holding Blacks down—do not adequately explain why Blacks initially made large gains before falling back in the 1980s and 90s.

58 Darity and Mason, "Evidence on Discrimination in Employment," 83–84.

59 See generally Carnoy, *Faded Dreams*.

60 Letter from James L. Westrich, Massachusetts Institute for Social and Economic Research, to Marta Russell (April 23, 1999).

61 Tomaskovic-Devey, "Race, Ethnic, and Gender"; see also David M. Gordon, Richard Edwards, and Michael Reich, *Segmented Work, Divided Workers: The Historical Transformation of Labor in the United States* (New York: Cambridge University Press, 1982).

62 Tomaskovic-Devey, "Race, Ethnic, and Gender."

63 Ibid.

64 Ibid; see also Paula S. Rothenberg, ed., *Race, Class, and Gender in the United States: An Integrated Study*, 4th edition (New York: St. Martin's Press, 1998).

65 Tomaskovic-Devey, "Race, Ethnic, and Gender" (emphasis added).

66 Galbraith, *Created Unequal*, 37–49.

67 Adam Smith, *An Inquiry into the Nature and Wealth of Nations* (1776; reprint, Oxford: Oxford University Press, 1993).

68 Ibid.

69 Karl Marx, *Capital: A Critical Analysis of Capitalist Production*, Vol. 1 (1867; reprint, New York: International Publishers, 1967).

70 Ibid.

71 Darity and Mason, "Evidence on Discrimination in Employment," 86–87.

72 See West, *Race Matters;* Oliver Cromwell Cox, *Caste, Class, and Race: A Study in Social Dynamics* (Garden City, NJ: Doubleday and Company, 1948).

73 United States Commission on Civil Rights, *Helping Employers Comply with the ADA: An Assessment of How the United States Equal Employment Opportunity Commission is Enforcing Title I of the Americans with Disabilities Act* (Washington, DC: US Government Printing Office, 1998), 4–5.

74 Sixty-nine percent of employers that provided accommodations spent nothing or less than $500, 9 percent spent between $2,001 and $5,000, and 3 percent spent over $5,000. President's Committee on Employment of People with Disabilities, "Costs and Benefits of Accommodations," July 1996, pcepd.gov.

75 There are exceptions, such as when compliance would create an "undue hardship" on the business's finances. Americans with Disabilities Act, 42 USC. § 12112(b)(5) (a) (1994).

76   American Bar Association, "Study Finds Employers Win Most ADA Title I Judicial and Administrative Complaints," *Mental and Physical Disability Law Reporter* 22, no. 3 (May–June 1998): 403, 404.

77   Colker, "Americans with Disabilities Act," 101.

78   Ibid., 101–2.

79   See, e.g., Matthew Diller, "Judicial Backlash, the ADA, and the Civil Rights Model," *Berkeley Journal of Employment and Labor Law* 21, no. 1 (2000): 19.

80   This was the situation in *Cleveland v. Policy Management Systems Corp*, 526 US 795 (1999).

81   See Matthew Diller, "Dissonant Disability Policies: The Tensions Between the Americans with Disabilities Act and Federal Disability Benefit Programs," *Texas Law Review* 76, no. 5 (April 1998): 1003, 1007–8.

82   526 US 795 (1999).

83   Ibid., 974.

84   Ibid., 977–78.

85   Ibid., 977.

86   Ibid., 976.

87   527 US 795, 119 S. Ct. 2139 (1999) (corrective lenses and myopia).

88   527 US 795, 119 S. Ct. 2133 (1999) (medication-controlled hypertension).

89   527 US 795, 119 S. Ct. 2162 (1999) (monocular vision).

90   119 S. Ct. 2153-54 (Stevens, J., dissenting).

91   Ibid., 2154.

92   National Chamber of Commerce Litigation Center, news release, June 1999, http://uschamber.com/media/releases/june99/062299.html.

93   Brief Amici Curiae of the Equal Employment Advisory Council, the US Chamber of Commerce, and the Michigan Manufacturers Association in support of respondents, 527 US 795, 119 S. Ct. 2139 (1999), 4.

94   "NAM Urges Court Not to Expand the Americans with Disabilities Act," NAM news release (National Association of Manufacturers, Washington, DC), March 24, 1999.

95   Gene Koretz, "Economic Trends: Which Way Are Wages Headed?," *Business Week*, September 21, 1998.

96   Ibid.

97   See Mishel et al., *Working America*, 7.

98   *Cognetics Annual Report on Job Demographics* (Council on International and Public Affairs, 1997): 2.

99   Mishel et al., *Working America*, 221.

100 Ibid., 8.

101 Ibid.

102 Thomas Amirault, "Characteristics of Multiple Jobholders," *Monthly Labor Review Online* 120 (March 1997).

103 Mishel et al., *Working America*, 21.

104 Ibid.

105 See generally US General Accounting Office, "Workers at Risk: Increased Numbers in Contingent Employment Lack Insurance, Other Benefits," *GAO Report*, HRD-91-56 (1991).

106 See Sheryl L. Lindsley, "Communicating Prejudice in Organizations," in *Communicating Prejudice*, ed. Michael L. Hecht (Thousand Oaks, CA: Sage Publications, 1998), 187–205.

107 Since January 1993, the number of people on welfare rolls has fallen 48 percent to 7.3 million nationally with three-quarters of the drop coming since the measure became law in 1996. "Clinton Asks Business to Hire More from Welfare Rolls," CNN, August 3, 1999.

108 Forty-two point seven percent of disabled people enrolled in high school do not graduate. H. Stephen Kaye, "Education of Children with Disabilities: Disability Statistics Abstract, No. 19," US Department of Education (July 1997), 2. Only 6.3 percent of all students enrolled in undergraduate post-secondary institutions (1992–1993) had a disability. Of these, 46.3 percent were attending school full time (compared to 52.9 percent of non-disabled students). See Thomas D. Snyder, *Digest of Education Statistics, 1996*, NCES 96-133 (Washington, DC: US Department of Education, 1996).

109 Public Law 104-193, 110 Stat. 2105 (August 22, 1996) (codified as amended in scattered sections of 7, 8, 21, 25, & 42 USC.).

110 John E. Roemer, "Divide and Conquer: Microfoundations of a Marxian Theory of Wage Discrimination," *Bell Journal of Economics* 10, no. 2 (1979): 695.

111 Jon Jeter, "Room for Working Poor in Welfare's New Deal?," *Washington Post*, March 15, 1997.

112 Ibid.

113 Ibid.

114 See ibid.

115 Electronic mail from Laura L. Riviera to Thomas Kruse, June 1, 1998.

116 Ibid.

117 Steven Greenhouse, "Many Participants in Workfare Take the Place of City Workers," *New York Times*, April 13, 1998; see also Steven Greenhouse, "Union to Sue Giuliani Administration Over Use of Welfare Recipients in Jobs," *New York Times*, February 4, 1999.

118 Ibid.

119 Ibid.

120 Jeter (referring to statement by the building's custodian, Joseph Nollie), "Roo for Working."

121 Ibid.

122 Nina Bernstein, "New York City Plans to Extend Workfare to Homeless Shelters," *New York Times*, February 20, 1999.

123 One example: New York Governor, George Pataki administration has quietly built up a $500 million surplus in federal welfare money over the last two years as a result of the dramatic decline in the number of people on public assistance, and expects

that sum to grow to $1.4 billion. Raymond Hernandez, "New York Gets Big Windfall from Welfare," *New York Times*, February 9, 1999. The surplus can then be converted into tax breaks for special interest lobbies such as housing developers.

124 "Job Creation and Employment Opportunities: The United States Labor Market, 1993–1996," Council of Economic Advisers, www2.whitehouse.gov/WH/EOP /CEA/html/labor.html.

125 Wolman and Colamosca, *Judas Economy*, 87–138.

126 Ibid., 53, 141–66. See generally Bennett Harrison, *Lean and Mean: The Changing Landscape of Corporate Power in the Age of Flexibility* (New York: Guilford Press, 1994). Harrison says income polarization is a "by-product" of the post-industrial society.

127 See John Dewey, "Democracy is Radical," in *The Later Works 1925–1953*, ed. JoAnn Boydston (Carbondale: Southern Illinois University Press, 1987), 296. Dewey argues against the Lockean notion of atomic individualism, suggesting instead that political philosophy must take seriously the social as a category. The individual, he says, can only be properly understood in the context of society, and must be understood this way to achieve progress.

128 See Dean Baker et al., eds., *Globalization and Progressive Economic Policy* (Cambridge: Cambridge University Press, 1998).

129 For an example of what a radical democratic planned future might look like, see Dewey, "Democracy is Radical," 296-99; Martin Carnoy and Derek Shearer, *Economic Democracy: The Challenge of the 1980s* (New York: ME Sharpe, Inc., 1980); Daniel Singer, *Whose Millennium?: Theirs or Ours?* (New York: Monthly Review Press, 1999).

130 Mantsios, "Class in America."

131 See Harrison, *Lean and Mean*.

132 See Wolman and Colamosca, *Judas Economy*, 144–45.

133 See Michael Yates, *Why Unions Matter* (New York: Monthly Review Press, 1998), 135–40.

134 Jerzy Osiatynski, ed., *Collected Works of Michal Kalecki, vol. 1, Capitalism: Business Cycles and Full Employment* (New York: Oxford University Press, 1990).

Chapter 6: What Disability Civil Rights Cannot Do

1 During the pre-ADA research phase, Congress found that "two thirds of all disabled Americans between the age of 16 and 64 [were] not working at all." Hearing on H.R. 2273, the Americans with Disabilities Act of 1989: Joint Hearing before the Subcommittee on Select Education and Employment Opportunities of the House Committee on Education and Labor, 101st Congress, 1st Session (July 18 and September 13, 1989; two hearings). S. Rep. No. 101–116.

2 R. V. Burkhauser, M. C. Daly, and H. J. Houtenville, "How Working Age People with Disabilities Fared Over the 1990s Business Cycle," in *Ensuring Health and Income Security for an Aging Workforce*, ed. P. Budetti, J. Gregory and R. V. Burkhauser (Kalamazoo: W. E. Upjohn Institute for Employment Research, 2001).

3   D. E. Lewis, "Access and Closed Doors: Despite Federal Act, Number of Disabled with No Job Is Rising," *Boston Globe*, July 4, 1999.

4   Linda Levine, *The Employment of People with Disabilities in the 1990s* (Washington, DC: Congressional Research Service, Library of Congress, 2000), 12.

5   H. Hahn, "Towards a Politics of Disability: Definitions, Disciplines and Policies," *Social Science Journal* 22, no. 4 (1985): 87–105; I. K. Zola, "Towards Inclusion: The Role of People with Disabilities in Policy and Research Issues in the United States—A Historical and Political Analysis," in *Disability is Not Measles*, ed. M. Rioux and M. Bash (North York, Ontario: Roeher Institute, 1994), 49–66.

6   42 USC. § 12101–12213 (1994).

7   42 USC. § 12101(a)(8)–(9) (1994).

8   American Bar Association, "Study Finds Employers Win Most ADA Title I Judicial and Administrative Complaints," *Mental and Physical Disability Law Reporter* 22, no. 3 (May–June 1998): 403, 404.

9   Ruth Colker, "The Americans with Disabilities Act: A Windfall for Defendants," *Harvard Civil Rights-Civil Liberties Law Review* 34, no. 1 (Winter 1999): 99.

10   United States Commission on Civil Rights, *Helping Employers Comply with the ADA: An Assessment of How the United States Equal Employment Opportunity Commission is Enforcing Title I of the Americans with Disabilities Act* (Washington, DC: US Government Printing Office, 1998), 5.

11   Matthew Diller, "Judicial Backlash, the ADA, and the Civil Rights Model," *Berkeley Journal of Employment and Labor Law* 21, no. 1 (2000): 23.

12   Arlene Mayerson, "Restoring Regard for the 'Regarded As' Prong: Giving Effect to Congressional Intent," *Villanova Law Review* 42, no. 2 (1997): 587, 612.

13   Robert Burgdorf Jr., "'Substantially Limited' Protection from Disability Discrimination: The Special Treatment Model and Misconstructions of the Definition of Disability," *Villanova Law Review* 42, no. 2 (1997): 409.

14   Ibid., 413.

15   Bonnie Tucker, "The ADA's Revolving Door: Inherent Flaws in the Civil Rights Paradigm," *Ohio State Law Journal* 62, no. 1 (2001).

16   Ernest Mandel, *Marxist Economic Theory*, vol. 1 (New York: Merlin Press, 1962), 151.

17   Ibid.

18   Marta Russell, *Beyond Ramps: Disability at the End of the Social Contract* (Monroe, ME: Common Courage Press, 1998), 109–11; Marta Russell, "Backlash, the Political Economy, and Structural Exclusion," *Berkeley Journal of Employment and Labor Law* 21, no. 1 (2000): 341.

19   J M. Washington, *A Testament of Hope: The Essential Writings and Speeches of Martin Luther King, Jr.* (San Francisco: Harper Collins, 1991), 250.

20   Martin Luther King, Jr., "Showdown for Nonviolence," *Look* 32, no. 8 (April 16, 1968): 24.

21   Marta Russell and Ravi Malhotra, "Capitalism and Disability," *Socialist Register* 38 (2002): 211–28.

22   D. A. Young and R. Quibell, "Why Rights are Never Enough," *Disability & Society* 15, no. 5 (2000): 757.

23   Classical political economy was practiced by theorists such as Adam Smith, David Ricardo, Karl Marx, and John Keynes who accepted politics as an inherent component of economics. Neoclassical economists reduce economics to an ahistorical and apolitical mathematical technique.

24   Samir Amin, *Specters of Capitalism: A Critique of Current Intellectual Fashions* (New York: Monthly Review Press, 1998), 134.

25   John M. Keynes, *General Theory of Employment, Interest, and Money* (New York: Harcourt, Brace and World, 1936), 249; Michal Kalecki, *Studies in the Theory of Business Cycles 1933–1939* (New York: A.M. Kelley, 1966), 131; Karl Marx, *Capital: A Critical Analysis of Capitalist Production*, 3 vols. (1867; reprint, New York: International Publishers, 1967), 589–92.

26   M. Friedman, "The Role of Money Policy," *American Economic Review* 58 (March 1968): 1–17; G. A. Akerloff, et al., "Near-Rational Wage and Price Setting and the Optimal Rates of Inflation and Unemployment" (2000), http://eml.berkeley .edu/~akerlof/docs/inflatn-employm.pdf.

27   Alan Greenspan, *Federal Reserve Board Humphrey–Hawkins Report*, February 26, 2000, http://federalreserve.gov/boarddocs/hh/1997/february/reportsection1.htm.

28   Michel Kalecki, "Political Aspects of Full Employment," in *Selected Essays on the Dynamics of the Capitalist Economy*, (Cambridge: Cambridge University Press, 1971), 140–41.

29   Michael Piore, "Unemployment and Inflation: An Alternative View," *Challenge* 21 (1978): 28–34.

30   R. Pollin, "The 'Reserve Army of Labor' and the 'Natural Rate of Unemployment': Can Marx, Kalecki, Friedman, and Wall Street All Be Wrong?," in *Political Economy and Contemporary Capitalism*, ed. R. Baiman, H. Boushey, and D. Saunders, (New York: M. E. Sharpe, 2000), 98.

31   M. Conlin, "The New Workforce: A Tight Labor Market Gives the Disabled the Chance to Make Permanent Inroads," *Business Week*, March 20, 2000.

32   Disability Policy Panel, National Academy of Social Insurance, "Rethinking Disability Policy: The Role of Income, Health Care, Rehabilitation, and Related Services in Fostering Independence," *Social Security Bulletin*, June 24, 1994.

33   Sheila D. Collins, Helen Lachs Ginsburg, and Gertrude Schaffner Goldberg, *Jobs for All: A Plan for the Revitalization of America* (New York: Apex Press, 1994), 10.

34   Americans with Disabilities Act, *Hearings Before the Subcommittee on the Handicapped of the Senate Committee on Labor and Human Resources*, 101st Congress (1989): 22.

35   J. W. Mashek, "To Cheers, Bush Signs Rights Law for Disabled," *Boston Globe*, July 27, 1990.

36   Russell, *Beyond Ramps*, 114.

37   R. Shogun, "Halt Bush's Tilt to Left, Conservatives Tell GOP," *Los Angeles Times*, July 14, 1990.

38 "Given a choice between two equally productive workers, one requiring the expenditure of significant sums in order to accommodate him and one requiring no such expenditures, the profit-maximizing firm would prefer the worker who is less costly to hire." John Donahue, "Employment Discrimination Law in Perspective: Three Concepts of Equality," *Michigan Law Review* 92, no. 8 (August 1994): 2609.

39 *Vande Zande v. State of Wisconsin Department of Administration* (1995) 7th Circuit, 44 Federal 3d, 538, 543.

40 Russell, "Backlash," 351.

41 See Michael Stein, concluding that biases against hiring disabled workers based on inflated costs constitute a market failure deterring employers from making rational decisions, and Peter Blanck, reporting a beneficial "ripple effect" to hiring disabled workers; in part, accommodation costs are "minimal." Michael Stein, "Labor Markets, Rationality and Workers with Disabilities," *Berkeley Journal of Employment and Labor Law* 21, no. 1 (April 2000): 333; Peter Blanck, *The Emerging Role of the Staffing Industry in the Employment of Persons with Disabilities: A Case Report on Manpower Inc.* (Iowa City: University of Iowa, 1998).

42 Amin, *Specters of Capitalism*, 144.

43 Ibid.

Chapter 7: Supreme Injustice

1 "'The Indian Enron'? Hundreds of Boxes of Documents Destroyed, Charges of Contempt of Court, Billions of Dollars at Stake, Millions Paid to Arthur Anderson: Native Americans Sue the US Government," *Democracy Now!*, April 29, 2002, http://democracynow.org/2002/4/29/the_indian_enron_hundreds_of_boxes.

2 [Gina Holland, "High Court Weighs Disabilities Cost," Associated Press, April 22, 2002.—*Ed.*]

3 [Ruth O'Brien, *Crippled Justice: The History of Modern Disability Policy in the Workplace* (Chicago: University of Chicago Press, 2001), 195.—*Ed.*]

4 [Michael Kinsley, "Genetic Correctness," *Washington Post*, April 18, 2000.—*Ed.*]

5 [Michael Parenti, *Democracy for The Few*, 6th ed. (Boston: St. Martin's Press, 1995).—*Ed.*]

Chapter 8: Handicapitalism Makes Its Debut

1 Joshua Harris Prager, "People with Disabilities Are Next Consumer Niche," *Wall Street Journal*, December 15, 1999.

2 Jeremy Kahn, "Creating an Online Community—And a Market—For the Disabled," *Fortune Magazine*, February 7, 2000.

3 *CBS* Infomercial, February 12, 2000.

4 [Prager, "Next Consumer Niche."—*Ed.*]

Chapter 9: Disablement, Prison, and Historical Segregation

1 Dorothy Otnow Lewis, "Neuropsychiatric, Psychoeducational, and Family Characteristics of 14 Juveniles Condemned to Death in the United States," *American*

Journal of Psychiatry 145, no. 5 (May 1988): 584–89.

2   James D. Watson, "President's Essay," *Cold Springs Harbor Laboratory 1996 Annual Report* (Cold Springs Harbor, NY: Cold Springs Harbor Laboratory, 1996), 14.

3   Christian Parenti, *Lockdown America: Police and Prisons in the Age of Crisis* (London: Verso, 1999), 238.

4   See Victor Finkelstein, *Attitudes and Disabled People: Issues for Discussion* (New York: World Rehabilitation Fund, 1980); Michael Oliver, *The Politics of Disablement* (New York: St. Martin's Press, 1990); Marta Russell, *Beyond Ramps: Disability at the End of the Social Contract* (Monroe, ME: Common Courage Press, 1998); and Joanna Ryan and Frank Thomas, *The Politics of Mental Handicap* (New York: Penguin, 1980).

5   Pauline Morris, *Put Away: Institutions for the Mentally Retarded* (London: Routledge & Kegan Paul, 1969).

6   Michael Oliver, "Capitalism, Disability and Ideology: A Materialist Critique of the Normalization Principle," in R. Flynn and R. Lemay, eds., *A Quarter-Century of Normalisation and Social Role Valorization*, Evolution and Impact, ed. R Flynn and R. Lemay (Ottawa: University of Ottawa Press, 1999).

7   Louis Harris, *The 2000 National Organization on Disabilities/Harris Survey of Americans with Disabilities* (New York: Louis Harris & Associates, 2000). See also the 1998 Report.

8   "When Punishment is the Crime: The Privatization of Prisons," *Out of Time* 31 (February 1996), 3.

9   The authors wish to credit the psychiatric survivors' movement for a large body of literature examining America's social policies with regard to people who have been labeled "mentally ill." Among its sharpest commentary has been the movement's critique of language; analysts point out that such terms as "the mentally ill" are highly charged, pejorative cultural constructs. They observe that such labels have been assigned to them by an entrenched power structure, relying for its authority on the DSM—the Diagnostic & Statistical Manual of Mental Disorders—a reference book that has repeatedly and justly been challenged for the subjectivity and bigotry underlying many of its socially constructed "diagnoses." Psychiatric survivors point out that throughout history, individuals who have been identified by the dominant class as "mentally ill" have in many cases been iconoclasts and mavericks whose behavior has been provoked by social injustice. In a paper which examines the situation of people who have been incarcerated—whether in prisons, nursing homes, or mental institutions—we particularly want to avoid the assumption that those labels which have been used to justify incarceration are appropriate or just. Readers are referred to Support Coalition International of Eugene, OR, http://MindFreedom. org, and to its newsletter, *Dendron News*.

10   Heather Barr, *Prisons and Jails, Hospitals of Last Resort: The Need for Diversion and Discharge Planning for Incarcerated People with Mental Illnesses in New York* (New York: Correctional Association of New York; Urban Justice Center, 1999).

11   Jean Stewart, "Life, Death & Disability Behind Bars," *New Mobility* 9 (June 1998).

See also Jean Stewart, "Inside Abuse: Disability Oppression Behind Bars," *The Disability Rag* 15 (November–December 1994).

12 US District Judge Wilkie Ferguson Jr., "Prisons: An American Growth Industry," *Miami Herald*, April 9, 1995.

Chapter 10: Stuck at the Nursing Home Door

1   [Sabin Russell, "Hospital Workers Bask in Bond Victory / Unions helped get out the vote for Laguna Honda," *San Francisco Chronicle*, November 4, 1999.—*Ed.*]

2   [Ibid.—*Ed.*]

3   [Lennard Davis, *Enforcing Normalcy: Disability, Deafness, and the Body* (New York: Verso, 1995).—*Ed.*]

4   [While the eugenic politics of Rockefeller and Bell were more straightforward in that they categorically opposed marriage and sex between disabled individuals (with the former going so far as to fund sterilization programs to this end), Goldman's were more contradictory. Goldman biographer Clare Hemmings writes, "Goldman endorsed an early eugenics movement's focus on quality of offspring, in what makes for quite uncomfortable reading from a contemporary feminist point of view. . . . Although I would not want to minimize the dangers of eugenics arguments emerging out of Goldman's development of her quality arguments with respect to women and birth control, then, it is important to bear in mind that she never supported [a] eugenics view that privileged propagation as a mode of national or racial belonging, but rather as a route to women's freedom." Clare Hemmings, *Considering Emma Goldman: Feminist Political Ambivalence and the Imaginative Archive* (Durham, NC: Duke University Press, 1998), ebook. For the eugenic politics of Rockefeller, see Edwin Black, "North Carolina's Reparation for the Dark Past of American Eugenics," *Guardian*, June 28, 2011. For Bell, see "Signing, Alexander Graham Bell and the NAD," *Through Deaf Eyes*, PBS, March 2007, http:// pbs.org/weta/throughdeafeyes/deaflife/bell_nad.html.—*Ed.*]

5   [*Ed.*—See, e.g., Fred Pelka, *What We Have Done: An Oral History of the Disability Rights Movement* (Amherst: University of Massachusetts Press, 2012), 11.]

6   [*Ed.*—*The Chicago Code of 1911* (Chicago: Callaghan and Company, 1911), 645.]

7   [*Ed.*—Marta Russell, *Beyond Ramps: Disability at the End of the Social Contract* (Monroe, ME: Common Courage Press, 1998), 96–108.]

Chapter 11: Targeting Disability

1   [The President's Commission to Strengthen Social Security, "Strengthening Social Security and Creating Personal Wealth for All Americans," December 21, 2001, http://ssa.gov/history/reports/pcsss/Final_report.pdf.—*Ed.*]

2   [See "Memo on Social Security," *Wall Street Journal*, January 5, 2005, http://wsj.com /articles/SB110496995612018199.—*Ed.*]

3   [Ibid., 149.—*Ed.*]

4   Linda Fullerton (Social Security Disability Coalition), statement before Subcommittee on Social Security of the US House of Representatives Committee on Ways

and Means, September 30, 2004.

5   [General Accounting Office, "Potential Effects on SSA's Disability Programs and Beneficiaries: Report to the Ranking Member, Subcommittee on Labor, Health and Human Services, Education, and Related Agencies, Committee on Appropriations, US Senate," January 2001.—*Ed.*]

6   For data on benefits see "Benefits Awarded—Time Series for All Benefit Types," Social Security Administration, http://ssa.gov/cgi-bin/awards.cgi; http://socialsecurity .gov/OACT/FACTS/fs2004_12.html; and http://ssa.gov/policy/docs/statcomps/ssi _monthly/2004-12/table1.html.

7   Edward D. Berkowitz, *Disabled Policy: America's Programs for the Handicapped* (New York: Cambridge University Press, 1987), 118, 121.

8   ["Memo on Social Security."—*Ed.*]

Chapter 12: Between Dependence and Independence

1   [Laura Hershey, "SSA Still Punishes People with Disabilities Who Work—and Their Advocates," *Crip Commentary*, August 17, 1999, http://cripcommentary. com/cc081799.html.—*Ed.*]

2   [Mollie Orshansky, "Counting the Poor: Another Look at the Poverty Profile," *Social Security Bulletin* 28, no. 1 (January 1965): 3–29.—*Ed.*]

3   [Patricia Ruggles, *Drawing the Line: Alternative Poverty Measures and Their Implications for Public Policy* (Washington, DC: Urban Institute Press, 1990).—*Ed.*]

4   [Louis Harris, *The 2000 National Organization on Disabilities/Harris Survey of Americans with Disabilities* (New York: Louis Harris & Associates, 2000).—*Ed.*]

Chapter 13: "Crips Against War"

1   [See Ewan MacAskill, "George Bush: 'God told me to end the tyranny in Iraq'," *Guardian*, October 7, 2005.—*Ed.*]

2   [In 1982, Disabled Peoples' International (DPI) adopted a Peace Statement at the Peace Memorial Park in Hiroshima Japan. In 2002, DPI held its Sixth World Assembly in Sapporo, Japan, where it reaffirmed and updated its original Peace Statement. "DPI Peace Statement," Disabled People's International, Hiroshima, Japan, June 24, 1982; updated, Sapporo, Japan, October 2002, http://ccdonline.ca /en/international/policy/newsletter/2003/01a.—*Ed.*]

Chapter 14: Disability and the War Economy

1   [Paul Krugman, "Stating the Obvious," *New York Times*, op-ed, May 27, 2003.—*Ed.*]

2   [Jonah Goldberg, "Baghdad Delenda Est, Part Two," *National Review*, April 23, 2002.—*Ed.*]

3   [Elliott Abrams et al., "Statement of Principles," Project for the New American Century, June 3, 1997, http://bit.ly/1LD2sSV.—*Ed.*]

4   [See Disability Rights Education and Defense Fund, "Individuals with Disabilities Education Improvement Act of 2003: Many Improvements but Ongoing Con-

cerns," News Release, June 24, 2003, http://dredf.org/2003/06/24
/individuals-disabilities-education-improvement-act-2003/.—*Ed.*]

5   [George W. Bush, "Speech to the Council on Foreign Relations" (Washington, DC,
December 7, 2005).—*Ed.*]

6   [John Spragens, "The Faces of TennCare," *Nashville Scene*, November 24, 2005.—
Ed.]

7   [As of March 2018, the total cost of the ongoing US wars and military operations in
Iraq and Afghanistan since 2001 had climbed to an estimated $1.8 trillion. "Cost
of National Security," National Priorities Project, http://nationalpriorities.org
/cost-of/.—*Ed.*]

Chapter 15: Un-Natural Disasters

1   [See Lex Frieden, "The Impact of Hurricanes Katrina and Rita on People with Disabilities: A Look Back and Remaining Challenges," National Council on Disability,
August 3, 2006.—*Ed.*]

2   [See Associated Press, "Video Shows Bush Was Warned Before Katrina," *New York
Times*, March 1, 2006.—*Ed.*]

3   [See, e.g., John McQuaid and Mark Schleifstein, "The Big One: A Major Hurricane
Could Decimate the Region, But Flooding from Even a Moderate Storm Could
Kill Thousands. It's Just a Matter of Time," *Times-Picayune*, June 24, 2002; and
Mark Schleifstein, "Bush Budget Cuts Levee, Drainage Funds; Backlog of Con-
tracts Waits to be Awarded," *Times-Picayune*, February 8, 2005.—*Ed.*]

Chapter 16: The Affordable, Accessible Housing Crisis

1   [Eugene T. Lowe et al., *A Status Report on Hunger and Homelessness in America's
Cities, 2000* (Washington, DC: United States Conference of Mayors, 2000).—*Ed.*]

2   [Marca Bristo et al., "Reconstructing Fair Housing," National Council on Disability, November 6, 2001, ncd.gov.—*Ed.*]

3   [See Jennifer Loven, "HUD Lax in Upholding Anti-Bias Law," Associated Press,
November 5, 2001.—*Ed.*]

Chapter 17: The United States versus the World

1   [In 2003, as a representative of the American Association of People with Disabilities, Marta Russell participated in a series of meetings of the United Nations ad
hoc committee charged with taking preliminary steps toward the drafting of what
would become the UN's official Convention on the Rights of Persons with Disabilities (ratified by the UN General Assembly in 2006). As of 2018, the US has still not
ratified this convention.—*Ed.*]

2   [Dave Reynolds, "U.S. Will Not Sign U.N. Disability Rights Treaty," *Inclusion
Daily Express*, June 18, 2003, retrieved online from Minnesota Governor's Council
on Developmental Disabilities, http://mn.gov/mnddc/news/inclusion-daily/2003
/06/061803unadv.htm.—*Ed.*]

3   [As of 2018, the US remains the only UN member state that has not ratified the

UN Convention on the Rights of the Child; is one of only a handful of states which have not ratified the UN Convention on the Elimination of All Forms of Discrimination against Women; is neither a signatory nor a ratifying party to the UN Convention on the Prohibition of the Use, Stockpiling, Production and Transfer of Anti-Personnel Mines and on their Destruction (i.e., the Land Mine Ban Treaty); is not one of the 124 member-nations of the International Criminal Court; and has not ratified the Kyoto Protocol (nor subsequent Doha Amendment) of the UN Framework Convention on Climate Change. "Multilateral Treaties Deposited with the Secretary-General: Status of Treaties," United Nations Treaty Collection, http://treaties.un.org/Pages/ParticipationStatus.aspx.—*Ed.*]

Chapter 18: Dollars and Death

1   ["[I]n the final analysis, economics, not the quest for broadened individual liberties or increased autonomy, will drive assisted suicide to the plateau of acceptable practice." Derek Humphry and Mary Clement, *Freedom to Die: People, Politics, and the Right-to-Die Movement* (New York: St. Martin's Press, 1998), 313.—*Ed.*]

2   [Jack Kevorkian, Written Statement to Oakland County, Michigan, Superior Court, August 17, 1990, quoted in Nat Hentoff, "Not Dead Yet," Washington Post, June 8, 1997, A15.—*Ed.*]

3   [Charles Krauthammer, "A Critique of Pure Newt," *Weekly Standard*, September 17, 1995.—*Ed.*]

4   [Linda Peeno, "Managed Care Ethics: A Close View," written testimony accompanying oral statement for the US House of Representatives Committee on Commerce, Subcommittee on Health and Environment, May 30, 1996.—*Ed.*]

5   [Kurt Vonnegut, *God Bless You, Dr. Kevorkian* (New York: Seven Stories Press, 1999).—*Ed.*]

6   [Diane Coleman, "Disabled Activists Outraged by Kevorkian's Media Circus," news release, *Not Dead Yet*, November 23, 1998.—*Ed.*]

7   ["'What they apparently did was pull up his sweater . . . cut the belly open and pull the kidneys out,' said Dragovic, likening the technique to a 'butcher at your corner store.' Tushkowski's sweater was blood-soaked, said Dragovic, emphasizing that the removal of the organs was not sterile." Ellen Warren, "Kevorkian Controversy Sheds Light on a Problem," *Chicago Tribune*, June 10, 1998.—*Ed.*]

8   [Quoted in Pam Belluck, "Prosecutor to Weigh Possibility of Charging Kevorkian," *New York Times*, November 23, 1998.—*Ed.*]

9   [Hemlock Society USA, "Mercy Killing: A Position Statement Regarding David Rodriguez," news release, December 3, 1997.—*Ed.*]

10 *Final Exit*, directed by Derek Humphry (1999), VHS.

Chapter 19: Eugenics and the "Sole Possible Economic Order"

1   Alfred Hoche and Rudolf Binding, *Die Freigabe der Vernichtung lebensunwerten Lebens* (Leipzig, 1920) in *Racial Hygiene: Medicine Under the Nazis* ed. Robert Proctor (Cambridge: Harvard University Press, 1988), 178.

2   Herbert Spencer, *Principles of Biology*, vol. 1 (D. Appleton and Co, 1914), 530.

3   Charles Darwin, *The Descent of Man and Selection in Relation to Sex* (New York: P. Appleton and Co., 1922), 136.

4   Proctor, 29, 98; and Robert Jay Lifton, *The Nazi Doctors: Medical Killings and the Psychology of Genocide* (New York: Harper Collins, 1986), 24.

5   Darwin, 632.

6   Lifton, 30.

7   Proctor, 96.

8   R. C. Elmslie, *The Care of Invalid and Crippled Children in School* (London: School Hygiene Publishing, 1911); Lifton, 23.

9   Lifton, 30.

10 Proctor, 117.

11 Friedrich Nietzsche, *Twilight of the Idols* (1889; reprint, Indianapolis: Hackett Publishing Company, 1997), 70.

12 Proctor, 185.

13 Ibid., 183–84.

14 Ibid., 66.

15 Lifton, 65–66.

16 Proctor, 186.

17 Ibid., 187.

18 Description by Reich chemist August Becker, quoted in Proctor, 190.

19 Hugh Gregory Gallagher, *By Trust Betrayed: Patients, Physicians, and the License to Kill in the Third Reich* (New York: Henry Holt, 1990), 146–47.

20 Ibid., 243.

21 Alexander Mitserlich, *The Death Doctors* (London: Eleck Books, 1962), 239.

22 Gallagher, 259.

23 Michael Parenti, *Democracy for the Few* (New York: St. Martin's Press, 1995), 10.

24 Adolph Hitler, *Der Führer*, US edition (1926), 287.

25 Walter Russell Mead, "Long After War, Taint of Nazis Remains in Europe," *Los Angeles Times*, November 3, 1996; Howard Zinn, *A People's History of the United States* (New York: Harper & Row, 1980), 401.

26 Baker quoted by Alexander Cockburn, "Eugenics Nuts would have Loved Norplant," *Los Angeles Times*, June 30, 1994.

27 Proctor, 180.

28 Ibid., 16.

29 Rockefeller and Carnegie quoted in Richard Hofstadter, *Social Darwinism in American Thought* (Boston: Beacon Press, 1971).

30 Ward quoted in Hofstadter, 82.

31 Charles A. Murray, *Losing Ground: American Social Policy, 1950–1980* (New York: Basic Books, 1984).

32 Gallagher, 78.

33 Proctor, 22.

34 Ibid., 259.

35 Ibid., 265.
36 Carl N. Degler, *In Search of Human Nature: The Decline and Revival of Darwinism in American Social Thought* (New York: Oxford University Press, 1991), 11.
37 [Roy Cohn was a notoriously reactionary federal attorney during the 1950s. J. Edgar Hoover was the FBI Director who spearheaded a massive campaign of repression against civil rights, labor, and socialist activists in the 1960s. Michael Milken was a top Wall Street financier indicted for racketeering and fraud in 1989. Charles Keating was a banking executive repeatedly convicted of racketeering and fraud in the 1990s.—*Ed.*]
38 Figures reported by the *Los Angeles Times*, April 17, 1996.
39 United Nations 1996 Human Development Report. [As of 2017, there were 2,043 billionaires in the world possessing a combined wealth of $7.6 trillion; this is equivalent to the combined wealth of the bottom 70 percent of the world's adults, or roughly 3.5 billion people! See Kerry A. Dolan, "Forbes 2017 Billionaires List: Meet The Richest People On The Planet," *Forbes.com*, March 20, 2017; Credit Suisse Research Institute, *Global Wealth Report 2017* (Zurich: Credit Suisse Group AG, 2017), 21.—*Ed.*]
40 Karl Polanyi, *The Great Transformation: The Political and Economic Origins of Our Times* (Boston: Beacon Hill Press, 1944), 57.

Index

Printed in the USA
CPSIA information can be obtained
at www.ICGtesting.com
JSHW080544061023
49668JS00003B/3